The Whistling Wind
the true story of a black man's struggle

John T. Hope

The Whistling Wind

Published by The Conrad Press in the United Kingdom 2023

Tel: +44(0)1227 472 874
www.theconradpress.com
info@theconradpress.com

ISBN 978-1-915494-43-6

The Conrad Press logo was designed by Maria Priestley.

Printed and bound in Great Britain by Clays Ltd, Elcograf S.p.A.

When I first became unwell, and started to write,
I was treated by Dr Lester at Highgate Mental Health Hospital
and an outpatient in the care of Dr Odutoye from Southwood
Smith Health Centre. I would like to take this opportunity to
thank them, their team, for their care, and support.

I would also like to thank The Conrad Press, and Margaret
Shenton for helping me to be published, and believing in my
abilities as a writer. My mother Hyacinth Shirley Minott, my
sister Anne Marie Minott for their love, and support.
To the one Most High, God of Love, Nature, and our *Lord
Jesus Christ* who has been my inspiration when drafting

Introduction

The Whistling Wind documents the life and time of an ordinary single black man driven by government monetary policy from the philosophy survival of the fittest, and the ideology the capitalist system endorses. Unable to find consistent work, I fell on the wrong side of the law to be released from prison a change man. Due to constant financial stress, I became mentally ill, then I was diagnosed with bipolar affected disorder, who is a high functioning philosopher.

I don't consider myself a writer, I don't normally read, and before the explosion of social media, I very rarely wrote a word. So, when I woke up one morning in 2009 with my laptop in my hand thinking, *I want to write.*

I learnt more about myself through my writing, and my mental health problems that helped me come to terms with my lifelong condition. It comes as a total surprise to write words that rhyme and flow. I'm compelled to tell my story, and the events around my life that make me, me. In a secular society, some do not understand or perceive they're on a spiritual journey into becoming aware there is more to understand than self-preservation, the capitalist system promotes. At the end of this novel, I hope you can understand the message that is conveyed in *The Whistling Wind.*

Preface

Just after the second world war, there was an influx of migrants to the United Kingdom in 1948 known as the Windrush generation. Since I was educated during a period when an education policy to dumb down ethnic minorities was implemented by the British government, until the mid-eighties. When I started drafting this book in 2009, I've had to unlearn everything I have learnt, and use what I see as writing therapy to re-educate myself.

This book doesn't just underline institutional racism across all public offices and private sectors, in a society that should be equal. It also proves economic exploitation of the labour force, how love can be cruel when it should be kind, and along with my mental health condition, how I have used the artform of writing to overcome and understand my mental health problems.

I've never taken an interest in the written word, I'm compelled to tell my story after a mental awakening, and the fact I never read, the content of this book may not be of a high standard in writing technique or conveyed in a conventional manner, it also tends to slip back and forward in my lifetime. This novel was not conceived for entertainment purposes, but tells the tales from some fictitious events, and fact-based stories within my life that could be beneficial to anyone reading the content.

Although this book involves the criminal world, it conveys a message for spiritual education, and my sincere words of love for humanity. As the author, I'm not looking to make a profit, but to voice what I consider to be balanced opinions and confront controversial issues society rarely discusses.

After being brought up by a single parent, serving a prison sentence, and not leading a model lifestyle. I believe my experiences as a young man, ex-offender, and a single parent, can give others a positive insight to their own spiritual journey.

The title of this book *The Whistling Wind* is a symbolic representation of an entity that is everywhere and nowhere, but it is within your mind.

Contents

The whistling wind intro

As my mind drifts aimlessly, empty in my thoughts with a clear conscience, I wander the wonders of a wonderful universe. I look up at awe, at the clear dark evening sky, stars flicker, twinkle like fairy lights, and sparkle brilliantly, as if they were fireworks in the distant night sky. In that same moment, my vision sweeps down, the whistling wind flies in a circle, when a cool breeze tickles the hairs on the back of my neck and whispers sweet nothings in my ears.

The windy whirling wind flows along elegantly, welling up over the River Thames through the city it takes a tour. The chilled wind is whipping up a whistling whirlpool, as the windy whirlwind twirls, it thrashes, and lashes the empty plastic bags in the air. It twists all over tall bright lampposts and turns around bends. The whistling wind flutters along majestically, blowing down dual carriageways, surging around houses, flats, across open fields of local green parks. The whistling wind drifts, then it whisks you up in the air. When you look up, you feel as small as a pinhead, just like a black ant, totally insignificant as you stand dwarfed by the size of the huge skyscrapers standing alongside tall tower blocks.

A silent gust whips up the whistling wind, it spins around, up, and down, it blows on the city concrete streets, it's cram packed with a diverse mixture of cultures, living in the centre of a metropolitan city. The whistling wind whips around dirty old bag ladies, drunken madmen barking, graffiti urban areas, and gentlemen's gentrified manors.

Suddenly, the windy wind thrashes harder, it brings a waft of delicious mouth-watering Turkish delights, and continental foods. As the windy wind hurdles over obstacles, it swirls around cars, rotates around parked lorries, and busy red double decker buses sway from side-to-side with rhythmic splendour. The noise from the hustle, and bustling rush in the traffic tend to drown the sounds of Nature, but if you listen really carefully at the right time in the day, you can hear Nature's symphonic orchestra playing a love song in your ears.

In the glow of a full moonlight, it's not twilight, an owl can be heard hunting, or calling for a mate, twit, twit a hoot, twit, twit a hoot.

In the darkness it couldn't be blacker, quiet can never be loud, and relaxed isn't busy, there's a wind whipping up a whistling whirlpool blowing on the ground.

It's quite late in the midnight hour, as the whirlwind blows the whistling wind ruffles evergreen leaves that dance on trees. The night air was cool, and refreshing, as the spring chilled wind blew gently, rattling the old Victorian sash windows, as it vibrates, it plays a rhythmic tune. Then there's the pitter patter pitter patter a light amount of rain, it's the sound a piano plays when tap tapping on the windowpane.

As I sit at the kitchen table in my open planned flat, all that could be heard is Natures orchestra playing twit, twit a hoot, twit, twit a hoot, pitter patter pitter patter, and the soft sound of the windy wind whipping up a whistling whirlpool. Blowing in between the branches of a few budding trees from the back of my apartment, overlooking the university campus, home alone with a little bit of rain, and the whirl from the whistling wind made Stoke Newington's church bells sing, ding dong, ding dong, ding dong.

The silent whirl from the whistling wind was soothing, like Barry White groovy, as comforting as a lullaby, and peace is replaced with tranquillity. But my mind is disturbed concerning society, unsettled in my work, and stressed about money. My thoughts are not made up, I'm still not sure what's up, the chilled wind factor is whipping up a whistling whirlpool in my mind.

Chapter 1

How one feels

My last thought, before going to bed.

'Oh, Good God, why? All I ask for is free will, stability, peace of mind, and a fair share of the resources. I can't go on like this, it's too much for my mind. Why should I change who I am, so I can survive in a world that is trying to destroy me, in order for them to survive. Other than my mother's love for me, my mother, and my mind are the only things I can trust. Lord, help me find the strength, Amen.'

Morning all,

As always, the red London bus brakes furiously at the bus stop, and the engine roars away like a lion calling for his mate, the noise wakes me up for another mundane day. It's a lovely spring morning, birds are singing, fluttering, cars braking, stopping. The day's rush is on, the city's need for cash begins. Happy to be home, no work to be done, being unemployed is no joy, there are pure hopes, it's never won.

A confusing thought when one wakes up, wanting to do something for the day, but not that, for that. Feeling happy with yourself, yet still empty, lost, and sad. The most unusual thing about this morning, my mind wants to write, I never want to write. So, I do as my mind tells me, like going to the bathroom, you feel the urge, you go, or if you want a drink, you drink, your mind tells you. Hence, with no pre-thought on the subject matter, I sit, and write.

13th. April 2009, (some dates denoted refer to edited publications on a social media platform.)

Where do I start? At the beginning is always the best place. How would anyone understand unless I could prove it! Maybe, finding something universal like mathematics. Having a question using the right formula, you can never be wrong.

I was born on the 18th, December 1966 Manchester, England at St. Mary's Royal Infirmary. Christened, Fitzroy Brian Edwards, I have many names; my workmates call me Fitz, or Eggy to my close friends. Deejay Man Egg when I first became a deejay, then much later on Deejay Fitz E. My step grandad Mr. Ernest Walker is the only person who calls me John, only because that's what he wanted to name me. Since my father was never there, my step grandad, dad as I called him, was very much my influential father figure. Although he had high morals with old fashion Jamaican principles, my grandad enjoyed a weekend drink in the Iron Duke, a local pub in Hulme, he was also someone I looked up to with high regards and utmost respect.

Now I'm an unemployed time served carpenter, living in North London, Islington for the past seven years. I was educated in the U.K. at a substandard level with a first B-Tec Diploma, in business and finance, which has not been much help in my chosen profession. I love music, T.V. and most importantly, I love people, people who don't love me, and that's the problem. If it weren't for love, believe me we would not be here. What do I mean?

Well, if it's one thing Thatcher's government did, was stabbing the socialist movement right in the heart for the capitalist ideals. This leads to mismanagement of social needs, corruption, fraud, the unemployed, and a total malfunction in social order. The environment and the want of the resources causes wars. Everyman for himself, you're on your own kid, and survival of the fittest is the capitalist ideology in a free market, where one seeks to be number one. A primitive train of thought, which is very much the expression of a woman's love, defensive, protective with a self-contained greed, otherwise and scientifically known as the selfish gene. Social needs requires a community collectively thinking and providing for an individual's essentials.

The main reason why I became a sole trade carpenter, it seemed more profitable. It was also the way the building industry was moving, and it fell in line with Thatcher's government thinking. A job I love to do, free I thought, and independent.

The end result of my labour, gave me a sense of achievement, knowing my work could be standing for twenty years minimum. Yeah, I felt great, at the end of a day, proud, and happy to be alive. As usual, there is always a spanner thrown into the works. For example, there is a mix up over the plans between the designer of a roof, the main carpenter contractor, and his sole trade carpenters. Six subcontracted carpenters fit the roof as first planned, only to find the drawings were amended without the carpenters being informed, who bears the loss?

The subcontractors, secular law is set against them just getting their weekly wage. It's easier for the employer to find loopholes within secular law where they can duck out, fail to pay or default payments. Better still, sack the subcontractors, and find fresh staff. This is an exercise where Magna Carta wins over Natural Law.

It's amazing, how communication skills plays a key role in my profession. That and the fact, I could be employed by six to ten different companies in a year. More often than not, I'm re-employed by past employers, but because there isn't any sense of long-term loyalty, I'm exposed to what is called underhand business, short change, and no respect for my social needs.

John T. Hope

After posting the above blog, the following morning 14th April 2009.

Ring, ring, ring. That's unusual, 9.56 a.m. I'm in my bed looking at the ceiling feeling bored, I'm not sure what to do with my unemployed day, fed up with life, and I get a call from a withheld number. I answered, 'Hello.'

An excited salesman's voice extends greetings, 'Hi there, could I speak to Fitzroy, it's Alan from Breeze Employment.'

Still feeling tired after a restless night, fed up because I don't know what to do with my time, and no interest in work, I replied, 'Fitzroy speaking.'

Barely awake, being disturbed by the call with a bitter morning taste in my mouth, and a lump of eye matter blocking my vision, I could hear him babble something about a job. Stopping his speedy chatter, I interrupted, 'Sorry mate, I'm not interested, I've sold all my tools.'

With a surprised tone in his voice, Alan curiously enquired, 'Why have you done that mate?'

My reply was sharp, as if I were in a speeding police car taking a bend, as loud as a foghorn, like a ballistic missile, I was direct to the point, then I exploded with a bellow, 'You don't get paid.'

I hung up the phone without waiting for a goodbye. That's not like me, there would be a time, I'd try to fit it into my working day, or pass the work onto a mate. I figured it's best looking at the four walls in my third floor two-bedroom flat, other than working for nothing. Able and willing to work, a person feels isolated from the pleasures of society, if one cannot trust members of that public to uphold, what is a moral right. The right for one to have means, and access to a fair share of natural resources when the labour is done. To have a tool which is used to overpower another is inhumane.

I can no longer take part in this game, economics. As a consequence, being bored as the day is long, broke as a bank that as just been robbed, this isn't a joke, feeling empathy for men, and women alike. I do, as my mind wants, nothing at all, but most of all, write when I never write a word.

Chapter 2

In the beginning

I can't say I had a troubled childhood, the only difficulty I had was with my neighbour, Peter Patterson. We were the same height, same age, he was dark just like me, he had a husky voice, with two front top teeth missing in his head, a bit like Bugs Bunny gone wrong from *Loony Tunes*. His first comment when we met, 'The world's going to end in the year 2000.'

In my Bay City Rollers flared chequered green, yellow, and black pants, not forgetting my brown turtle shell five-inches platform shoes, at five years old, I could just about count, I made a fast calculation, which was wrong. My thoughts rung out in my mind, *'Hey, I just got here, I'm too young to die.'*

Peter lived at 128 William Kent Crescent, and we went to the same educational facility, Royce County Primary School, built on the original site of Rolls Royce. Although we were friends we were always fighting for one reason or another. Mainly by his will, wanting things that did not belong to him, and not sharing anything of his own, he was a bit of a bulldog bully in school. He was always throwing his childlike weight around at the other kids in the playground. We were separated as much as possible in primary, and secondary school. Peter was seen as a bad influence on me and is now doing life.

As for my mother's relationship with my father that was a problem. 129 William Kent Crescent, Hulme, Manchester was where I lived, with my loving mother. My mother is only five foot five inches, slightly overweight for her size, which is an understatement. My mother has a lighter complexion compared to me, she may have come from the Caribbean when arriving in the United Kingdom in 1964 at the tender age of seventeen, but she speaks better English than the queen. I always remember, my mother cooking up her one and only son, a little black boy's favourite food, rice, peas, and fried chicken.

I have two younger sisters, Sharon I found difficult to have a good relationship, she would challenge me, or confront me when I made decisions as the older brother, and timid little Anne Marie being the younger of the two, always looked up to her big brother with respect.

The three-bedroom house was situated in the middle of the crescent shape tower block of flats, on the first floor. As you approached my home, walking along the public veranda, over-looked large patches of green playing fields, where we played football, or cricket. Two paths led to a small park in the middle of the crescent for younger kids, climbing frames, swings, a slide, and a seesaw. The two paths led out towards Royce Road with four fields, two on either side of the tarmac path. Walking along the veranda to my home, there was a balcony above the walkway, which only gave access to the family living within that house.

To my memory, my father would usually come around at some late hour, when my family were sound asleep. He would climb to the veranda like a black leopard, which gave entrance to our home, smash the window as if he was a wild deranged bear, frothing from his gaping jaws. Then beat nine bells and ten more out of my mother, it was hell at my door.

There have been many times with fear in my heart from the tender age of seven, I've had to physically fight, punch my father with my skinny arms and small glass fists, in the defence of my family. Along with my step grandad, Mr. Ernest Walker who was a well-built disciplined patient ex-boxer in his youth. He lived with his second wife after being a widow. Mrs. Gertrude Walker, a small woman who was round in shape, a regular church goer, and a fantastic cook. On my birthdays, every year I would receive a birthday cake, and a Jamaican fruitcake with icing for Christmas. Mrs. Gertrude Walker, or Gee was the name my step grandad would call her whenever she lost her patience, was my mother's mother. My grandmother would take me and my sisters to Sunday school, at Saint John's Church in Longsight every Sunday, opposite the market on Dickenson Road. The hustle and bustle of diverse cultures buying Caribbean foods in the market, the smell of the tropics was delightful. Until I was about eight years old, I stopped going to church.

My grandparents lived on the third floor at 513 William Kent Crescent, where they could hear my mother and father fighting. As the chaos of a frantic woman shout, scream from pain inflicted by a monster, cries of agony yearn for help, echoed as if you were in a deep cave reverberated around the crescent. To enforce order, like water flowing over a bitterly cold waterfall, the police would rush into my home battens ready to inflict bruises and pain. Equally my father would try to fight them off. I always understood my father was strong as a big brown American bear, when I saw him punch through a wall like soft butter, when he fought off four or five police officers. I later realised, the difference between a brick and plasterboard when I tried the same as a kid. Children will only do what their parents show them and defend themselves by whatever means necessary like anybody else. As an intelligent society we should not have to be in fear of ourselves.

What surprised me the most, after my father had been to a mental institution and jail, the council moved him into a flat six doors away from my council home. My mother would sit at home looking out of the window in fear of my father, and whenever my mother did see him, similar to James Bond ordering a drink, my mother would shake not stir, or was it shivering, as if she just come out of a cold shower, and shudder, like a leaf in a vicious storm. For weeks, my mother would not go out, and she had a five hundred yards court injunction on him. He lived less than one hundred yards away. I remember, on the one and only occasion when my tall skinny looking father came knocking on the door to say hello, carrying bags of food, which my mother was not agreeable with, what could she do. Fortunately, it seemed like he got better, he wasn't much of a problem.

My step grandad had a tall heavy weight stature with broad shoulders, slightly grey, a slim moustache, low cut hair, and a deep gentle reassuring voice. He always advised and expressed to me, 'John, give your father a chance, he is not a well man. You must remember, for all his might and strength, no man is greater than you, no man is lower than you, we are all equal. Now don't forget that John.'

With his words of wisdom, I always forgave my father for the wrongs he has done to my family. I hope he can forgive me, as I got older, I became stronger, feeling no fear for my father, I defended my family.

This all occurred, when I was around six, or seven years old, feeling adventurous, I'd walk to 146 Great Western Street Moss Side, my grandmother's home on my father's side of the family. As I walked, I would look up at the tall high-rise flats in Hulme, pass my school, crossover what was a busy road, Chichester Road. I'd approach one of the many unsafe adventure playgrounds in the area, depending on the weather or my mood. If I didn't walk round, I would walk through the busy Moss Side shopping centre locally known as the precinct.

In the market hall, the variety of colourful interesting products, diversity in cultures, people from all over the world seem to be in one place. Indians, Irish, Caribbeans a few Africans, and the one or two Chinese selling a wide range of exotic tropical food. As a young boy I would pass a record shop along the mall at the Limbeck Crescent entrance, where my mother bought my first track from Murray's Record shop, much later on he moved to Princess Road. When I was much older, about nineteen years old, there was another record shop I discovered in the market hall, and the first time I heard Oliver Chatman, *'Get down Saturday night,'* I had to buy the track.

Upon entering the shopping centre, walking towards the main square hall to your left led to the sports hall, where my primary school took us for swimming. To the right, led to Kwik Saves, opposite was a library I never used as a kid, the library was a joined to the Moss Side Community Centre where activities for the area were made available. I personally didn't use the facilities; it had the bad boy gangster element outside. About this time, in the early nineties, a new concept in business started up called Chicken Run, they delivered Caribbean food to your door. On the odd occasion I'd attend one or two promotional events from big London sound systems, such as Saxon Sound System. They had one of the deepest bassline that was not dissimilar to a creeping rumbling earthquake. Many other sound systems played at the Community Centre, Taurus, Baron, Mega Tone, all good Manchester reggae sound systems. On the odd occasion I would attend when R & B was being played by the biggest sound system in Manchester at the time, Soul Control from Longsight.

As I walked through the precinct there was an upper level in the main square that was not used much, no shops, no conveniences, no facilities, nor services, just empty shops a sign of recession, decline, and downturn in economy. Can't you tell its Thatcherism, a woman with an iron will.

Walking straight across the large square shopping hall, the walk way led pass a few shops, and out of the building towards the right, but if you turned to the left, the precinct walk way turned like a dog's leg back on itself. This is where drug dealers, and other bad boy business would unfold outside the bookmakers. I'd walk pass the betting shop to see my father on the few occasions to say, 'Hello.'

Although he was a sick violent man when I was younger, now he's older, he has mellowed out, and he takes his medication, I have always shown him respect. After all, he is my father.

On my way out of the shopping centre to your left you could walk to the sports hall, but if you turned right, below the walk way there was an underground garage, and a short walk away down towards Moss Lane East, at the Princess Road junction there is the fire station. Back then in the early seventies, next to the fire station there was what was the Big Alexander pub. Big, it was a very old Victorian boozer, I never went in, I was just too young when it stood proudly as a local landmark.

Across the dual carriageway of the A5103 on the opposite side to the Big Alexander pub, there's the brewery, adjacent to that, you would find notorious gangsters, and upfront R & B played in the basement club called, the Reno. Up above was the Nile club, they tended to bust reggae, I preferred the Reno. Way back in the day, in the seventies, as you walked up Prinny Road locally, or Princess Road on the map, Barry's Men's Shop was where my step grandad would take me to buy my suits, clothes, and school uniforms. It was a busy road, as I remember, before part of the Arndale Shopping Centre opened in 1975 and the Manchester, Moss Side riots June 1981.

After the civil unrest that part of the road was the start of degradation, all that was left after the demonstration were burnt out shells of vibrant businesses made waste. The only shops that weren't damaged were the Reno, Murray's record shop sold reggae, a cobbler's shop run by Barry who was later one of our sound system members. A petrol station, one or two hairdressers, and taking into consideration there's just been a riot, what the criminal elements are going to need is a solicitor. Turning left away from Prinny Road, I'd walk over to Recreation Park, but the kids in the area called it Reck Park, just before you would pass the two West Indian Centres social clubs, known locally as the Old People's Home. As you walked around the West Indian Centres you would cross the quiet road of Raby Street, looking down the street, you would see the big yellow brick church, just after Moss Side youth club, across Recreation Park is grandma's, on Great Western Street.

In that part of Moss Side, it's quite a nice fragrance or aroma, to smell drifting in the air of the whistling wind, hops, oats, barley, and any other ingredient needed to make beer ferment in the local brewery. This is where my other grandparents lived, on my father's side, grandfather and grandma or Mr. Buster & Mrs. Bee McCoy. We didn't do much together, mainly because of the relationship my father had with my mother, but that did not stop me from knowing my wider family, which didn't extend further than my first cousins on my father's side.

Boney M, *'Brown girl in the ring,'* Bay City Rollers, Burning Spear were the types of music that reminds me of my childhood. Champagne, *'How about us'* was the first track I asked my mother to buy for me. When times were good with my mother and father, I can remember them having late night parties with the sound of the bass rumble like a snowstorm avalanche in my home, which my grandparents Mr. & Mrs. Walker, did not approve. When my father was not in jail or in a mental health institute, I remember my father as a deejay, busting reggae, lovers rock, the early seventies tracks.

It was difficult for black people to host clubs, and they were not allowed house parties, *'disturbing the peace'* was the most commonly used phrase by the police. It was hard finding fun as a black adult in the seventies from what I, a child could see. The black and white issue was not apparent to me as a young boy, the school I attended was mainly black populated, and I played with black kids.

Living with what seemed to me a normal family surroundings, we cohabited with hundreds in what was the height of architectural design in the early seventies. William Kent Crescent was among four or five storey crescent tower blocks, which had hundreds of families living one on top of the other. I noticed I was one of the few black kids who was fortunate enough to have grown up knowing their grandparents, from both sides of the family. I was born from one of the first wave of Jamaican migrants that came to the United Kingdom in the late forties, early fifties known as the Windrush generation. In the eighties, nineties, Hulme, and Moss Side became a lot more violent with drugs and crime taking its toll on society, or does it all become more noticeable as you get older?

Responsibility was on my shoulders at an early age, and as a single parent, my mother would work when she was able, had the time, and could get a job that paid. So, money was always an issue, and the electric, *'The meter has ran out'* was the phrase, like you could run after it. Overall, my mother is a great woman because of the way I was raised, I'm still here today.

By my thirteenth birthday, there's been no trouble from my father, when we moved from Hulme to 40 Aston Avenue, a semi-detached house in Fallowfield housing estate. My sisters had to share, one of the three bedrooms with a garden front, and back. Six days after moving in, on my fourteenth birthday, my mother has to take Sharon back into Hulme, so my sister could perform in a school play, they never got there. As the advancing lorry aggressively applied its brakes, my mother was runover by a container lorry, on Princess Road, Platt Lane junction at a set of pelican crossings. Dazed, semiconscious, my mother repeated to any question, 'I can see the green man, I can see the green man.'

Luckily, for Sharon, my mother took the full blow, protecting my sister from getting injured.

From what I can remember, my mother's head received twenty-five stitches, her leg had severe bruising around the hip, and my mother's left shoulder ligament pulled out of its socket three inches. She was very severely injured from the accident.

My mother spent one week in intensive care, and a further four weeks on a recovery ward. I've always had to have responsibility for my two younger sisters, whenever my mother could find work, or if she were out and about. More so now, she was in hospital. I had to make sure my sisters were ready for school, when my step grandad, would pick them up, take them back to Hulme, where their school was. I would walk to Moss Side, where I attended Ducie High School. I'd help out as much as I could, until my mother was on her feet.

That year, my mother asked me to work on the garden, the backbreaking labour involved made it the first, and last time I would do that kind of work. My father asked me many times, where I was living, but my mother told me not to tell my father, I never told him where.

Chapter 3

In need of help

It's the 16th, April 2009, this isn't right, I should not be feeling like this, every morning watching the news, all this death with rotting flesh, it's not like I've not seen it all before. It's an everyday thing, death, murder, rape, war, there's always more, corruption, and fraud. It's sad and depressing just thinking like that, an everyday thing. My mind, I'm not well, my mates have been showing a bit of concern about me, and I've noticed. I've lost a few of my so-called friends on social media because of my blogs. This is not a good sign, the only reason for joining the site six months ago was to promote myself as a deejay promoter. I thought, *'I should just go down to A & E at Euston General Hospital, just to see what the doctors say.'*

First of all, my thoughts for a plan of action, *'Pop in the pub, checkout my mates in my local.'*

The Edinburgh Cellars, the largest Edwardian pub in Newington Green didn't have a garden, but around the back end of the boozer was a large function room. I thought, *'I'd just go to see how my friends react to me.'*

From time to time, I do some work at the Edinburgh Cellars, as their carpenter, deejay promoter. As a result, I'd say I'm popular with a good few in the area in connection to this pub. I can't afford to go anywhere else, and as always, the landlord has a slight hang up with black people, but tries, bless him. He declares he's hard up for cash, or they're a hard business team Simon and Neil, partnered landlords and more likely hard businessmen. Funny enough, I don't know much about Simon's past when he took over the pub, but he was a slim white guy who liked to be bossed around by his girlfriend, he had a soft gentle persona who was easily misled. As for Neil, as time passed, I learnt he was an ex-accountant, and one who like to use cocaine, very arrogant, self-centred and loves himself. In one of our conversations I had with Neil, he did mention, 'My father is racist.'

His comment raised my eyebrows similar to *Spock* with suspicion, guarded as if I were a soldier guarding Buckingham Palace, I stood to attention, and I was a cautious Sunday driver who needs bifocal glasses.

Just after evening rush hour, I decided to go ahead as planned to see the doctor, but as I made my way down the main street to the pub, I noticed my mate's new Audi convertible, belonging to an old friend, Tom Moore. A stubborn black Mancunian living in East London, he's generally a straight-forward in your face to the point type of guy, if you rub him up the wrong way. He exhaled a deep thunderous like voice with an intimidating persona, a tall stature, well-built, and a good laugh when he has a wee drink. Usually, he'd phone before passing by to see me, but not on this occasion. Above the noise of the rushing city traffic, I could hear him shout, 'Where you going?'

His greeting was in his normal rude manner with a deep northern twang to boot. I shouted over the noise of the traffic, 'The pub, you coming?'

He waved me over to cross the bustling panic of the busy traffic to his car. Sure enough, I did the green cross code bit, approached, and entered, the leather wrapped red interior, just as he started up, the heavy ended rumbling engine, vroom, vroom, vroom. He explained how a concerned schoolfriend Edwin Blair who lives in Manchester, asked him to pass by to see how I was doing. I've known Edwin since I was eleven years old, to understand his persona is to know he was the captain of most team sports in school, always a calm composed leader of men. To cut a long story short, Tom took me to the hospital, after a drink in the pub.

As we cruised with the traffic down the busy highway of Euston Road, I felt a heavy warm swelling around my mind. It was so overwhelming, as if a flow of liquid were being injected into my brain. It forced me to sit further back in my seat, I had to hold my head with both hands, there was no pain, it was amusingly pleasing, as if I were watching Robin Williams in *Morning Vietnam*. My mind was filled with an elixir of an indescribable sensual pleasure. The only way to express or imagine the sensation, is the subtle feather touch flow of warm water over my mind. I declared, 'Tom, I know everything, oh my word my brain feels like it's dancing.'

I've never felt such a feeling like this before. Ripples of waves were running over my brain; it tinkled my senses with joy. It felt as if, my brain was jumping with excitement, and laughter at the unbeknown. A perplexed husky voice reverberated when Tom answered, 'You alright Eggy? Which way do I turn? Eggy, which way?'

I looked in between my fingers that were holding my head, to see we'd just passed Warren Street Tube Station heading towards Camden, and the traffic was moving at a fast pace.

Tom was getting a bit flustered, him not knowing the local area. I replied, 'Take the next right and right again.'

In that moment, I lowered my head and went onto add, 'Tom, this is unbelievable, oh my word, Tom, I know everything, oh my word. Tom, how am I going to tell seven billion people this? Oh, my word, Tom, oh my word.'

Thereafter, we parked the car, and went into see the doctors at Euston General Hospital to explain my thoughts concerning humanity's plight to survive, and creationism, (Omni's wordsmith mantra) how I broke my left leg in 1993, then I offered the other cheek, and received a broken jaw when I was in prison in 1996. They just didn't get it or understand what I was saying. Reading the expression on the doctor's face, I talk sense, but the doctor and his medical team looked puzzled. Their faces suggested they were questioning themselves, why have I come to the hospital talking about my stress in work, society's philosophy survival of the fittest and my thoughts on creationism! The doctor proclaimed, 'You're fine, you can go home.'

What was I to do?

Half the things I was expressing to the doctors are thoughts I've never had the time, inclination to think, ponder or consider, only when I'm mentally ill, so it seems. This being the second time in my life I've had a mental health problem, the first was back in 1993. Tom drove me home and the last thing I said before leaving the car was, 'Thanks Tom for the ride, and your concern, see you when I see you again.'

Then I went home and wrote the following edited version for my blog 16th April 2009.

Helpless hands

I'm out of work, nothing planned, just leisure at my pleasure,
no fun, a cost my budget could not stand.
So, I stay at home instead, write a line before bed, in the hope
we don't see the dead, the sacrifice just to get fed.
Yet I stay awake, at 6 a.m. just to take in the news at 8,
stressed because there is nothing I can do.
Starving hands, flies in their pans, no one's love is at hand,
what can I do?
My head is in my hands.

John T. Hope

Chapter 4

Not feeling the same

Waking up to another wet dull Friday morning on the 17th April 2009, today is a bit out of step. My giro cheque from the benefit agency did not arrive in the post. I'm not using my bank account, I have no income to honour my creditors, which totals £25,000. Penniless, hungry, cupboards empty and dry, at 1 p.m. it was time to go to the benefit line. I got myself dressed, grabbed my laptop, I'm never without, so I could publish my blog of the day, which I did in a café on the way to the jobcentre. If anything, in my mind I'm saying, *'I could get a counter payment.'*

The weekend was here, waiting until Monday before I could buy some food was too long a wait. I won't get into the politics of being attended to by a civil servant, smug as a bug in a rug, impolite with bad manners, they treat you with disrespect, not courteous, and very unhappy when doing their job. Their unpleasantness rubs off, creeping up your back, depressing one's day like a cold red rash, when I'm normally chirpy never grey. I had to wait for ages to be seen. After speaking to a member of staff I was reluctantly informed, 'I have to wait until Monday before I could report the cheque as missing.'

I had to leave with nothing.

As I walked home my thoughts were, *'What can I do? How do I survive without food?'*

Heading towards home, the hope of a Saturday post kept my stomach in. As I walked up the slope on Matthias Road, my thoughts were, *'Patience is the best solution.'*

Approaching closer to my home, I could see my friend Sarah Smith, meaning princess, she's a lot more than that she has a heart of gold, but like most of us in this area, and around the world, having been beaten, and battered as a young mother, she's had her share of so-called bad luck. It doesn't come easy for an English cleaner, getting work at a rate one can live on, demanding work.

As we got closer, we greeted one another with a hug, and a cosmopolitan kiss on her rosy-red cheeks. I was happy to see her, but not happy with myself. We said our hellos, with that Sarah added, 'There's a good few policemen on Green Lanes, looks like something major.'

I suddenly felt so much rage flowing through my body. This feeling was a new experience, the need to demolish someone's face, the wanting to harm another, but the feeling was not towards Sarah, I wanted to punch a police officer, the urge to act on it was great. With her sentence said, I just turned away from her, and like an Olympic speed walker about to win the race, I walked furiously at a rapid pace towards the incident, which was in the same direction as my home. I could hear Sarah's voice in the growing distance along with the busy bustling traffic of city life around Newington Green, shouting, 'Fitzroy, Fitzroy, Fitzroy.'

I wasn't interested in what she had to say, my intention was to get that copper, and smash his face in. Luckily I snapped out of it, I came to my senses before seeing an officer, I stopped in my tracks, turned round, and made my way to the bus stop. Feeling in such a way as to want to harm someone was not the right emotion to be expressing when just walking down the road. I felt the need to see a doctor. As a result, I got on the 73 bus, to A & E Euston Hospital.

Upon arriving at the newly built hospital facility, I was seen by a doctor shortly after entering the building. I was led into a large hospital box treatment room with a doctor, two other medical staff and a security guard. In what seemed to be a stage play, the scene was set, and props were in the room with just four hospital chairs. We all sat down with the security guard standing at the one and only door. The atmosphere in the room felt as tense as a bicycle spoke. I deduced the security guard was intimidating, as he stood there looking over his glasses with his electric blue eyes, stabbing me in the chest with his beady stare. I began to explain to the doctor how I was feeling angry for no good reason, full of rage at nobody but myself, and totally distressed about being knocked. It wasn't before long I had to explained the term, 'Non-payment, for work I've done.'

To have such a term as the afore mentioned *knocked* shows and proves, the everyday exploitation of the workforce. The injustice within society, I did not understand at the time, why I was feeling in so much rage. I mean, we live in a world where we know most of the rules, and we seek advice in the law when needed, so why do I feel so aggrieved, I ask myself. As always when talking with anyone of an official capacity like Members of Parliament, solicitors, or civil servants, they tend not to have any emotions similar to *Spock,* they eternally have a blank expression. The doctor told me, 'I'll be back in five minutes.'

All four parties got up and left the room. So, I sat there waiting, and waited, and waited.

It was Friday around 4.30 p.m. I was hungry, and I was beginning to lose my patience, having waited for the doctor for one or two hours. I decided to make my way home. As I was leaving the treatment room, I could see two large security guards in black uniforms, sitting outside the door of the treatment room I was in. I pulled the door wider, to walk into the corridor, the two guards stood up speedily like stiff soldiers to attention. One asked, 'Where are you going?'

Seeing them stand up in such a manner, made me feel unsettled, like a cautious mouse, or an insecure rabbit being stalked by a vicious wolf, nervously shaking similar to a fast spin washing machine, I answered, 'I'm going home.'

To my immediate left there were the double swinging fire doors that led to the exit. When I reached for one of the doors, the first security guard who was slightly shorter than myself, had a slim build, stood in front of the doors, and grabbed my left forearm. While the other guard with his protruding gut, stood very close up behind me. I politely asked the first guard, who was in front of me, 'I want to go home, could you let go of my arm please?'

The first guard was no doubt Asian from India, in a very authoritarian, impolite, disrespectful manner, responded, 'You're on a section, you cannot go anywhere.'

Identical to a combustion engine clogged choking its last breath suddenly, bang, I spontaneously exploded, resembling a wild uncontrollable Tasmanian devil. My rage was clear, I barked, 'No doctor has placed me on a section, let go of me.'

With my sentence said I pulled my arm away from the first guard, but the second guard grabbed me from behind, in a bear hug, engulfing both of my arms in his grip. I could feel my weight slowly lift off my feet, as the second guard tried to pick me up. Looking directly at the first guard, I lined up my vision for his forehead, and lunged with an almighty head buck, like a big cast iron ball from a demolition truck. I felt totally relieved with my outburst of rage, then I resigned to my predicament, akin to a dead rose drooping, my body wilted and became lifeless in the arms of the guard behind me.

As suddenly as the situation arose, as quickly as three other guards found their way into the corridor to apprehend me, without resisting I was forced back into the treatment room. Whereby the four guards lifted me up in the air, one grabbing each leg, the other two held an arm each, spreadeagled. In the rush and tumble of it all, my laptop, slid to one corner of the room, I did not want to fight, I was outnumbered, and I am not a violent man.

The first security guard was hands free, hovering with joy, dancing eagerly, he reminded me of the bear Ben from the T.V. show the *Grizzly Adams,* or the bear Winnie the Pooh, excited at finding honey. He was prancing keenly from the excitement of the situation, as the adrenaline rushed through his rotten red blood. I could see the first security guard's eyes glowing like an owl in the night, taking pleasure in the thrill, as if he were on a roller coaster. The control he had over me, and the power to do has he pleased, licking his lips in delight, like a hungry dog, he was joyous at getting his supper. I sensed he wanted to hit or kick me in some way. I held up my drooping head, and I looked straight into his bloodshot eyes. I shouted, 'You're enjoying it too much.'

With a look of guilty surprise on his face he looked straight back at me, his eyes were wide eyed, his pupils dark in daylight, and devilishly hungry to inflict pain, he turned to leave the room. As he walked out, two doctors walked in with a syringe needle in one of their hands, declared, 'Fitzroy, we're just going to give you an injection.'

As I was being held by four men spreadeagled, hovering in the air similar to a bedsheet on a washing line, flapping in the wake of the whistling wind, calmly I replied, 'Okay.'

The guards placed me on the floor where I found myself near my laptop. I scrambled along the clinically dirty ground to where it was, then I grabbed hold of it and opened it up. I always have my laptop on standby, all my windows were up, and ready. I went straight to I Tunes, and played, the Isley Brothers, *Harvest for the world.*'

Upon hearing the track, it was soothing similar to a child's bedtime song, more relaxing than a massage, disarray exchanged to being calm, and I was moved from apprehension to comforting. The track fit the occasion, but they're not aware of subliminal messages. I heard someone say, 'Keep still Fitzroy, we're about to administer the medication, and you will feel a slight prick.'

Feeling like a prick was the contrary, I felt confused, mixed up and alone, I answered, 'Okay.'

They gave me an injection, as I curled up in a ball over my laptop, then I passed out. I woke up the next day, my usual, happy go unlucky self, in a hospital ward. After speaking to a doctor that morning, he informed me, 'I was not on a section.'

Which makes me wonder, why would the guard lie, and what was the drama all about if I wasn't sectioned! The doctor went on to ask, 'Could I stay for a few days?'

I'm not sure, or can't recall my feelings about this proposal, but I do believe, there was no harm me staying so I said, 'Okay.'

On reflection, the feeling of rage is not something I ever express. Of course, we all get angry, but I always walk away before the situation escalates. I know how I feel, yet I feel different in my mannerism, and I don't feel myself. For one, I don't write, and I sign every blog John T. Hope. I've tried to explain to the doctor, there is another with me, but I don't think he understands what I'm saying when I refer to John T. Hope, my subconscious or conscience. They discharged me a few days later, then I wrote Monday 20th April 2009 edited blog.

Chapter 5

Trying to tell

After being in a mental health hospital for a few days it was nice to be home, my lovely, sweet home. Upon returning, the welcome of a cheque from the benefit agency put a big smile on my black Lancashire cat face. Now I could do a bit of shopping, cash is in my pocket, feeling comfortable with myself, having money to do as I choose. I've lived in Newington Green since 2002, which is mainly a Turkish Islamic community. I know a good few people, but it's a face one says, 'Hello.'

I don't seem to know their names.

I try to shop as local as possible, reason being, I have no car, and to keep the local economy flowing. Some of the shop owners complain, how times are hard, and business is slow, or is it greed, one just doesn't know. A mini-Tesco has just opened up, handy for me. However, for what the likes of Tesco do to the small traders, and new starter businesses, they do not stand a chance.

There is one shop, whereby my friend Beste Aydin runs a second-hand shop, she is a nice woman, late forty, Turkish with good intentions, but when it comes to making money, she is a clever businesswoman, dominates her British ex-husband, and is a forceful older sister. I've known her for as long as I've lived in the manor. Of late, I seem to be getting closer to her as a friend. From time to time, she would stay in my spare bedroom, whenever her boyfriend Mehmet Cetin came over from Turkey, or was it Holland. Her love life is complicated, but we won't go into that. I happened to walk pass her shop, on my way to Tesco when she pulls me up, 'Hello Fitzroy.'

The spring sunshine shone on her warm glowing smile, asked, 'I have some concerns about your health, is it okay for me and my man to stay with you in your spare room for a few days?'

It was free.

So, I informed her of the fact, and with that, she continued, 'Could I move back in on Friday?'

When I heard that, I was slightly elated, I replied, 'Yeah not a problem.'

Thinking to myself, *'I could do with the company.'*

Then I went onto do my shopping, after the shop, a tap on the keys, writing some words in the hope I am heard, please stop the fighting. On the next page is an edited blog published on a social media platform on the 22nd, April 2009.

Boring song

The most boring thing is this boring song.
What can I do when there is so much to be done?
No cash, nothing can be done, no fun, love, not even a holiday
in the sun.
Just four corners of a room, the curtains are always drawn, does
that ceiling need paint?
No money, nothing can be done, not a bit of fun.
A promise on a promise, what a philosophy, corruption,
robbery, and unemployed, the pensions fraud, murder isn't that
an illegal war, a sacrifice that should never be made.
I pace, I walk, I walk a pace, thinking a thought, achieving
peace is no disgrace.

The glory of war

Control creates disorder, your logic is out of order.
Justifying the truth in secular law that rewards dishonesty
within natural morality, this isn't humanity, isn't that the truth?
If a murderer gets a brave medal, the reward is but a cold heart.
Proud of winning a war, where is the sorrow for losing a soul.
Feeling good you've killed a heart, just to inherit gold.
Honours for courage are dreams of a living nightmare.

John T. Hope

Chapter 6

Wordsworth

The spring morning of the 22^{nd,} April 2009 was warm like the Caribbean heat. The low clouds covered the blue sky with a light fresh city breeze, blows the whistling wind as it drifts like a sailing boat, it twists as if it were a princess dancing, and twirls from the excitement from a rollercoaster. The day was damp, as a fine mist of rain wanders aimlessly out of the sky, you could be stood at the edge of a waterfall, it was very humid and muggy. I felt on top of the morning, bright, and chirpy, with a step to my walk looking around at the girls as I bopped, watching them tits rock, cars going beep then stop, the rush for the bus, while others walk, somebody shouts, 'Look out, the bike!'

It's bloody mad, the panic, trying to get across the road, the drivers put their cars in gear, racing off before the green, go. Money hungry, doesn't it drive you crazy, if not maybe.

I'm in no rush to get to my appointment with Awareness Workshop Working Links, a new government back to work plan. I was intending to use any grant offered to start a new promotional company, come deejay agency as a long-term proposal. Since I made the appointment on the 22^{nd,} March 2009. On the day, I had mixed feelings about how I would be received once I had my say. I just needed people to hear my views, it's vital, the urgency, importance, and the necessity was clear to me. People around the world were suffering and dying needlessly.

Since I walked from my flat up to the jobcentre on Mare Street, Hackney, I found myself late upon arriving at the office. After signing in, and getting directions to the meeting room, upon entering, they were in full swing, and were about to handout application forms for a business plan, again.

I was pissed off the minute I saw the words, business plan on the top of the page. I could not help myself; I stood up for everyone to hear me shout as loud as a ghetto blaster, and clear like bathwater, 'This does not work. I've done this three times.'

There must have been sixteen trainees in the room, plus two members of staff, who were presenting the course.

They all looked around at each other, as if they were meerkats looking suspiciously for a predator. When one of the staff queried my response, 'What do you mean it doesn't work?'

In a manic manner, I explained in five minutes, the chances in probability, and the ratio of a small business competing in a market that is overpowered by big business, the small man doesn't have a chance. After my slight burst of rage, and frustration with the same old thing by a different government, I walked out dismayed with financial forecasts, disillusioned like I've just seen a mirage, and very disappointed with government policies. In that split second, I made my way to the bus stop, lost in thought thinking, *'How can I get to speak to the masses.'*

I must have stood outside Hackney Town Hall, at the bus stop watching the busy bustling traffic for about an hour. My bus must have passed me four or five times, as I gazed into space, thinking, *'How I could tell seven billion people what was on my mind?'*

At that moment, inspiration hit me when *Flash Gordon* appeared, go to the town hall to see my M.P. which was opposite the bus stop to where I was standing. With brand new hope and a mission, I made my way over to Hackney Town Hall, picked up a leaflet, which gave the days for surgery. When I came home, I wrote what you the reader is about to read dated on the next page and published my blog before bed. Sure enough, I arrived at my flat to see the news report on the Taliban. The death of more British soldiers, both sides losing so many lives. The sorrow I felt, it's oh, so depressingly sad. So, I wrote for the next day's blog 23rd, April 2009, I had a lot to say.

Heart, head and hands

My heart, head and hands bear a pain one's soul cannot stand.
A heart that aches, minds makes hands inflict pain.
A head that yearns, a heart beating relentlessly for tender hands
coming with a concerned mind.
A hand that aides, a heart is filled with delight, a conscious
mind is pleased.

Pride

A sense of pride, there is work to be done.
A sense of pride when the day is done.
A sense of pride, a mother for her son.
A sense of pride is the love from everyone.

War correspondent

While writing a letter to the world leaders about the war, it
comes to mind that I am blind.
So, I sit and imagine in my mind writing a line.
It slipped my mind, I have no hands; this will not stop me, I
will walk to the United Nations, and have my say.
Then it hit me, I have no legs, I feel around to have found,
there is no body.
Happy are the governing bodies members, safe in their beds,
knowing there defended.
Where is my head?
Oh no, I'm dead.

John T. Hope

Chapter 7

Sense of self

The first time I became aware of any conflict between black and white was at the tender age of seven years old. I was stood on the veranda of William Kent Crescent with my mother. In the distance, yet close to my home, there were seven tall high-rise flats, grouped together, locally named after the constellation of cosmic stars, Seven Sisters. At the time for modern seventies buildings, they had character, stood tall, elegant, and proud on the Trafford side of Greater Manchester.

From behind the flats a crowd appeared, marching in uproar approaching where I lived. I could see hundreds of white people holding banners getting closer to the crescent, marching down Stretford Road, shouting abusive racist language. It was a hot summer's day, out of fear all the parents on our crescent called their kids in from the fields and park. When I asked my mother, 'What's going on?'

Looking worried, and a concern expression on my mother's face explained, 'The march was from a group called the National Front. They do not like the fact that black people were living in England.'

That brought a question to my mind, 'Where are you from mum, if not England?'

With her loving warm brown eyes, and a big glowing smile my mother answered proudly, 'I was born in Jamaica.'

After watching the march, a few evenings later, I was deep in slumber when my mother wakes me up to watch a T.V. drama, *Roots*. The drama documented the history of a black family tree when they first became slaves in 1750 to the present day. Kunta Kinte, the first slave from this family tree was always trying to escape from his slave master.

Finally, the slave master tired of playing cat, and mouse then hide & seek, offered Kunta Kinte an option, 'Which one do you want chopped off, your penis or your foot?'

They chopped off Kunta Kinte's left foot. I found it very educational, horrifying, and somewhat upsetting, watching a black man lose his foot because he ran from his slave master, very demeaning. But now I see it, as a subliminal message from the collective subconscious mind. It was a good job I didn't have many white friends at the time.

The morning after watching the show, made me very angry towards white people, a feeling I did not like to express. In fact, I hated myself for hating them. At an early age, I knew, one couldn't tar everyone with the same brush.

Racism is very inconspicuous in England today. Marching on the same issues as the National Front is not socially accepted in today's society. Nevertheless, racism, if not in your face, it is very much discreet, and is the main reason why young black people cannot achieve.

Things seemed very much normal as a kid, I went to school, doing okay, appointed leader in secondary school, and I was not getting into trouble. It was about this time, having been a long time, since my first encounter with racism, it shows its ugly self. We were playing a school football match in North Manchester; it was the first time I'd been to Moston. At fourteen years old, being on the football team, gave me a chance to see Manchester without my mother. In the changing rooms on the wall, in mainly a white populated school was written, *There are three million unemployed, not one million niggers.*

The team came out of the changing room fired up, and ready for a brutal game of football. Every player on their side, came off injured. We won 13 nil.

Chapter 8

My Mind

In 2008, it's been six, seven months into joining a social media platform. In that time, I've not put a picture of myself up, which seemed to naturally work well with what I was doing, mysteriously. I was using YouTube music video's eighties, nineties, R & B, hip hop selections linked to my page. I was also creating links with other groups and inviting strangers to join my party groups None of D Above, and Fully Fledge Funky.

Confused, I couldn't call it paranoia, or was I delusional, my perception on the following was questionable. The fact a social media platform was suspending my page, and the company was having file sharing copyright problems. Then, after I sent an email to the Prime Minister and the President, the Labour party email scandals came to light, and a music site called Pirate Bay music, didn't help the efforts I was making as a promoter. It was making me wonder if Pirate Bay were linked to my page, and if I was part of the social media company's problem. With the emergence of Swine flu in the air, I felt that the powers that be were getting prepared for what I had to offer the world. So, I waited patiently for an official to contact me, which didn't occur, but I still kept on doing what my mind says, which was to keep writing.

Frustrated here waiting, tedious yet patiently hoping praying, if only someone could hear what I'm saying, we could achieve peace with a bright new rainbow. Being kind with a new frame of mind, feeling fine, now we are wise.

Chapter 9

First night's raving

Academically, if I did not fail, I averaged out on most subjects. Music a lesson I wanted to take up in primary school was taught by a teacher, who was as impatient as a hungry dog held back from its dinner bowl, like a donkey that doesn't want to move, she was pig headed, and a British bulldog bully. Miss Morris, a tall white greying blonde woman smelt of stale cheap perfume, in her fifties. The worn-out poor excuse for a teacher, slammed the piano lid down on my small six-year-old black hands, quick reaction kept my fingers on my hands. I was very reluctant to take up music thereafter. Looking back, could that have been a racist act!

Being a six-year-old black boy, what am I to know or understand about a white adult's motive.

When my mates invited me to a party, many years later, when I was thirteen, they were involved in the high school steel band, performing a show. Timidly with a few other schoolmates, I arrived at one of their gigs where they laid on nights of exciting pulsating entertaining weekends, at community centres, garden parties for members of staff, and vibrant carnivals in Manchester when it didn't rain. During a lively party I attended, the young school girls were hot to trot, and the steel band was stealing the crowd with an energising musical vibe.

It all went tits up, when one of the band members mentioned, he'd seen Mr. Brown, a proud tall Scottish man, a history schoolteacher, coached the football team and was also the steel bands event's organiser, receive cash one night after the band's performance. When the band confronted Mr. Brown, he looked over the group of small adolescents with his tense beady eyes, and an imposing tall adult stature. He told the band members in a defiant manner, '£200 paid goes to the school fund.'

The band disagreed, rightly so, never being paid for any event performed, entertainment done for free and fun, the group split up.

During school hours, you would see students dancing in corridors, dub stepping to UB40, Madness, Two Tone, roots reggae music, from ghetto blasters echoed deep rumbling bass around the hallway, and gymnasium.

Irate teachers look like hungry snapping piranhas, rushing around the corridors screaming blue murder for order in the midst of unruly chaotic kids, in time the students would settle down to lessons.

It wasn't before long, the music scene was calling me, and my friends to youth clubs. New musical sounds such as Extra T's *'E.T. Boogie,'* Grandmaster Flash, *'White lines,'* were entertaining my eardrums. Some of my mates formed a Jazz Fusion group. Then bang, on the scene, electro dance groups, body popping in shopping centres, and with the added past time of playing pool at youth clubs, adventure playgrounds were getting boring. The lure of the city clubs at sixteen was too much of a pull, just before leaving school.

On Wednesdays, we would walk to Legends nightclub one of many venues at the time was situated on Princess Street, central Manchester. The big spacious mirrored venue, provided along bar, quenching the thirst of five hundred plus party people, spinning glitter balls, reflected laser lights giving a futuristic scene from *Star Wars.* Deejays Greg Wilson, Chad Jackson, and Mike Shaft, fifty pence for members to get in. Being young, inexperienced, girls were not the first thing on my mind, dancing to the riveting drumbeats, heart beating bass, and futuristic electronic sounds was all I was interested in.

Wednesday nights brought coaches to Legends from Birmingham, Liverpool, and Leeds, parked up, to hear high tempo jazz fusion. Art Blakely, Miles Davis, tunes from Loose Ends, Luther Vandross, and Leer. Men sweated vigorously, displaying street fusion tap dancing moves.

Admiring flocks of sexy ladies flirted with any guy who smiled back. Throbbing beats and the pounding bass, brought on a vibrant atmosphere, which was an eruption from an enthusiastic crowd. I was amazed and hooked to the club scene.

Chapter 10

The body's role

My mother's name is Hyacinth Shirley Minott, a cousin to the late great reggae artist Sugar Minott. Hyacinth is also a beautiful flower, but my mother's friends called her Shirley. I recently discovered the flower was named after a Greek goddess who was hit in the head by a discus Zeus threw. When my mother was not dragging me and my sisters to school, which is not all together true. Although I had trouble getting out of bed, I enjoyed education, and messing around with my schoolmates, so I was always looking forward to going. I remember my mother being a dinner lady in my primary school, when I was nine to eleven years old, and in the playground supervising the kids. Later on in my mother's career, she was a sewing machinist in a sweat shop located on Bloom Street.

One afternoon, my mother was shopping after work in Manchester city centre at Woolworths, where they had a four-storey department store, near her factory. Fire took hold in the furniture department, the foam used to upholster the sofas had toxic chemicals when on fire. This caused customers in the store to inhale deadly fumes and substances, causing the death to a number of people. Luckily, my mother was thrilled to bits to escape, unharmed, and be rescued safely by beefcake firemen.

Government health and safety laws were introduced thereafter, to ensure such substances are not used again. Looking back at that, governments always act too late when it comes to health and safety at the hands of business, where the many do not think of the one.

My mother's friend Rita Taylor had a fifteen-month baby girl, who modelled chubby fat cheeks, big glowing hazel eyes and a giggly smile, the child loved life.

Rita was distracted when she was washing the kid's clothes in her brand-new top loader. She placed the young child on top of the washing machine to answer the front door. When she came back, the young baby fell in when the machine switched to a fast hot spin. The burns on the mother's hands in her effort to drag her daughter out of the washer are too horrifying to mention. The young child died from eighty percent burns. Only when too many lives are lost, governments place importance when public safety is the government's first priority.

Another example, how many years has the car been invented before public pressure, forced car makers to fit safety belts. Before unleashing the best tool in the world, the internet, no one thought about placing any kind of international law. Now we have sex rings preying on our kids at home from a screen in a supposedly safe environment. Intelligence thinks, is society thinking?

Chapter 11

Lessons in love

It's about 1982-1983, I was going to a number of clubs and venues in Manchester city centre, one or two all day parties known as all dayers held in various cities, once a month when I was still in school. They were nice tastefully interior designed discos, strobe laser flashing lights, and packed with girls wearing as little as possible. The ladies modelled pink string vests with the odd no bra, welcomed one's eyes. The occasional jeans cut too short, up to the bumper line, and beyond in some cases. Lovely sexy women dressed in fishnet tights in varied colour leg warmers.

At sixteen, I just started attending Saint John's College on Quay Street, Manchester to re-sit my exams for English and mathematics. I was more interested in the club scene, and my love for the latest music. Electro hip hop, jazz, R & B, breakdancing, body popping, fusion is a form of street tap dancing, it was the rave for my generation.

This was the same year I met my future baby mother, Alice Barnaby. Like some young men, after many times trying with other girls, Alice was my first. At twenty-one she lost her virginity to me, and she was a practicing Christian, I was not. As our relationship grew Alice became more involved in the club scene.

The parties never stopped, one of the best nights ever was when I first pulled on a bighead spliff. This particular night was different, as me and my friends planned to go to the Reno, on Princess Road, known as the frontline nightspot. The underground scene for upfront, fresh as a daisy music, drugs, and guns. The boys were excited, like fluffy black bunny rabbits running around a tree, and as joyous as a black church choir, it was our first time attending the venue.

While in an enthusiastic mood, some of the guys got into gangster character, not being thugs. One of the four guys pulled out a fat £2 bag of weed, before I knew it, they were smoking laughing and joking. They offered me some, but I refused, many times, I knew the effects of drugs when looking at my father, and his serious mental health issues. No, was not good enough for my mates. After an hour or so, they all jumped on me like a pack of wolves about to feast on a deer, and similar to a bunch of rotten police officers, they ganged up against me, forcing me to have a blowback. This is where, they'd hold one's nose, blow the smoke into one's face, what can one do?

I didn't fight back because I'm not violent, not that I can remember most of that night, but what a laugh.

After that I became distracted in college, six months of further education, I dropped out. Putting me on the road in the catering industry, as a trainee chef, at Swan Street Youth Training Scheme, paying a weekly wage of £25 plus bus fare. Things haven't changed much in over twenty-five years. It may be a different name for another government scheme, Education Maintenance Allowance, E.M.A. get £30 per week in 2009. After the Y.T.S. scheme was completed, I started working for various catering establishments.

Eighteen months into dating Alice, my love for her was growing with each day. Other women may have been interested in me at the time, but my heart and mind was on Alice. One evening, Alice invited me to a party, which was being held in Hulme on Limbeck Crescent. We both arrived at the party at various times with our friends. Upon arriving, I found myself there before Alice, and the party was in full swing. About 2 a.m. Alice appears with her sister, and a few of her friends soon after. The heavy reggae bass rumbled in the packed house party, we lined the walls, having a few slow dances together. The heat was building up when Alice exhaled, 'I need some fresh air.'

Then she went outside with her sister. A few moments later, Alice returns uttering, 'Why don't you come outside and join us?'

I followed her outside, the evening was warm, and the night sky clear as day. There seemed to be more people outside the flat than in the party, the area was buzzing with chatter, fun, and laughter. Drinks were flowing, and weed was being smoked. We stood outside on the public balcony to where the party was being held, the night air had the aroma of oats hops and barley, coming from the local brewery. The delicate scent drifted in the calm soothing silence of the whistling wind, as it waft gently in the background. In the backdrop, across Princess Road, light running engines from the night time city traffic could be heard, vroom, vroom, vroom.

Alice noticed the door next door was open, as various people seemed to be welcoming themselves, in and out of the flat. Alice declared, 'Let's have a look!'

Sure enough, I followed her into the eerily creepy dark hallway of the flat. All that could be heard was the boom, boom, boom in the background, as the deep rumbling reggae bass from the party next door played on. As we walked casually down the hallway I could see a three-seater sofa, from a crack of light emanating from the open living room door. I entered the room first to see an acquaintance Dan Redbridge, five foot six, a short black guy with a very short temper. He was sat in an armchair opposite the three-seater sofa, looking up at me and Alice. I sat down on the deep leather brown three-seater sofa to hear Dan say to Alice, 'Come over here and sit on my lap.'

His comment came as a surprise to me, I didn't know Alice, and Dan knew one another. I thought *Dan didn't show me much respect, talking to my woman in such a manner, and as a second thought, where does Alice know him from, for him to be that forward!'*

Alice turned her head to look in my direction, feeling confident with our relationship I said, 'Come over here.'

Alice looked at me plain and square with a cold blank expression, then slapped me down like a baseball when she replied, 'No.'

I felt totally humiliated and didn't feel I was getting respect from my girlfriend. After Alice's short abrupt rousing speech, I stood up, left the flat and the party, then went home. Not knowing what happened, never asking a question, I never found out what happened that night between Alice and Dan. My trust was shattered, I learnt from then, women will instigate, or provoke jealousy with their female charms to test love. In time, my love faded away for the attention of other women.

In the poetic prose, there are two types of text *italic,* and plain italic, representing two voices, *John,* and Fitzroy, or two minds in one head.

Remember memories

'To see me, you wouldn't want to be me,
from all that I can see of me.'
*'It is a tragedy, all the misery, why there is unhappiness was there
love lost with all the friends you have loved?'*
'Tragic it may have been, but there was no love lost,
my happiness is that they still live, so they can give love,
isn't that how you live?'
*'There is only us, one should only forgive,
remembering one's love, painful it maybe, why hate the harm,
embrace how love felt, not how you feel.'*

John T. Hope

Chapter 12

It happens

Seven months before leaving the cosy comfort of my mother's home in Fallowfield to face the big cruel world, on a hot summer's day, in the early evening, me and Alice were listening to Alexander O'Neal's first album in 1985, Alice tells me, 'I'm pregnant.'

Similar to a freshly made snowman with a cold uncaring concern. I told her, 'It was over between us.'

Cruel I know that now, I was unsure if the child was mine, and I just met another woman, Beverly Carter. Beverly lived in Longsight with four other sisters, a lovely mother, and a niece. She worked for a company in Ardwick, and we met at a packed house party a few weeks earlier in Moss Side. Beverly had a soft persona like a bed of red petal roses, gentle hands reflected a generous heart, very attractive with a subtle manner to her personality, and a laugh a minute.

When we first encountered each other, Beverly was stood alone in the packed house. I offered her a drink, which she was more than happy to accept, we danced the dance, talked the talk, and went for a walk and strolled in the Recreation Park on Great Western Street. In the bright light from dawn light, the warm crisp summer air came with the whistling wind. The windy wind blew a gentle breeze in her Nubian hair, her perfume smelt of a sweet rose, or was it fragrant lavender oil. We exchanged numbers, and kept in contact, we later became close, close friends.

It was about this time at eighteen my father asks me again, 'Can I come over to your house to see your mother?'

He was intent on starting a relationship with my mother, all kids want from their parents is to be together, and something he played on. There are some relationships, we walk into we want to run away from. Who said society is right to say, 'One should work on a relationship.'

You tell them that when they've been beaten up, used, and abused. After many times of my father asking, I thought, *'There could be a chance.'*

Subsequently, I approached my mother, she was against the idea, but came around to my way of thinking. My mother added, 'It was okay, as long as you were there.'

When my father did come to my house, I left them both talking at the front door, while I watched the T.V. in the living room. A few moments passed when I heard my mother's cry of agony, pain, and distress, 'Ah oh my God, FITZROY.'

I dashed out horrified, as if I were running out of a house that was on fire, to see my mother covering her head and face with both hands. My father's hand was raised to hit my mother, I ran over to my father and gave him a right-hand punch to his left cheek. As I did that, I began to push my father away from the front door, and down the garden path. My father turned round, running out into the road, I gave chase, just to see one of his legs reach out to kick me. I caught his foot, pushed him to the floor, giving him four kicks to his head, one for every member of my family and warned him away from my mother's home.

Then I felt a sudden jilt forward, a strong grip grab hold of my body, engulfing my arms like a big bad grizzly bear. It was Charlie Monroe my mother's neighbour, a doorman for the big city clubs and pubs, embracing my body from behind. He was talking in my ear whispering, as if he were the silent whirl from the whistling wind, 'Calm down Fitz, calm down.'

I was in control, and composed, in an effort to calm the situation down, Charlie held me in his firm grip, picked me up, then swung me away from my father, similar to a construction crane. It did not give me much comfort, doing that to my father, but I could never see my mother feel pain from anyone inflicting misery, harm, and distress.

That summer, when I met Beverly, the first woman of three ladies I've had the pleasure of living with, and my longest relationship to date, eleven years on and off. My relationship with women, isn't meant to be a kiss and tell. Life isn't much of a life unless it revolves around sex and the one you love, it's just part of my life. There have been many women, who I have loved being lovers, I've loved every one of those loves, all in different ways. Women who know I'm with my queen, women who have a king. It makes me wonder, then I conclude, some women and a lot of men are lying to themselves. In so many ways, they go against what they believe is a natural paired love. Something we deny when the statistics suggest, society is not naturally conforming to what we believe within Christian, Islamic, and many other cultures that endorse marriage values between two people instead of concentrating their love, concerns, and responsibility on the child.

My son was born on the 19th, December 1985, by the 2nd, January 1986 my mother tells me, 'It's time you leave home, you're not contributing enough of your wages.'

By this time, I'd already done one or two government schemes for little or no money. Working in the catering industry as a canteen cook, and a commis chef, which was part of the training, while I was on a Youth Training Scheme and a Youth Opportunity Program at Manchester University, but at this moment, I was just receiving benefit when my mother said, 'I must leave.'

I was starting a new catering job in the morning, my mother wanted all of my wages. At the time, my benefit was the only bit of money I was getting, £49 every two weeks. What my mother was asking for sounded unreasonable. Sure enough, I left.

Upon leaving my mother's home, walking lost within my mind, the whistling wind was churning around in my thoughts like a whirlwind of confusion, and I was as penniless as Charlie Chaplin. I had a brown box leather suitcase in my hand, with little, or nothing in it. Just a few clothes was all I had with nowhere to go.

A few years after the 1981 Moss Side riots, my first personal encounter with a policeman was upon leaving my mother's home. I was walking down the path along the main carriageway of Princess Road, Moss Side, into town. The red brick pre-war terrace housing estate partly sheltered me from the bitter cold from the whirling whistling wind. On the opposite side of what is a motorway cutting through a housing estate are the big open fields of the posh boys Grammar school, the Y.M.C.A. adjoining Alexander Park then on pass the bus depot on the right-hand side. Opposite the fields are the lemon, yellow brick houses of Alexander park housing estate. The thrash from the whirling whistling wind had so much force it was pushing me into the gardens, driveways, and homes of Mancunian red brick post-war houses.

Of course, police presence was quite high, an officer stopped me in my tracks asking, 'What do you have in your suitcase?'

At 6 p.m. it was a cold winters night; a freezing artic gale was whipping up a whirlpool with twirls and loops as the whistling wind blew down Princess Road, at the junction to Claremont Road. The highway was lit by tall streetlights, which brighten the dual carriageway, and walkway. Innocent of any crime and as calm as the deep blue sea, I replied, 'A few clothes and my knives for work, I'm starting a new job in the morning, I've just left home officer.'

The police officer looked me up and down with a cold white face. Similar to Lurch from the *Addams family* he had a blank spooky expression written on his mug, and he had a deep dark empty stare emanating from protruding eyes, responded with an order, 'Open the suitcase.'

Which I did, he had a look, then sent me on my way.

I was confused in my mind, like a wild whirling windy whirlpool in what to do, where to go. I found myself at 146 Great Western Street, my grandparent's home on my father's side of the family, Mr. Buster & Mrs. Bee McCoy. They brought up my cousin who is a couple years older than me, Richard Campbell. Being the first grandson to my father's parents, he had favour over the rest of their grandkids. Not that it was a problem to me, the point was underlined discreetly, whenever the need seemed to suit. I found myself knocking grandma's door, I entered shouting, 'Hello grandma.'

Her front door was always open, only the family were aware of the fact, which led into a hallway, the stairs were right in front of you as you came in the three-bedroom terrace house, on the left there were two doors next to one another. I made my way to the last door, as the first door led to the front room. This is where the crown jewels of the family's pictures were situated, there were none of me, or my family. Only special guests were allowed into see and have a private chat.

I entered the second room with the warmth of the gas fire burning on a low flame. I could see my gran sat in front of the fireplace, relaxed in the warmth on a comfy sofa, watching the start of Sunday Praise. My grandmother was surprised to see me, I never called round as late as that. Grandma answered, 'What's wrong? Where you going with that suitcase at this hour?'

A bit lost in my mind, my thoughts thrashed and twirled, as if it were the whistling wind, swirling with misdirection in a mazed cave, and I was feeling apprehensive about my future. I declared my situation, 'I don't know grandma, my mother has just kick me out, I don't know what to do or where to go.'

Grandma was gob smack shocked, her false teeth nearly fell out of her head, she had to push them back in her mouth, and the surprised look on her face, her eyes bulged out like a giant squid, after hearing what I said. She looked into my eyes proclaiming, 'You can't stay here, there is no room, go to your father's flat.'

In my mind, it seemed like a clever idea, my father was in hospital with mental health problems. The one-bedroom flat in Hulme wasn't too far from where my new job was in Whalley Range, a district less than a mile away. I replied to grandma's suggestion, 'Okay thanks grandma, I'll see you before the weekend.'

I was about to turn and leave when grandma cried out, 'Fitzroy, here take this.'

I turned to look, grandma was reaching into her handbag, at that moment she pulled out a fiver. One thing about grandma, when I was in need, she never let me go without giving me a pound, God bless her soul. I thanked her, then left for my father's flat in Hulme.

William Kent Crescent always brought back bright fond memories of my childhood. Five or six years after leaving the area to live in Fallowfield, Hulme was not the same environment. When you passed a flight of stairs it was dark as a glum dungeon, rubbish piled up invited all kinds of vermin, it was drip, drip, dripping wet like a concrete rain forest. The area was damp similar to clammy socks and smelt of urine. The flats were not as welcoming, the area was well known for late night parties police were always trying to stop. Vandals occupied vacant flats and hardcore drugs part of everyday life, something I did not know much about, weed was something my father did, so it's one thing I could call part of my culture.

Approaching my father's flat, it occurred to me I didn't have a key, so I was left with no choice, but to kick the front door in. When I walked into the flat, it smelt smoky, musk, and damp. I wedge the front door shut with some letters that were on the floor, the hallway suddenly became dark. I felt around the wall for a light switch, but once I'd found the button there was no electric. I made my way down the dark hallway, I passed the front room, and bathroom, to where his bed was situated in a room next to the kitchen. I pushed open the door into the living room, from the window the street amber lights brightened up the accommodation. Again, I tried to switch on the light to view no light, there wasn't much there. All I could see was a double bed with no bedding, a record player from the sixties, a few vinyl tracks, and a wooden school chair. It was about 7.30 – 8 p.m. no T.V. So, I bedded down, prepared myself in mind for a new job, and a day's work. The future still looked bright, as long as I have a job.

The following morning, it was cold with frost on the roads, at 5 a.m. it's dark, I'm on my way to work with my knives and chef's clothes. There's no traffic on the roads, the pavement felt sticky, as I peeled my feet off the ground from the cold ice that acted like glue. There was no noise, I could have been in a library it was that quiet, and the wintry weather was similar to a warehouse freezer.

As I approached the Victorian Mancunium red brick hotel, it stood isolated on Withington Road that was lined with shops. The hotel was surrounded by a three-foot red brick wall in the middle of a car park. Entering the front door of the warm Victorian hotel, slept 50 people. My start time was 6 a.m. with breakfast starting at 6.30 a.m. I arrived at 5.30 a.m. a bit early; I was keen because it was my first day, I wanted to get changed, prepare the menu, set a good impression, and get to know the kitchen.

I was welcomed by Dave at the reception, the same guy who gave me the interview a few days earlier. He was tall, had a soft tone to his voice, and a Billy goat beard. We said our hellos, then made our way down along corridor with a ceiling that soared forever up. Purple and mud brown fur like paper covered the walls, old fashion fifties figure eight lampshades brightened by funny looking bulbs, dimly lit the creepy dark hallway, it all resemble the *Adam's family* home.

We turned left, then a quick turn to the right, a flick of a switch, gleaming silver steel from the equipment I sighted. Dave showed me the layout of his large kitchen, steel was everywhere, equipment I've not seen before. It all glittered similar to *Aladdin's treasure trove.* This being my first job that was not a government scheme, he informed me, 'The customers would come to the hatch, take their order, and put the meal slips in this box.'

With that, he left, I got changed, and the hatch door was open at 6.30 a.m. till 10.30 a.m. The day got off to a very slow start, after one hour there wasn't a customer in sight. I'd cleaned half the kitchen equipment, it seemed not. I was beginning to wonder if there was anyone in the hotel when I heard a ping, a ping from a bell. I looked up from the cooker I was cleaning, to see a large well dress man in a well pressed dark blue suit, a clean white shirt with a lovely colourful summer tie in the middle of winter, stood at the service hatch. I said, 'Good morning sir, how can I help?'

He informed me of his breakfast requirements, which I promptly made to order, then I cleaned up, washed his plate once he had his fill. The day was really great with a bounce to my step, I proudly walked, by 11 a.m. I was at my father's place that was the end of my day, perfect. For ten days I did that, it wasn't hard I was getting £80 a week, which was good money for my age back then.

On the tenth day, payday you know, it was very much the same as the first day. I was cooking breakfast for myself, which was a lifesaver, since I had no money, a cup of coffee for Dave, and one full breakfast for the one customer, then I'd clean that's all I did. The kitchen was spotless with that at about 9 - 9.30 a.m. I'd stop to have a smoke, seated at the backdoor, which overlooked the kitchen. I could still see the kitchen hatch if anyone came, which seemed unlikely, and never did. However, on this occasion I sat there smoking when the kitchen door crept open, in came a short stout man, bald around the top with flakes of grey hair along the sides and back. I stood up to attention not knowing who he was to the establishment. I greeted him with, 'Hello, can I help you sir?'

He angrily shouted out some verbal words I couldn't understand, he was speaking in another language. After hearing his uplifting and deepfelt inspirational speech, he left the kitchen as quick as he came in. I went onto finish my smoke; I looked around the kitchen to see what could be done. I placed one foot forward to approach a job that came to mind, the kitchen door swings open, appearing from the door, Dave accompanied by the same stout man. Dave's expression was not his cheery chirpy self, he had a very serious manner along with his stout little friend, Dave questioned, 'What's been going on in here?'

In most puzzle games and quizzes, if you're clever you can solve the problem, but on this occasion I was lost to what could unfold, I'm wishing I had a crystal ball. Like a contestant in a quiz show I answered, 'Nothing. I've cleaned the kitchen, served the one breakfast, and had a smoke. Then he came in shouting, why I don't know.'

Dave looked at his little bald friend, nothing was said, but he did turn to me, stating, 'You have to go, pack your gear, and leave.'

I was taken aback, slapped in the back, shocked, I don't mean *Spock*, rocked, and there's no prize, I was surprised, it was not what I needed to hear, I wasn't sure, if I was sacked. Smoking back then was not as serious as today, you could still smoke on a bus, in some public places, and even in hospitals. So, I went onto say, 'What about my pay?'

I looked directly at the little bald man, from out of nowhere along feather tip black bullwhip appeared from behind his back.

Suddenly, like a cold wet shower a sense of fear came over me, I was wondering what he was going to do with the whip! Dave declared like an army officer, 'You'd better leave now.'

All of a sudden the atmosphere in the kitchen felt hot, sweaty and the cooker wasn't on, like a stubborn rhino, and in need of my wages, I replied, 'I'm not leaving without my pay.'

I was not prepared to leave without my money. In the time I was working there, I'd moved from my father's flat into a hostel, since the council sealed up my father's place, when I was at work one day. The rent at the grubby hostel was £40 per week plus, two meals a day. They allowed me to stay at the smelly hostel with the understanding and assurance, I would pay two weeks rent once I received my first wage.

Dave's little friend unrolled the whip, gently onto the floor like a feather falling on a mattress. Dave asserted his authority, 'If you do not leave, we'll call the police.'

Startled as if I'd seen Freddie Krueger from *Nightmare on Elm Street*, I felt braver than a frontline soldier in the Falkland Islands war, and bold, akin to the British roaring lion, I didn't do anything wrong, if they hit me, there's a lawsuit. I replied with confidence, 'Fine, get the police, I'm not leaving until I get paid.'

Silence filled the room, the only thing heard was the whistling wind drifting in the air, and the gentle creaks from the swinging backdoor. The tension was high, high as Mount Everest, and the quietness eerily haunting. It all reminded me of the house built on a hill in the black and white film, *Psycho*. They both looked at one another for a moment, then a sudden snap out of the silence into a storm of movement, they turned, and walked out of the kitchen.

With a sigh of relief, I got myself changed, by the time I came back into the kitchen from the changing room, two large and very intimidating police officers were there, a very quick response. One officer pulled me to one side, while the other officer spoke to Dave. I explained the situation to the officer, who listened keenly to what I was saying.

After speaking to his fellow officer, the policeman approached me, then told me with no terms or conditions, 'You're going to have to wait, until the end of the month to get paid, could you leave the building until then?'

This seemed so unfair when the agreement was a week in hand. So, I had to leave with no pay, which made me homeless. To top that, I never got paid my £160 before tax. This was the first of many situations, where I've worked for no pay. I didn't take them to court, being young, and naïve, I didn't know any better. Besides, the hotel closed down for one reason or another soon after. I learnt from an early age things happen when it's least needed.

I landed on my feet, finding somewhere to live in Rusholme, next door but one to my very dear loyal friend, Edwin Blair, and where we took up the new artform as deejays. After the birth of my son, my baby mother Alice becomes mentally ill with post-natal depression.

Six months after his birth, my mother is made guardian of my son making things easier for me when it came to seeing him, and I was able to take care of him on the odd weekends, without the headache of one's baby mother.

Chapter 13

Am I well or not?

After watching late night T.V. news, not unlike the tap dancer Rhapsody James tapping on the dancefloor, I tap away on the keyboard, incessantly writing, and posting blogs in response to current affairs. This particular day on the 2nd, May 2009, I found myself getting up later than usual in the afternoon. Feeling hungry with a bit of cash, after a clean, and a shave, I was on my way to the Edinburgh Cellars to have some breakfast.

It was a lovely warm spring afternoon, the London city traffic around Newington Green was quiet, and the birds could be heard chirp, chirp chirping in the built-up area, as I walked down the road. Passing old re-modernised Victorian and Edwardian shops lining the streets, looking above the off licence, greengrocer, and the cobblers shop, old sliding sash windows for flats above, standing tall and proud above all, one or two council tower blocks. This makes for a humble community in a district at the centre of a metropolitan city.

I arrived at the boozer to see no one was in the pub, and it was 1.30 p.m. As I looked out of the large window of the bar while I was waiting to be served, Terry Yoruba caught my eye from the street corner, and waved me over. I left the pub, greeted one another with two fists touching, we said our hellos, then I asked, 'Terry have you got a moment for a chat?'

Terry is a man on a search to understand, what are the causes for all the wrongs in the world, he's determined to succeed in life, love's the ladies, and he's a laugh a minute. Born in the United Kingdom he's mixed race, African descent. After inviting me into his flat, offering a drink, getting comfy, I conveyed to Terry what was on my mind concerning creationism, mankind's plight, and the compassion I was expressing towards humanity.

He sat there and listened intently, then offered up some political and religious questions to me, which I answered with an agreeable response from Terry. We saw eye to eye on most points mentioned, needing time to think about others. Then I made my way home.

Somewhere along the way to my flat, I decided it was time to go to parliament. Subsequently, I retrieved my pushbike from home, and cycled to Westminster. Only to return home having seen no one of importance.

Somehow I found myself at Sarah's flat, which is not too far away from my home. The chances are she may have called me on my mobile inviting me over for dinner, she's good like that Sarah. She made me something to eat, then we sat down on the sofa, had a few joints and a chat, about what was on my mind concerning humanity's plight to survive. What surprised me the most, I started crying for no reason that comes to mind in Sarah's lap. After a very tearful moment, I wrote the blog for the 2nd, May 2009.

Following that, I left Sarah's place for the police station to give them a copy of what I wrote for my blog. When I spoke to the duty officer at Stoke Newington police station, she questioned, 'What am I to do with this?'

I felt quite mystified with what I was doing. I answered, 'I'm just following my mind and it tells me to give you this note. Just give it to your superiors, my details are on the top of the page.'

I left the station for home and to bed, below is what I left at the police station, and my blog of the day.

2nd May 2009 7.23pm

I decree incompetence in secular, Islamic, and communist laws. I have defined logic, in so doing, I decree absolute, I rule the world, game over.

John T. Hope

Chapter 14

What's happening?

On the 3rd, May 2009, my body seemed to be doing the weirdest thing. This could only be a psychotic episode, where I lose control of my body and speech. I'm only aware, or understand this fact, after the incident, which is a statement I proceed to state.

Unlike most mornings the 3rd, May 2009 was different from others. I found myself sat at the kitchen table with my laptop open. A bright hazy sunlight beamed through the kitchen window; the room was filled with the ambiance of a church hall. In between the noise of the bustle and rush of the city traffic, a song bird sings with the soothing sound of the whistling wind gently blowing rustling leaves in the background. Subsequently, I wrote the definition for the word symbolic with my personal details for the blog of the day, but I was unable to publish until the 8th, May 2009.

After writing the unpublished blog of the day, I suddenly stood up from the chair I was sat on around the kitchen table, knocking over the chair I was sat on. I then screamed like a wolf howling at a full moon, why I just don't know. I fell to the floor where I was stood, screaming, and kicking the air in uncontrollable panic. Sensing the feeling I was being whipped or beaten, but there was nobody there to do the hitting or strike me in anyway, and I felt no pain. I was just kicking wildly in the air and screaming out loudly, 'No, no, no, oh my word, no, no, no.'

I repeated my words, crying out with no tears from my eyes, 'No, no, no, oh my word, no, no, no.'

As suddenly, as my screams started as soon as I'd stopped. I stood to my feet facing the kitchen table with the window in front of me, I could feel every single muscle within my upper body flex up tighter, and my legs felt as firm as a tree trunk. At that point,

I began growling like a big bad black grizzly bear, at nothing but thin air. I felt so primitive, furious anger but controlled, and focused at one single point. Throughout all of this, I do not believe I was asking my body to act in such away. I was asking myself, *'Why am I acting in this manner, what's going on?'*

I couldn't understand what my body was doing.

By this time, Beste had moved in with her boyfriend Mehmet, they were asleep in the spare room. I picked up the chair that I knocked over, then I sat down. At that point, similar to a bellowing whale reciting his love song, I repeatedly shouted, 'Beste, Beste, Beste.'

Banging on the wooden Ikea dinner table, each time I called her name. Very soon after, I heard a male voice with a Turkish accent, 'Fitzroy.'

I turned away from the table I was banging with my fist, to look behind my head to see Mehmet stood at the hallway door, in his red Micky Mouse boxer shorts, and a blue tee shirt. I stood up straightaway with my laptop in my hand, rushed over to him feeling excited in confused panic. I said, 'Mehmet read this, read this, give it to Beste, tell her to read it.'

Now, this was not like me, to be calling Beste in such a manner was damn right disrespectful. After giving the laptop to Mehmet, I placed myself back on the chair to start banging on the table once again, shouting repeatedly again, and again, 'Beste, Beste, Beste.'

Banging on the dinner table each time I called her name. Mehmet looked puzzled, not dissimilar to a child doing a complicated mathematical problem, and he could have been lost bewildered in the woods, he was at odds with my actions. Following that, I heard a soft female Turkish accent gently exclaim, 'Fitzroy.'

I looked behind to where Mehmet was stood to see Beste standing next to him, 'Fitzroy.'

Again, came from an even more baffled Beste looking as if she were a drunken moth flying into a wall. She held out her hand, as an offering to me to hold her hand. I felt mixed up, bewildered like a blindman in the desert, totally perplexed at what I was doing and saying. Confused, hesitantly with lack of trust, I did not replicate the gesture. Upon hearing a concern soft subtle Turkish accent, Beste verbalized, 'Fitzroy, Mehmet come downstairs to the shop, Fitzroy could you help me open the shop?'

She was so nice and gentle towards me; I could see she was trying to understand what the drama was all about. I said nothing, I was trying to comprehend what was going on myself, then they both left my flat. I sat there for a minute or two, maybe longer. I then decided to pick up my laptop and make my way to the shop downstairs.

Upon entering the shop, Beste was stood in front of the shop window on the phone, Mehmet was standing in the middle of the display area, looking towards me with the same confounded expression on his face. As I entered, I placed my laptop on a nearby coffee table that was on sale. I noticed Mehmet kept a close eye on my movements, as I passed him, and went to the back of the shop. When I got to the back, I turned to face Mehmet, at that point, I crouched down towards the floor, like I was about to leap frog out of a mystic lake. Then I started swaying from side to side, as if I were a rocking chair, I could have been rocked to sleep, weird or what. In his broken English-Turkish accent, Mehmet asked, 'Fitzroy, you hungry, you want something to eat?'

I didn't say a word, I was just crouched there rocking from side to side, looking straight at Mehmet's eyes but staring past him. I stood up suddenly, to walk behind the counter in front of the till, Mehmet was directly in front of me, on the other side of the counter, offering me a cigarette. Now, what I found really weird, as a smoker being offered a cigarette, one takes the cig, and smokes it. I never smell a cigarette, after all it's not a cigar, which is what I did, I slid the cigarette across my nose like a sliding trombone. I knew I was not myself. I was trying to make sense of what was going on in a windy whistling whirlwind of confusion in my mind.

Ring, ring, ring, the ring tone from my phone sounded off, it's my mate Edwin Blair, or Eddie as we call him from Manchester. When I answered the phone, I felt elated to hear from him, but in panic, as if there could have been a fire, puzzled, this wasn't a quiz, and excited with my situation like I was on a merry go round. Speedily I responded, 'Hello Eddie, something isn't right, I don't understand what's going on. It's really not a suitable time, my head's all over the place, I'm not myself.'

From the front of the shop, I heard Beste cry out, 'Fitzroy, should I phone for an ambulance?'

A quickfire reaction to Beste's question, I replied, 'Yes.'

In that moment, I switched conversation to state, 'Eddie I can't talk right now mate, I just do not understand what's going on. I'll call you back when I can.'

I hung up the phone, I didn't want to hear what he had to say, I was confused as if I were trying to complete a crossword puzzle, panicked not dissimilar to chickens being chased by a fox, and nervous with the whole palaver I was creating. At the very far end of Beste's shop, there is a storeroom, I made my way to the back with Beste in tow behind me, I entered the room to stand in the middle. Beste grabbed hold of my right hand asking, 'Fitzroy, are you alright?'

Beste is only five foot six inches as she looked up into my face, I stood like a giant at six-foot one inch. She was so attentive to my needs, the concern in her voice was comforting to me. When she asked again, 'Are you okay Fitzroy?

Suddenly, within my mind a sense of fear for authority came over me, something I've never felt before. To a great degree, it had a commanding presence as it got closer towards me within my mind. I straighten my back as stiff as an iron board to attention, then I cried out, 'Beste, he's coming, oh my word, he's coming now.'

Feeling proud like a father for his son's achievements, bold as a pick pocketer, panicked I'm a rabbit, bewildered is this magic, and fear of a dark creepy forest, I looked down straight into Beste's eyes, she looked up staring back. In that moment I repeated my words, 'Beste, he's coming, oh my word, he's coming now.'

In that split second, he was there, the weight of the world engulfed my head, pressing down on my shoulders, and my mind was in a wild windy whirlpool of wondrous wonder. I was asking myself, *'What is going on?'*

I felt the presence of the Good God Almighty, how do I know it was God?

Because my mind told me, like a sixth sense, my mind is the only thing I can trust. My forehead burnt from heat of an unknown source, I looked up to the ceiling, then struck a stiff pose like a lamppost, as Beste looked up into my face. At that point I cried out, 'Logic correct, logic correct, logic correct.'

Repeatedly stamping my left foot on the wooden floorboards each time, bang, I shouted, 'Logic correct.'

In between each sentence, very randomly, I stamped hard on the wooden floor, at that point I bellowed out, 'Probability incorrect.'

Throughout this psychotic episode, I heard no question, and no one was in sight. The funniest thing to my mind, while in the presence of God, one would think a man would fall to his knees, I didn't. I question, why I did not?

I was unaware how long I was saying, 'Logic correct, logic correct, probability incorrect, logic correct.'

In this time, Beste had made her way to the front of the shop, I could hear her in the distance shout out my name, 'Fitzroy.'

I stopped stamping my left-foot and crying out logic correct, then I came out to where Beste could see me from the front of the shop. I stood at the storage room door answering, 'Yes?'

She was stood at the far end of the shop in front of the window, looking worried and concerned. Beste came back with, 'The police and ambulance are here.'

I dashed over to the front of the shop, leaping over display furniture's like a graceful gazelle being chased by a vicious lion, just as a police car zoomed pass the shop window with flashing blue emergency lights, and the sound of the sirens interrupt the Sunday silence with whoop, whoop. I cried out, 'Authority.'

It's not a word I would use when referring to the five oh, or dibble, as we say up north. Everything I was doing and saying was not right, it wasn't me. I turned away to run into the changing room of the shop, which was situated pass the till but not pass the storeroom, I nearly knocked over Mehmet as I passed. I found myself in the changing room, pinned my back against the wall, eyes wide open in the dark shivering in fear of the authorities. I was only in the dark room for a moment, but the sense of fear was overwhelming.

I soon overcame my suspicions and trepidations, I came out of the changing room to see two ambulance crewmembers, and two police officers walk into the shop. Their presence filled up the large shopping display area with their size. The ambulance team asked me a few questions, before I knew it, I was on my way to the hospital.

When I came out of the shop, I looked up at the clear blue morning sky, I felt sublimed at the beauty in colours, a wondrous world, and spellbound with what I could see. The two or three grey pigeons were flying with no effort, aimlessly in no direction, and the sun beaming brightly. I was spinning around and around with a spring to my step with my hands in the air, praising our *Lord Jesus Christ.* At the same time, the ambulance crew were trying to control oncoming traffic whilst I was spinning across the road. A joyous moment, my actions, and words were not mine, I never spin around when crossing the road, I'm not stupid. In the ambulance there wasn't much that happened on the journey, I was inquisitive, looking around and out of the ambulance window, just repeatedly commenting like a curious kitten, 'What is it? What is it?'

Everything in my vision I reacted with, 'What is it? What is it?'

Knowing full well in my mind, what it is I'm looking at. I was even questioning screws to the body of the ambulance, 'What is it?'

A comforting soft female's voice from an ambulance crewmember interjected, 'Fitzroy, how old are you?'

She was nice but a perplexed sound reverberated in her voice. I sat there strapped to the chair in a safety belt, swivelling my head around similar to Stevie Wonder playing his piano. If I can, I would describe myself as an owl, wide eyed, looking at everything

74

fixed in the ambulance, and anything that moved. Calmly as I've always tried to present myself, I replied as quick as I heard the question, 'Forty-two.'

After answering her question, I went straight back into repeating, 'What is it? What is it?

Suddenly a thought occurred, I looked up straight into the female ambulance crewmember's blue eyes. In that moment I proclaimed, 'Oh my word, he's just calculated how many cars are on the road all over the world.'

At that juncture back to saying, 'What is it? What is it? What is it?'

I felt so childlike in my mannerism, and robotically stiff in my movements, it's a really weird experience, hearing words you've not thought of saying, feeling emotions you're not aware of having, saying things, you would never utter. It's bizarre watching your own body moving at its own will, and you know, you've not asked yourself to do or say that. All seeing all knowing, aware I'm not doing it.

When I arrived at Whittington hospital A & E, I was led into the reception of the hospital calmly by the three ambulance crewmembers, two police officers and a policewoman. I sat down with quiet composure in the waiting hall of A & E. As I sat down, I looked up to see waiting patients on beds, chairs, hospital equipment, doctors and nurses going about their everyday business. Suddenly and quite abruptly, I stood up shouting, 'Abomination.'

It follows, I made a quick dash for the exit, leaving the surprised police and the ambulance team standing, they soon gave chase. As they got closer in their aggressive misunderstanding manner, I could have been playing rugby, I was tackled by all parties, and escorted back into the reception area of the hospital, placed into a side room where I waited to be transferred to a ward and given an injection. You should have seen and heard what I was saying to the police officers who were watching my performance. I, it, whatever came over me, was like a staged play. I felt as proud as a peacock prancing up and down the treatment room displaying his feathers, as I paced back and forth in the box room. I was very respectful towards the police who are my equals, inquisitive like a mad scientist, wondrous as if I were watching a magician, very flamboyant, not dissimilar to a pink flamingo strutting elegantly in a sky-blue lake, and I was ever so flirtatious with the female police officer. None of this persona was me.

I could not understand at the time, I was totally confused, not panicked because I was now in a safe environment. I was just watching myself, and I, let whatever was happening, happen, what could I do. I was totally out of control of my own bodily actions. One maybe two hours after arriving at the hospital I fell asleep. In the morning, seemed like any other day, a lovely, bright spring day. I didn't understand at the time, but in the morning, I felt as if I gave birth to a new mind, or I was possessed by another. It could only be my subconscious or my conscience, John T. Hope. No longer confused, I'd like to believe a form of mental self-defence is becoming aware of one's surroundings, a sixth sense. I was without my laptop, but I was still feeling the urge to write. I asked the nursing staff if I could have a pen, paper, and the dictionary, then I incessantly started to write.

It was not until this admission into hospital, when I met with Dr Lester, and the rest of his team from Highgate Mental Health Hospital Opal Ward. I explained, what was on my mind concerning my working life, how with every attempt to do the right thing, something gets in the way of me getting paid for the job. I also informed him of my beliefs, and thoughts concerning humanity, I never knew I had. Dr Lester stated, 'We could have an interesting debate, and philosophise on creation, but there is not enough time. You just need a few days rest in hospital, and you should be able to go back to work.'

The rest sounded very inviting but going back to work I thought, *'There is no chance of that.'*

I proclaimed, 'Dr Lester, I'm not working under these conditions, it's designed so people like me, don't get a fair share of the resources. I will not take part in a game that is constructed to destroy me as well as society.'

I stayed in hospital for a few days, putting my points across to the nursing staff, and stressing them out with my reasoning, while they observed my behaviour on Opal Ward.

On the 7[th,] May 2009 I was discharged. Thereafter, I published what I wrote while I was in hospital, below is the edited blog.

8[th,] May 2009.

This should have been posted on the 3[rd,] May 2009.

Symbol stands for a sign, or a thing that stands for something else. Symbolic adjective symbolically adverb is a representation of something by symbols; movement in the arts, and literature using symbols to express abstract, and mystical ideas.

Fitzroy is an old French, or German word.

Fitz meaning bastard.

Roy meanings royal, or king.

Brian, switch I, and A, spells Brain.

Edwards is my economic slave name.

DJ Fitz E, a bastard son with two brains aka Man Egg.

My left leg has been broken at the ankle, and my jaw, has been broken. Someone came up behind me, then punched me on my right cheek, I offered the other cheek, and it was taken. I have decreed absolute.

Who

'Who is who, in your mind?
Who are you if it's not your mind?'
'A mind of its own.'
'When you sit, you just do it, or is it your mind.
If your mind is not yours, whose mind is it?'
'Saying irrational things, is that me, or is that it?'
'Doing its own thing, I think.'
'A weird, and wonderful thing, is the mind.'
'A mind of its own.'
'Even acting it out, doing illogical things.
It's an interesting mind I think.'
'That really does make me think!'
'Who is who in my mind?
Who am I?
Who could be there?'
'Inspiration; ideas, imagination, intelligence, and emotions, mainly
love for humanity, this is Nature.'
'You are the mind; I am the tool that brings it to reality.'
'A mind to do as free as I will.'
'Likewise, is my mind, and my free will.'

John T. Hope

Chapter 15

Stop writing.

It's Sunday 10th May 2009, having little or no money, I spend most of my day smoking weed when I can afford it, like I have been doing for the past twenty-five years and watching the news. Political shows broadcast 24 hours a day, reporting murder rape and war. Political indifference, influenced by the will of money and not the people. The sorrow one feels, devoid and drained of life, helpless as I watch the insane acts of humanity.

The days are so long and boring, October 2008 was my last carpentry work employment contract. That's another tale of how I've worked for four or five weeks with no pay, in the hope another job will come one's way. I still have not been paid for that job. The last I heard; the boss was on holiday, while I did the same thing for the past four Christmases. Home alone, my family lives in Manchester, I can't afford to go to my mother's home for the season. Mishaps, bad luck, or no job, sad but true, for every good luck there is twice as many with misfortune, or are the laws of probability at work?

What are the odds, this formula is used against the public by insurance companies, bookmakers, and stock markets etc. My blogs make me sound like I have a false impression of one's importance, I rant, and rave, rave, and rant, then continue to write in reply to what's said on the news of the day. Having been discharged from the hospital and putting forward ideas on how to share the resources, something in my mind was telling me, the fact I was born on the 18th, December 1966, my left leg was broken, and I have a broken jaw was important. How these things played a part in what I was trying to communicate with my doctor, didn't seem to make much sense to me at the time, as well as my doctor.

Chapter 16

Constant thoughts

Around Sunday 24th May 2009, posting blogs on profound subjects such as politics, religion, and the financial system, filled my mind with a slight paranoia when they suspended my page on a social media platform for the second time. Having Pirate Bay on the news with a link to my YouTube page, made me wonder even more, if I was being heard by the media, and having an effect on public opinion. I expressed how I was feeling to my mate Edwin, who has a wise head for his age, him being a few months older than me. He put my mind very much to rest, when he stated, 'There's lots of guy's doing what you're doing with social media linked to YouTube.'

At the same time, I was disappointed in the fact no one was reading what I was writing.

With nothing to do with my days, looking at the wonders of nature seem to take on a different point of view. I was debating in the Edinburgh Cellars whether or not, a tree thinks, comparing that with the early development stages of having the sense to close their leaves shut, or reacting like the Venus flytrap. I pondered on how each molecule of a spider's web worked as a team providing an effective weapon, home, etc. In nature, it seems chaotic, but there is natural order in chaos. I would sit at home what seemed like minutes were really hours, only realising a day or two later, I'd missed appointments at the jobcentre or doctor. I've been trying to register with my doctor for years, but for their inconvenient policies.

Since I drank and was a deejay in the Edinburgh Cellars, I became a bit more popular in the area knowing faces more than names.

There were a few people I could talk to, one of them who seem to want to know me more than me wanting to find a friend, Jeff Randell. He was reading my blogs and seemed concerned with my wellbeing. We had some debates on issues I'd posted, we agreed on some, and I left him to think on others. He explained, 'I have read a book, which was part of my course work.'

Jeff was a careers officer, his course work involved working with young adults, he added, 'You're going through a transition in your life, a new direction maybe in order.'

It seemed like good advice, but I still didn't feel comfortable with myself, people all over the world were dying, needlessly and senselessly, I make sense.

Chapter 17

Back in the day

Having been kicked out of my mother's house at the beginning of 1986 and received no pay from the hotel in Whalley Range, I was lucky to know a friend, who knew a guy, two years older than me, and went to Ducie High School, Michaël Biggs was his name, but we all called him Biggs. As is suggested in his name, he was a big muscle-bound bulldog bully in school. He was also known as Deejay Mick B, at 21, he'd just inherited the property, and was renting out a small box room. His aggressive manner reminded me of Donkey Kong losing the plot, and defensive stance comparable to a soldier in the red army. He mellowed out slightly to tracks such as *'Mellow, mellow right on'* by Lowrell, and due to the influence of his girlfriend June Clarke.

We lived at 8 Deramore Street, Rusholme Manchester, a three-bedroom red brick terrace house, where Biggs taught me the art of the turntables, along with my long-time schoolfriend, Deejay Edwin, or Eddie. He lived a door but one, at number four. Albert Reuben a fifty-year-old was a divorced road layer with his new live-in lover, and weekend drinking partner, lovely little Eve O'Connell, a part-time cleaner for the N.H.S. they both rented the second bedroom. Biggs was in the master bedroom with June, they'd been dating a couple of years.

We created a sound system with a few other mates called, the Main Attraction, building our own mid tweeters, eighteen-inch bass bins, and a number of amps to Maplin Electrical design. I became a hip hop, R & B, deejay with a bit of dance and house music thrown in. The most weed was being smoked, mates still living with their parents found number eight a safe house for top recent music and smoking the most weed.

We would travel by train with equipment in hand to Preston more often than not, due to the fact, one of our mates was attending Preston University, we were promoting house parties, in a short time we built up a reputation for playing good tunes. Then we were booked at Preston's carnival, and we took over a dancehall above a pub in the town centre. Lucky me, finding a girl for the night was never a problem during, and after the parties.

During this period, Alice was having mental health problems, it looked like the authorities would foster my son. I had to prove myself a worthy unemployed father with social services. I demonstrated this by walking from Rusholme to Salford General Hospital every day for a week, then my son Nicolas and Alice were transferred to Withington's mother and child baby unit for the mentally ill in 1986. After six months of walking in all weathers to the hospital, me and my mother applied for guardianship, which my mother won. The court thought, I was too young to look after my son, a fact that suited me.

I wasn't getting much work in the catering industry, it was not what I was looking for, and there was no social life as a chef. Having no money didn't seem much of a problem, I've never had it to be wiser. Looking back, my extended family were always at hand, whenever I asked. I was also making money selling mix tapes, plus a bit of cash from the promotions we did. The money always went back into buying music, and I was signing on, whenever I got sacked, relieved, or left a dead-end catering job.

After eighteen months living at Biggs, my eldest cousin Richard joins the army. Richard and grandma pulled me to one side to ask me if I'd move in, to keep an eye on grandma. They said, 'The extra cash from my rent would come in handy for the family.'

So, I moved in. At this point, I was still seeing Beverly, as well as other women, who knew I had a queen. When I first met Beverly, I was introduced to a guy called Fitzroy Russell, otherwise known as Russ, and his younger brother, Brian Russell. Their names are very much a coincidence, so it seems. Russ was seeing Beverly's younger sister Sherri. Me, and Russ became good friends. Club nights out with the two sisters was great fun, full of laughter, and if I can say myself, we were good looking couples.

My Grandparents Mr. and Mrs. Walker who lived in Hulme,

decided to go back to Jamaica, after Thatcher introduces the poll tax. My step grandad thought it was an unfair tax on the poor. The sound system broke up, after a year or so. When I moved into grandma's she could see that I had a love for music. When I wasn't with Beverly, or some other girl, most nights having no money, I'd stay at home. As a result, at a very low volume, I'd practice on the turntables, I managed to get from a member of the ex-sound system, Barry Oxbridge. Grandma wanted to see me work, or join the army, the army wasn't likely.

Grandma did find me a job, as an apprentice carpenter for a company in Stockport called C.S.C. Construction, advertised in the local church she attended. A three-year apprenticeship, over five hundred applied for three positions, part of the Moss Side and Hulme Task Force to regenerate the area. I was employed and doing a City & Guilds in carpentry and joinery. I studied at the John Unsworth College of Building on Quay Street, once a week, next door to Saint John's College, where I met Alice. Thereafter, I was placed on various building sites, doing on site training, and carpentry around Greater Manchester.

It was at this point Beverly's lovely mother sadly passed away. Having no father around, Beverly, and her four other sisters decided to sell the family home. Without talking to me about the matter, Beverly placed both our names on the council housing list. Upon getting an offer for housing, we both decided to live together at 38 Cadogan Street, Moss Side, a two-bedroom terrace house, just before my twenty second birthday. Grandma wasn't pleased, as I was falling back on the reason for being there. I was of the mind grandma was not there for me, when I left my mother's home, why should I care to stay now?

Besides, I was moving two streets away from where grandma lived. I took a step back from buying music, while I was living with Beverly. She didn't like me smoking weed, so I gave up using the drug. My new job as a trainee carpenter was not paying much and I was trying to buy tools for my new trade. I couldn't afford to buy technics turntables, so the boys in the sound system took the set I practiced on back.

Russ and Sherri moved in for a brief time, he was just as bad with the women. When his loudmouth Jamaican baby mother came knocking at Cadogan Street, one lovely evening I was having with Beverly. Beverly answered the door, to hear this Jamaican woman probe her, 'Where's my man Fitzroy?'

Believe me when I say Beverly shouted my name like Tarzan coming to the rescue, 'FITZROY!'

When I got to the door to see this woman, it took the strange woman by surprise when I replied, 'What is it? Who are you?'

She looked very stupid, as the correct Fitzroy, Russ was not there to answer questions. Russ and Sherri both moved out after a few months, when everyone found out I was not paying the rent. I was spending the money on nights out, come weekend Manchester was lively, and a man, had to look good. I cannot say, I was irresponsible with money. I've never had enough to act freely or to do as I choose.

Chapter 18

Music lovers

Day in day out, doing something isn't too bad, doing nothing is boring and sad. I'm sleeping irregularly with no plans, the alarms never on, so its bed when I want to, and up when I'd prefer not, 2 a.m. writing a blog, 3 a.m. let me start again. I've never been into the internet, or p.c. world, being a manual worker, power tools and music are my toys. With all my misfortune, and downturn in luck within the building industry, it was time for a change. Part of that effort was joining social media platforms and discovering YouTube in 2008. Most of the tracks I could remember, which were stolen from me back in 1993 could be seen on YouTube. This and a link with social media was a great tool as a way of promoting my promotional nights and venues.

Things were slow at first, but okay. As a new London promoter, it was to be expected with a goodnight in the Edinburgh Cellars, and a really good evening when I joined forces with another promoter in West London. The next two nights at two other venues went tits up, in a bad financial way. What really did my head in, was what occurred at the Edinburgh Cellars next time round.

I arranged a day in December 2008 with Neil & Simon to attend a meeting, to discuss a night I wanted to put on in the Edinburgh Cellars for 30th April 2009. We could not agree on a deal, they just offered the gate takings when I wanted eight percent of the bar, as well as the gate, for half the cost of the door attendants, and taking care of the promotion, deejays etc. Since we could not agree terms, I left the meeting with no deal.

A few days later, I was doing some repair work on the stair handrail of the Edinburgh Cellars when Neil approached me, offering the deal I wanted. Hence, I gave him £100 for the cost of the door attendants and arranged to have a thousand flyers printed. The lot cost me just under £200. Thereafter, I had the task of putting the flyers out, and around north central London on my pushbike. The promotional night didn't seem like a good deal, I was getting the impression from people that other deejays and promoters received a far better contract. It really didn't matter to me, I have a very good fanbase in the area, and my love of music made it worth the sacrifice. A lot of clubs and pub owners play on one's ego, to win you over to their terms. At the same time, I had little, or no money to find another venue.

The Edinburgh Cellars maybe a pub, but they had a late license until 4am. I could charge the customers after 11 p.m. given a decent price, which was £3 all night or £10 for a party of four people. Two lovely friends, Sasha De Val an aspiring artist, who is good natured, works hard, and Jane Shantell Harris the glamour queen of Newington Green, or should I say Black Diamond, took care of the guests and their coats. They worked in a very professional manner, the Hilton Hotel at the Edinburgh Cellars, lovely job.

The party animals slowly developed into a warm friendly crowd. While I, Deejays Tim, and Deejay Revenge, both very good friends took care of the decks raving up the dancefloor. Having had a good night, which I needed, I broke even on the gate after paying for flyers. The four staff I employed for the night, understood what I was trying to do as a small new business idea, worked the whole night for nothing, real good friends, there's love for you.

As the night came to an end, there is always one who starts something mischievous. Usually, a guy who cannot handle his drink, and can't get a girl for the night. It was about 1.30 a.m. and the nights going well. I'm on the turntables playing some R & B, Deejay Revenge was due to play at another venue, and Deejay Tim left the pub with my record box, leaving his records instead. An easy mistake, but the situation left me in a jam, as that box had all my house music, and I didn't know Tim's tunes. When I tried to explain to a customer who wanted to hear funky house, the guy was not happy, and went onto comment, 'The event was shit and a wasted effort putting the night on.'

I was not happy with his remark, neither his attitude nor his manner, as he swung from side to side waving a glass of beer. Neil did not put any door attendants on for the night cutting costs that I paid for. Most of my friends were there and aware of the fact. When I asked the pisshead customer to leave the venue, he didn't take it kindly. The next thing, the pisshead started shouting out a lot of verbal street words and kicking the deejay booth. My friends who were stood around the area came over with force, four or five men pushed the pisshead out towards the main pub door. It took a minute or so, but they managed to get him out. Amid the loud screams from party people, bodies pushing and shoving away from the men barging out, the situation calmed down after a few minutes.

Then I went onto play a track, things seemed to settle down, the crowd floated back onto the dancefloor like ducks to water. I had my eye on one or two ladies, three or four had their eyes on me. Things seem to get back to normal as quick as the uproar started. All the guys involved came back into the Edinburgh Cellars, laughing and joking about the drama. The two ladies I had my eyes on sat with their backs against the large pub window, which was alongside the deejay booth. The two women I had my eyes on were all smiles with me, rocking their bodies to the rhythm of the beat. They just sat there staring at me, it looked like I was in for a good night, and a treat with, which girl to pick, or could I have both queens was the sexual fantasy on my mind.

Suddenly out of nowhere, an almighty bang, like a clap of thunder echoed in the pub, bang, bang, bang in quick succession. I turned to look outside; all I could see was a lone figure running along the length of the pub, smashing four very large windows of the boozer from outside. The two ladies who were sat in front of the window were so lucky the windows did not shatter all over them, as they dived to the pub floor for cover in fear for their lives. An eruption of panic came over the customers, loud screams, bangs from tables chairs falling and glasses could be heard breaking. People were running chaotically in misdirection, looking frantically for the main door and fire exits. Neil, Simon, and my mates dashed outside, chasing after the lone figure that was running in the distance. All four windows that faced the main road were smashed, and fragmented.

Seeing that no one got hurt, the first thing on my mind was who was going to pay for the damage. When Neil and Simon return to the pub, the lights were on, it was half empty, and put a premature end to a goodnight with the two women I liked gone, out of sight. I expressed to Neil who was slightly exhausted after his hundred metre dash after the lone stranger, I proclaimed, 'I know a window fitter who could do the job.'

Panting heavily as if he just missed the bus, Neil was trying to catch his breath, still panting quite deeply he asked, 'How much would it cost and when could he do it?'

Not being a glass fitter, I answered, 'I couldn't give a price for the windows, but I can call him first thing in the morning to see when he could come round.'

There was a slight pause then Neil responded, 'Okay.'

I was feeling a bit concerned about my pay. I needed to feel reassured I could give something to the good people who tried to help me. So, I went onto confirm, 'Neil, this has gone tits up, no matter what, everyone involved gets a meal on the Edinburgh Cellars.'

There was a secondary pause for a moment, a bit longer than the first. Neil replied, 'Okay.'

That proposal of mines could have been a mistake, all the same. I turned to look around the pub, to see the staff cleaning, and clearing broken glasses around the bar. While Jay Fuller the head bartender was totalling the cash. I called him over in a quiet manner to ask, 'Jay, how did we do tonight?'

He walked over to where I was stood, on the opposite side of the bar, uttering, 'Not a bad night Fitz, £3360, we could have made a lot more but for an early end to the night.'

With that I shouted, 'Goodnight everyone.'

I made my way home feeling pissed off and apprehensive about how much I'd receive from the nights taking, now the windows were smashed. 8 a.m. that morning, I called my mate Preston Phillips, a body builder, and a window fitter to see if he was busy, he was not doing anything that day. I explained the night before. Preston responded, 'I will do the Edinburgh Cellars a cheap deal as a favour to you.'

After grabbing a bit more sleep, I found myself down at the pub to see what was happening about the windows. When I arrived, Preston was already there with two very big windows fitted and fitting the third. It was 5 p.m. the same day, I thought great, good man, he made me look good, dependable, and reliable. After saying hello to Preston, I asked, 'How much you charging them?'

He answered, '£500 for labour and materials. If they went to a company, they would charge £1,000 to £1,500 easy.'

I thought, *'Top man.'*

I then went into the pub to have a word with Neil and Simon, about my pay. Given the situation from the night before, I've done my part of the deal, but Neil and Simon didn't believe they owed me anything. Simon was not aware of the agreement, and no contract signed between me, and Neil. Yet they agree to pay for dinner to everyone involved. This is one of many ideas and plans made waste by someone else's actions. Where is my right to get paid for my efforts?

It doesn't end there. I found out a few weeks later, Neil's insurance company paid out £2200 for the damages to the window. If you believe this is what is good about the capitalist system, then you will understand, why there is so much crime. Neil and Simon knew what stress I was going through with my work, so the question is, do people help and enjoy your downfall if they know one is in need?

I believe yes, greed, over the need to feed. There's the demons deed, greed propagates, the devil's endeavours.

Chapter 19

Taboos cause and effect.

At twenty-one, my first Monday on a building site was the start of an enjoyable working life. When I had the task of screw fixing battens to the windows, by the time it was Friday, my hands were red raw from the hand screw I was using. There were no cordless drills back then. Do I sound old when I'm not. I was doing all aspects of my job fitting doors, window frames, and locks, all kinds of work, it was great.

A year or so into the job, I was working on a new roof with four other chippies in Whalley Range, just on the edge of Gooch Estate. The area was well known in Manchester for violent gang members selling their drugs, and shootings, which was never the scene me and my friends were involved in at the time. The district was well known for prostitutes.

From time to time, looking down from the top of this new building complex, we would see the girl's parade their assets to slow moving traffic, the odd car would stop. Dog whistles echoed out from the builders as a gust of wind rushed in, whirling and swirling. The whistling wind caught the moment like Marilyn Munro standing over a fan, we viewed the prostitute's knickers while she was peering into a car's window.

One day, all the builders watched a very attractive woman take off her knickers in the middle of the road, barely able to stand she was just about capable of controlling herself, she was more concerned for the can of beer she had in her other hand. Then she climbed into a car parked nearby.

The indignant way men and women treat the act, and the instrument of love is undignified, demeaning, owned when one cannot be owned, the pleasure it brings, is a desire that is forbidden, and despised, if over enjoyed, cheapened to be made worthless. People all over the world are very confused, and don't understand, it's a pleasurable delight, respect one another in the act of friendship, or a close bond.

A few years later, the same girl became one of my punters, heads, or drug users when I was involved in selling drugs. She approached me with no money, I felt sympathy, compassion, and uncomfortable at her clucking from withdrawal. I took her back to my house, sat her down, and gave her what she needed, crack cocaine and heroin.

I gave her some food, she looked unfed, as if she were from an African famine, underweight, someone with anorexia looked healthier, a worn-out tire had more use. While I prepared, cooked, and her eating a meal, I asked, 'How and what made you start using class-A drugs?'

I felt ashamed for being a man, bitterly disgusted of what some men can do when she retorted in a shamefully proud defensive tone, 'A guy gave me a Charlie spliff, unbeknown to me, I thought it was weed.'

She was honest when she mentioned she enjoyed the smoke. She continued to comment, 'This guy got me started on the drugs, I've been hooked on it for six years. He also took advantage of me; we went back to his flat, then he fed me more drugs, as a consequence, he had his way for six days, I was unable to leave.'

She added with a lot of contempt in her voice, 'He got his kicks out of tying me up.'

At sixteen she'd just left home to meet this guy with nowhere to go, she was running from her stepfather and her stepbrother's sexual exploitation. Soon after her mother's death from alcohol addiction, and terminal stress. The mother's condition was brought on by her husband who sexually, and psychologically abused her mother. Her mother wanted to leave him years before, but for the fears, stigma, and social values of the young girl's grandparents. Her mother stayed with her stepdad to have an early death. This young attractive girl sounded bitter, a sour apple could not have had a worst taste, twisted as a hurricane, and held deep seeded hatred for men to earth's core. I hope I showed her for that brief moment of two minds just talking, not all men are like that.

We send our kids out to an unsafe world. It starts from government ideology, policy, and philosophy. If there is no love from the governing body, it reflects in society, and individuals show no love or respect for one another, not even family.

Family ties

The sight of love, the warmth from my mother's eyes.
A deep tender voice, the advice from a father's conscience.
The sweet smell of a birthday cake emanating
from grandma's kitchen.
Tripping up, on your brother's love,
'Ahh, that bloody skateboard.'
Whose make ups whose?
Sisters lovingly fight, who is the prettiest sis.
The family love can be lots of fun on a Sunday afternoon,
distant family love comes but once a year,
many not seen, until that special day.
It's funny, love, and what distance does, memories of love,
and laughter.
Lessons in life can only be taught and
learnt through the labour of love.
Love can only be given then received, anything else is just a
selfish passion a desire your love would surely please.
There not the ones who should hear one's anger,
but the powers that be, who divide us.
The division of a family's love isn't a subject for the governing
bodies, they know they're the cause, divide,
and conquer is their daily chore.
Breakdown the community, install lack of faith and trust,
dishonour his holy name, then they try to claim
the fame that's the body's game.

John T. Hope

Chapter 20

Expressing self-awareness

Around mid-June 2009, after being released from hospital I met Joanna Huber at Drayton Park social services, off Holloway Road, London. Upon meeting Joanna, a southern, United States of American woman was warm, open minded, and tried to cater for my needs. Joanna always phoned me an hour or so before my appointment time, she was well aware I'd lose time lost in free wondering thought and busy writing. Joanna patiently listened for 30 minutes once a week, never having enough time, our appointments always ran over to 45 minutes or more.

I expressed my concerns for humanity's plight, how society was enslaved to the monetary system by the will of a tenacious bully on a community that loved, and how my life to date, has been an example of black exploitation of the labour force, which has caused my illness, or can I say, kick started me becoming aware of my subconscious.

Since I was not on any medication when leaving the hospital, it gave me the chance to understand, and be more aware of John's personality, or persona, as well as trying to distinguish my own thought pattern from John's. The time I spent with Joanna was invaluable, the subject matters I was referring to were profound topics. Joanna showed empathy for my concerns, not fully understanding who John was. When I tried to explain, how I was not in control of my body or speech. Joanna said, 'You sound like you're having an outer body experience.'

My friends were concerned but I didn't want to be an imposition by expressing my views, opinions people don't really want to hear, when there is not much anyone can do. Then, there's that clash of beliefs, but I needed some form of outlet. Joanna, sat patiently, and listened, which was far more than Dr Lester.

I was unable to pay my mounting bills from £83 a fortnight, the financial stress was a heavy load, I had no intention of playing the game economics. In my mind, any cash I received allowed me access to the resources, and to express very little free will. Joanna suggested we should apply for Living Disability Allowance.

I stated in a defiant mood, 'It may be a clever idea, if you paid my bills because I have no intention of paying what little benefit I receive on bills.'

Joanna just looked at me with a blank expression on her face, like a clown that doesn't know any good jokes, added, 'Could you sign this L.D.A. form, I'll fill out the details later.'

Nothing in the day is more important than listening to the news and current affairs. An unmovable tear would occasionally slide down my cheek, hearing the news of someone's death. I was beginning to have more control, or I'm able to separate the feelings of Fitzroy, from John's.

Another plane crashes, earthquakes in Italy, floods in Asia, G20 protests, and fires in America. It was all happening, all signs in my mind of God's hand at work, but the world is blind to his movements. As a consequence, I continued to write frantically, responding to world affairs, intuitively knowing how the leaders felt with the political indecisions. My compassion for the suffering was swelling, Fitzroy and John felt helpless, wanting desperately to be heard, believing in what he's writing because Fitzroy does not write.

Echo

'I hear thoughts from an echo, in my mind, no voice,
no noise, just an echo with no sound.'
'No one hears this voice, it's only the mind that knows.'
'I thought I said, it's left; my mind says, it's right.'
'An echo of inspiration, information from whose
mind is that sound?'
'An answer to a question that was never asked.'
'No one is aware what it's about.'
'There's one, no there's two, the echo's maybe three.'
'Look it's only me there, are you there?'
'An echo of an idea, a thought that came to my mind.'

John T. Hope

Chapter 21

Stress conscious related

This morning is no different than any other, looking at things from a realistic point of view, my situation is not very good. Over the years, irregular signing on for benefits, unusual working patterns, and wages not paid, caused escalating unauthorised overdrafts accumulating to £803. Mounting banking interest gave the impression I was swimming against a current that grew stronger at every bend. Housing benefit demanding repayment for their overpayments £1,479.

The Benefit Agencies now cross reference spent earnings against tax paid to date from benefits received over the years. This is the government's way of finding funds to balance their books via the backdoor. Whereby, people on benefit have to find money they haven't got. My rent arrears came to £650 with a summons to attend court on the 17th August 2009, gas and electric £3k, other bills like credit cards, and loans.

A sudden almighty thud, clap of thunder struck, the letterbox closed shut, mail landing on the floor, the banging noise within one's mind, bills, bills, bills. Right now, it doesn't matter to me, I'm fighting back, let the council take me to court. The state's action against me for bills unpaid when I have contributed to society only to be treated unfairly, in my mind this is an inhumane act. British secular law needed to be questioned at the cost of my home, what do I have to lose?

I have nothing whether I'm working or not. One of the main reasons why our ancestors became farmers is so the community did not speculate on an unforeseen future with the shared labour for love. This philosophy and practice helped to drive the primitive savagely demonic, primeval sense of being out of humanity.

A couple of weeks after the party on the 30th April 2009, Neil invited me over to the pub for a quote on a job, thinking to myself, *'Quote yes, doing the work, no.'*

When I arrived at the Edinburgh Cellars, Neil introduced me to an ex-soldier, Roland Pennington. As we talked the talk drinking beer, supping up and chatted, reasoned about war, being an ex-frontline soldier, I valued his conscious voice. I could hear confused pain of friends lost, life he himself took plagued on his mind, but it wasn't said in so many words.

He was trying to justify his actions with a poem he recited. The poem makes men feel fired up for war, causing the heart to beat harder, never racing fast enough with the excitement of rage, and hunger for the victory of seeing blood. I'm not one for reading, but I was beginning to understand increasingly, how powerful words on paper can be, if not used or understood can be mistaken and taken out of context from the real message, *'How senseless war is.'*

A few days past, when John proved to be too emotional when I had the pleasure of meeting the brave ex-soldier again. Roland confronted me over what was said between us in our previous conversation. But on this occasion, he seemed excitedly agitated, not being able to stand in one place, unsettled like a big baby not wanting to sleep, an annoyed supreme judge could not be as frustrated, and a tormented mind couldn't be more troubled. His guilt was apparent, his rage built up in misdirection, my direction. Roland found it difficult to justify his actions as a soldier fighting for the benefit of the British way of life.

In a deep subtle voice with a calm approach I argued, 'If your uneducated ancestors fought and won a war, where they may have been in the wrong, does that make the war today right if it seems your opposition is wrong?'

Roland was speechless for a brief moment, his eyes rolled round like a white bowling ball when he looked up towards the ceiling. He then lowered his head, wires of red blood streaked through the white in his eyes. The soldier looked straight into my eyes with a deep dark empty stare, as if you were in a cave full of rage. He replied, 'Look at my legs!

Are you saying me and my friends, fought, and lost lives for a way of life that maybe a lie?'

He straightened up his painted stained jeans to hide along deep trench of missing muscle from what was a tree trunk chunky sized leg. I could not take my eyes from his leg. Tears welled up blinding my vision, I turned to run to the toilet overwhelmed with tears and empathy for his confused psychological pain, I was shocked at his constant physical reminder. My uncontrollable emotional outburst embarrassed me, I ran to the toilet hearing the soldier mutter, 'What's wrong with him?'

In the growing distance from across the bar I heard Neil, who was overlooking our conversation respond, 'I don't know, he's been really weird for weeks now.'

What they didn't understand is how money, and war was being used to pull love apart.

Dead soldier's letter

'The sacrifice of the dead, I wonder what would be said.'
'Dear World Leaders,
Sacrifice was made for peace, lonely is our head, pain comes from a
cold heart, lost dark eyes, sight never gained, memories of forgotten
smiles, tastes very rotten, a smell that's not forgotten,
the sacrifice of the dead for peace in your bed.
Now that you're well fed, if the truth was to be told, we don't
believe it's worth it, it's lonely being dead for
a cause that wasn't worth it.
The advice from the dead that pest in your head, it's a conflict of
conscience those lives and your conscience,
talking the reason for your appointment, look now we're dead.
Yours sincerely, live in peace, dead soldiers.'

John T. Hope

Chapter 22

Crack lives

Although we went to the same secondary school, I did not spend as much time with Peter once my family moved to Fallowfield. By the age of thirteen or fourteen he was in detention centres for one offence or another. It's now 1989, so it came as a pleasant surprise to see him outside the betting shop on Moss Lane East, when I came off the number 15 bus after a hard-working day on site. We walked round to my house on Cadogan Street and had a laugh about the good old days in Hulme, then he went about his business.

A few days later, work in the morning, chilly winter nights always made it a very enthusiastic moment for me come bedtime with Beverly. Hearing a knock on the door was not something I encouraged my mates to do after 10 p.m. It was now 12.38 a.m. a few days after seeing Peter, and I was not very happy as I approached the front door. Upon opening the door, Peter was stood there looking innocent when he is always guilty, stating, 'Sorry Eggy, I know it's late, I need your skills as a chippy mate.'

Pissed off with the fact it's cold as the North Atlantic and screwing a ton because I'm not in bed with Beverly. I replied, 'What's the problem?'

He stood there with his fake big brown puppy dog eyes, but I know he's a wolf in sheep's clothing, yet loyal to his friends like a Taliban warrior. Peter muttered in the cold midnight air, 'Look out here Eggy.'

He pointed to a door on Normanby Street, which was at right angle to Cadogan Street, Peter continued, 'I've managed to damage a front door on that street and I've broken a glass door inside, I'll give you fifty quid, if you could fix it now!'

It was late, but fifty pounds was twice as much as I was earning in the day. Overjoyed for the extra cash I proclaimed, 'Hold up mate, let me get my tools, and let Beverly know the score.'

After telling Beverly what had occurred, I picked up my tools, I then made my way over to the house Peter pointed out. As I approached, the front door was slightly opened with the hallway light on. I pushed open the door shouting, 'Peter, Peter.'

All I could see on the floor were varying sizes of dogshit, decorated with bits of woodchip. I looked up to the door to see the mortice lock had come away from the doorframe, the damage wasn't too bad. Peter raced down the steps asking, 'Do you think you can fix it?'

This job look like a good earner, I replied, 'Yeah, not a problem mate.'

Within fifteen minutes the lock was fixed, looking at the floor helped to push my efforts in getting the job done, I just wanted to get out as soon as, quick. Job done, I shouted out, 'Peter, jobs done.'

Peter answered, 'Come upstairs.'

As I tip toed over the brown blobs blotted on the floor, I leapt up the flight of stairs like a show jumping horse. I was hoping I'd leave the mess downstairs just to find the same upstairs, but some of the brown blobs of shit had fermented turning white, sick at the sight. I turned my head to see a young blonde girl through an open door, seated on the floor, her face was pale, white as snow. Her legs were spread wide open, wearing filthy grubby dirty soiled pink knickers for the world to see, some show. In her right upper leg, looked like a syringe needle was stuck in her. Peter called out my name, 'Fitz, can you fix this window?'

I looked round to where Peter was pointing to the upper part of a door, which was a glass panel, and shattered. I reacted, 'I can fix it, but you'll have to wait until I come back from work before I can get the glass to repair the damage.'

He looked a bit pissed off, but he realised it would be very difficult finding a supplier at this late hour. Peter replied, 'Okay.'

As I turned to leave, I caught sight of the girl, it looked like she'd passed out when a tall dark male figure appeared from nowhere. He bent down on his knees over the girl, as I walked toward the stairs, I could see the man fondle the girl's crutch, and savagely rough up her breast with his big dirty shovel like hand. I turned my head in disgust, like a fighter jet I flew down the stairs. Drug users, are they low lives, or does society make them lowlife?

If there is no respect for life, why should our kid's think any different if we as adults cannot treat life with respect.

Chapter 23

Was it fun?

When I was living behind the frontline of Moss Lane East at 38 Cadogan Street wasn't so bad. Until there was a scene, and an outburst of aggression from Dan Redbridge, a bad-tempered, unknown idiot, and a troublemaker. I was at a late-night party in Limbeck Crescent Hulme near Moss Side shopping centre.

While I was enjoying the reggae music being played through the deep bass bins in an empty dark room, a slight crack of light shone from the toilet into the hallway. It was only 1.45 a.m. the clubs were still open, and people were due to full up the house party about 2.30 a.m. When Dan's face appeared from a crack of light produced from the toilet. He was one of the first to walk in, alongside two young women. They were shouting at one another over the loud music. I thought, *'It's time to leave.'*

When I began to make my way out, as I passed the three heading towards the front door, one of the girls shouted, 'Fitzroy, please help us!'

Looking at the situation, in my mind I knew one of the girls who happened to be a couple of years younger than me. I remember her from Ducie High School, but I couldn't remember her name, and I know Dan, but I was a closer schoolmate to his half-brother Donald Redbridge. I thought, *'I may be able to calm the situation down, since they both knew me.'*

Dan did not take it that way, he was very aggressive the moment I said, 'Hi Dan, what's happening man?'

He pushed the two girls out of his path as if they were pins in a bowling alley, forcing me to back up against the wall as he approached, before I realised, or could react to the drama unfolding, the Deejay was over to where we were stood, pulling Dan away. The Deejay told Dan, 'Come out of the blues party!'

Dan turned to walk out, but not before giving me the stabbing eyes of hate. Then the Deejay turned to me declaring, 'Give it a few minutes, then you must leave the party.'

A few moments went by when I could see in the distance the Deejay's eyes glow as red as a tomato, giving me the evil eye, like Dracula hypnotising his victims as he emerges from his coffin in the dimly lit room. I got the message; it was time for me to leave. Sure enough, I made my way home to Cadogan Street, I walked about two hundred yards from the party, under the dark passageway of the flats built above, a distant streetlamp lit up the area, but casted more dark spooky shadows than providing light. Silly me, walking home relaxed, carefree, and not thinking the situation could escalate, I heard a voice from behind me shout out, 'You think your bad.'

I turned to see who was behind me, as I did so, I received a sharp cut just under the left-hand side of my nose. I made a movement to stop the bleeding to hear from a distance, 'No.'

When I looked up to see Donald runover to Dan and pull him away. Smothering my upper lip with my hands to stop the blood gushing out of my face, within my mind I heard, *'Run.'*

In that moment, I made a quick dash for Moss Side police station, which was not too far away to report the matter. I arrived at the police station to be seen by W.P.C. Jane Kent. She took me to Manchester Royal Infirmary where I received four stitches. The officer then drove me back to the station, whereby I gave her a statement.

I couldn't help but notice how very attractive she looked with her long legs and tightly fitted black uniformed pants. Before I knew it, for every question she asked about the incident, I had a personal question for her. She liked the way our conversation was flowing as my words pitter pattered at her attractive allure. Her large breast were pressed tightly within her uniform, made her chest look similar to a puffed-up pigeon, and her pale white skin sparkled like a pearl coming out of the deep blue sea. I asked, 'How long have you been married?'

Her small cheap wedding ring was plain to see. She answered

readily, 'Five years.'

Her expression was a very unhappy despair. She continued, 'He's another officer and bit of a pig in bed.'

I was quick off my feet, a bit like Usain Bolt when hearing what she proclaimed. I rapidly responded, 'Do you give good head?'

At the end of the interview, after looking at a few mugshots, and seeing no pictures of my attacker Dan, she enquired, 'What time does your girlfriend go to work?'

As I looked into her big blue bulging eye's she gave me a smile of approval, I unwittingly stated, 'She leaves about 8 a.m.'

I made my way home arriving at 7.30 a.m. Beverly was half dressed for work, worried.

I came home later than usual; Beverly became even more concerned when seeing my upper lip in stitches, I then had to tell her about the drama between me and Dan. At ten past eight there's a knock on the door. After Beverly answers the door, she returns to inform me, 'It was a policewoman making sure you got home safely.'

Within my mind, I was gutted like a fish, I really didn't think W.P.C. Kent would knock on the door for the bed work. Since then, I've had many close encounters with Dan, him having knives or a gun on a couple of occasions, I was running in fear for my life. After speaking to his family, I was slightly educated about the new drug, crack cocaine, it was mentioned in Grandmaster Flash 'White lines,' and K Solo 'Tales from the crack side,' the tunes make a lot more sense now. Following a chat with Dan's family, it was decided the best solution was to press charges in order for Dan to get off the drugs. He was caught, about a year after the party, and was imprisoned for a period of time.

A few months later, I came home one evening to see a man in my house after 10 p.m. selling life insurance, while Beverly was in her night clothes. I didn't say anything, I just thought of Beverly differently, when one or two other things got under my skin. So, I started getting involved with a girl in Bury called Lora Wright.

At the same time, I had no future plans with the woman, her two overactive kids put me right off the idea of wanting to take things further. Beverly was number one, but I wanted more of I don't know what. This girl from Bury, enjoyed smoking a weed, and it wasn't before long, after eleven months drug free, I was back smoking weed again.

One Saturday night, I thought enough is enough between me and Beverly. When I came back to Cadogan Street after an evening out, I brought back a girl I'd just met while I was walking home. My intentions was to be a lot more intimate. Beverly wasn't very pleased when I woke her up to hear me say, 'I have a girl downstairs, I'm going to have sex with her, if you don't like it, there's the door.'

Let me tell you, it's a very good way to piss a woman off. A big shouting match broke out as Beverly flew down the stairs to kick the woman out, and sort matters out between the both of us. Beverly moved out a few days later. I ask myself many times, why I did that, but yet to find an answer, I just followed my mind at the time.

Chapter 24

Poetic flair

On the 28th, July 2009, my present mental health didn't seem to be much of a problem, until I went into Beste's shop that afternoon. The shop wasn't doing much business when I walked in, Beste was sat at the counter working on the computer. Beste greeted me with, 'Hello Fitzroy, how are you feeling today?'

As I walked towards the counter where Beste was sat, I thought, *'A warm greeting but the comment reminded me of what a nurse might say.'*

As I approached, I answered, 'Hello, I'm fine thanks.'

Now, the weird thing in my mind is how I then started to speak to Beste as I approached her. I turned so only the left-hand side of my face could be seen from her point of view, as much as I tried, I could not face her, face to face. I lifted up my left leg, suddenly there was an almighty bang on the wooden floorboards, as I stamped on the floor with my foot, causing Beste to jump as if she was a jack in the box. In a deep husky voice, I bellowed out similar to the echo of Big Ben, 'You are a witness to this cosmic event.'

Bang, an earthquake hit the floor again, as I stomped on the wooden floorboards with my left foot, I repeated, 'You are a witness to this cosmic event.'

Beste was startled like a scared little fluffy white bunny rabbit that's just seen a snake, and already under a lot of financial stress, lost her cool, blew her top off, identical to a volcano, her face was fiery red with rage. Beste pushed the computer screen onto the floor shouting, 'Leave me alone I don't need this shit Fitzroy.'

She didn't understand what was happening to me, I was fully aware I would say, and do things that was not me, or of my own will. There wasn't much I could do within my mind, I thought,

'As long as I don't hurt anyone, I'm no harm to myself.'

I went home only to go back five minutes later to say, 'Sorry.'

I startled Beste a bit, it's not something someone in their right mind would do. I then came back to my flat to continue writing.

Dee as a result for my English exam, showed up well when I look back at the first print published blogs. Not being much of a reader, only writing a letter if I had to, the blogs were full of grammar and spelling mistakes, which improved as time went on. At this point, I didn't know there was a dictionary on my laptop. As a consequence, I was referring to a pocket dictionary, which doesn't give anyone a full meaning to a word, like logic. I noticed within my writing, I rhymed words with poetic flare, prose someone suggested. Not that I knew what prose meant. I thought, *'It was a nice comment.'*

This needed encouraging, my efforts, think harder, it was all very surprising, my words seemed very powerful. If I can say myself words of wisdom, this really wasn't me. It was much later on when publishing my blogs, it came to mind to publish two books.

31st July 2009 the blog of the day.

PLEASE stop fighting, this has got to stop, this is because of money and resources, stop fighting. This is Fitzroy writing, *'I am very surprised, I am trying to get to grips with me writing, when I never write. Then I remember or I'm reminded John is doing all the writing, Fitzroy's hands are just the tools.'*

'You're back to John writing.'

I have always liked, Tina Turner, *'What's love got to do with it.'* Not one I would play in my set, but it just got me thinking, *'Who needs a heart when a heart can be broken.'*

We need our heart to pump the blood around the body, the feeling of love is in our mind. The heart would do anything for the sake of love, all for the mind.

So, the thought of love was of a love one had, it was a love for the mind, and what the mind believed, and wanted.

Is the love you have, the love you want, when love seems hard to find?

Is the love you have, not the one you want because for others it's easy to find?

Or is the love you want, the love you cannot have because the rules aren't the same for the other?

John T. Hope

Chapter 25

Can't help it!

We may not have been living together, but I was still seeing Beverly when she moved out of Cadogan Street to live with her eldest sister. About a year or so had passed, by the time she'd moved out of her sister's with the sale of the family home, and buying a house close to Great Universal Stores, Ardwick. It was a period when I was coming out of my apprenticeship, there wasn't much change on the employment front, unemployment was up, and construction was down. I had a young boy living at my mother's house to feed with no job, and no money. I needed to make some cash, at twenty-four years old with little finance saved on the small apprentice wage I was receiving, moving away was not an option, I wanted to be near my son, and the word on the street were men were not getting paid for one reason, or another. British men working in Germany reminded me of the T.V. dramas, *Auf Wiedersehen Pet,* and Yosser Hughes, *Boys from the black stuff.* The collective mind of the media and arts, tries to inform us of the exploitation, we just take no notice. Things had to change but I didn't know what, where or how. Then a friend understanding the situation I was in offered to rent my spare room, double the amount I was paying for my two-bedroom council house.

Come the day of him moving in, my friend Tony Riley was well-spoken and respected in the community. To see this big black businessman, you wouldn't think he was involved in drugs. Tony introduced me to his mate Pegleg, a tall chap, skinny, and confident for his youthful age. Tony went onto inform me, 'Pegleg will need a key, don't worry Pegleg will be in and out a lot, I'll see you next week with the rent, take this.'

Straight after our conversation, he handed me the agreed sum.

Being unemployed at the time, I sat, and watched Pegleg's movements. Within minutes of him arriving, there was a call on his mobile phone. The technology on mobiles had just hit the streets. Pegleg pulled out a black brick sized Motorola phone to answer, 'Hello.'

'Who?'

'What you after?'

'Be with you in five, in a bit.'

Pegleg had a small duffle bag on his shoulder, he tried to place the phone in his jacket pocket, but he was fighting with himself as the phone, and bag were too bulky for him to maintain balance. He dropped the bag, where I could see tins of air fresheners fall-out. Once he'd gained control of himself, he picked up the bag, placed the air fresheners in the bag then went into the kitchen. In and out every five minutes, his phone ringing, in and out of my kitchen.

Subsequently, after watching him for an hour or so, I had a look in my kitchen. I looked around to see his bag on the floor empty. I looked under the sink; all I could see were four tins of air fresheners I never purchased. I opened up one of the draws, and there, pure money. I don't know how much was there, but it was more than I'd ever seen before. I thought, *I've got to have piece of this action.*

Until then, I'd never broken the law, but if the government cannot ensure work through economics, why should I have less of the resources when I'm ready, and willing to work?

The next time I saw Tony, I enquired, 'Have you got any work for me?'

Tony was an ex-army man, at six foot two he was slightly taller than me with broad shoulders, and his big chest reminded me of Optimus Prime, muttered, 'Yeah, £300 a week for eight hours per day to answer the phone and deliver heroin.'

This was twice as much money as I was getting on my apprenticeship for doing little of nothing.

Now, money was flowing like dirt, I was clubbing every night in Manchester, and around the Northwest.

I was able to take driving lessons, later failing the test, but still having hired cars. I could afford to take up my hobby, buying my music every week, and I bought two technics turntables. All this impressed Beverly, with the money came more girls. It wasn't before long I'd raised enough cash to start finding my own drug network and started to work with a mate. Money was flowing, and the benefits to my family could be seen.

Chapter 26

Unaware conscious

Christmas week 1991, funds are flowing, and my pocket is phat with cash. I was buying my suits from St. Anne's Square, the upper-class shopping spot in Manchester, and where you were likely to see a famous footballer, or an actor from Coronation Street. Piccadilly Twenty-one, one of the biggest venues in central Manchester, two or three U.K. R & B acts were performing on the night. I can't remember who performed, I was captivated by a light brown skin girl, who reminded me of the young Lisa Bonnet, very attractive, and an understatement, her name was Cate Withington.

I approached her while she was dancing, we didn't speak much because of the loud music, yet a lot was said within our body language, as we danced the night away like a pair of black loves-truck swans. Cate looked sexy and confident, not shy yet innocent, stunningly welcoming, softer than snow with the warmth of the summer sun. She had her hair pulled back like Sade, wearing a black skin tight cat suit, modelling a coke a cola bottle figure, and her bumper were similar to two plump red peaches, God damn.

We hit it off straight away, the night was over, and it wasn't before long she was in the front seat of my car, which didn't please the mate I came with, he was forced to sit in the back seat of my new, used, metallic blue Ford Sierra. It wasn't before long me and Cate were sleeping together. Me, understanding Cate was eighteen, and living with her mother after her parents split up. As the weeks and months passed, I was spending more of my free time in her company. Cate was wholesome fun, full of joy and laughter, but my mates did not approve of our relationship. Only because they believed Cate was younger, sixteen.

One evening, when Cate left her many birthday cards in

my house, I questioned her about her age. Her big brown eyes dropped to the floor, and in a soft sorry voice, she confessed. If I'd known her true age now seventeen, sixteen when we first met, there could have been a stronger chance I would have had my fun, then sent her on her way, but I fell for her.

As time moved on, Cate wanted to move into my house, her home life with her mother was getting difficult, so she moved in, which meant I had to slow down with the number of women on my case. I wasn't able to take timeout to see Beverly.

My relationship with Cate did not make my business partner very happy, I was spending more time with her instead of finding other women and new punters with him. It was not before long me and my mate's partnership in the drugs industry ended up folding, after one or two mishaps occurred with drugs and money.

During this period in 1992, after spending a great deal of money on my record collection, four or five years buying, whenever I had the cash, I was invited to join a pirate radio station, Love Energy 99.75 F.M. This put me in the public eye, many of my friends did not know I was a music man. I was slowly building up a good fanbase, which exploded Boxing Day 1992.

The venue booked was too small for the numbers at the door, the night was rocking. After a misunderstanding with the manager, concerned with our late arrival, at the end of the night, at £5 per head, and the club was able to hold 150 easy, the manager ends up only paying us £50. The manager used the excuse, we came too late, paying us less than agreed, which was taking the door for promoting the night.

A few days later, I was in hospital with mental health issues, ignited by the death of a friend, Stanley Benji, he was only fourteen years old, and shot dead in a West Indian takeaway on Saturday 2nd January 1993. At the time of his horrific murder, I was presenting my radio show, the Fresh Egg show as Deejay Man Egg, playing up front hip hop, and R & B in a block of flats in Hulme.

At the time, I was overlooking the city of Manchester from a high rise flat around the time of his premature death. Unaware of this tragic scene, I noticed the rush of traffic gradually moved slower then stop. Movement from pinheaded people vanished from the streets below as the atmosphere suddenly dampened like a loudspeaker being muffled. The low rumbling noise from the choked air traffic below, usually vibrated around the blocks of flats, cascaded into a cold silence, embracing the city like a layer of thick snow.

It wasn't until I came home, I understood the ambiance that engulfed the city when Cate told me of his death, it hit me so hard. All I could think of was that could have been my boy, my son.

My mind was lost in bereavement searching in no direction, looking to find insight, needing to help his family, and wanting to find an answer to his death. Confused about the world, bewildered by the word humanity and angry with anyone opposed to my viewpoint, I attacked society, the church, government, and bankers whenever I did my broadcast. In so doing, the manager of the pirate station decided to physically remove me from my radio show.

My rage would flare up uncontrollably from the slightest thing that was in conflict with my opinions and reasoning, but I was never violent. I was becoming mentally ill, and I was the kind of guy who'd shout, or spoke loudly to get my point of view over in a manically excited manner. Edwin showed me how patient a friend he has been towards me, after I shouted my opinion in his face specified, 'We'll agree to disagree, but no one man can rule the world.'

Very wise words, from a very dear friend, I replied, 'As long as you think like that, we will always be friends.'

In my bereavement, and my first spell in a mental health hospital, I was told I am a Manic Depressant, and it was not good for my mental health to continue smoking dope. My illness showed me how sensitive I was towards the loss of life. During my very first six weeks stay in a mental health hospital I decided for the first time to put pen, to paper, and wrote a letter to my step grandad Mr Walker. Him and his wife were now living in Jamaica for the past six or seven years. I can't remember what I wrote, but it was the first and only letter until now that I'd sign the name John Thought Hope.

I may have been living with another woman, but Beverly showed me she really loved me. Beverly came to the hospital one evening with her sisters in tow, to get me out of hospital for an hour or so. It was while I was in hospital all my music and equipment was stolen. I made a speedy recovery, smoking dope the second I was discharged from hospital, which makes me wonder! Am I becoming mentally ill now, after fifteen years of good mental health, and smoking the most dope whenever I can. I'm talking in the same manner as then, about God, creation, politics, religion, and economics, but I'm making so much sense this time round. I understand the meaning to my existence.

Chapter 27

Is it really worth it?

Throughout my relationship with Cate, I was always trying to get her to find her own place in between our stormy arguments and our passionate lovestruck reunions. When I was discharged from Withington Mental Health Hospital in 1993, I found myself staying with her at a hostel in Crumpsall. She managed to get a newly built one bedroom flat soon enough in the same area, with the death of my young friend, I did not feel safe or at peace with myself at Cadogan Street. The loss of my music and the thieves having smashed the window in, then trashed the place, it was felt by my doctors at the time, it was best moving me to a new flat, and environment.

As a consequence, I moved to flat 4 Clarendon Road, Whalley Range Manchester. It was close to Great Western Street, but far enough away from the frontline of Moss Lane East. I was too popular in the area, and I felt vulnerable to gang members. The doctors were not aware I was selling drugs not to my knowledge anyway.

My new flat was situated on the top floor of an old converted Victorian, or Edwardian house. It was only a one-bedroom flat, which suited me, it was smaller making it easy to clean and manage. I had a slight cash flow problem, not as much as I owe today, being a local drug dealer, the cash flow would soon pick up once my punters knew I was back online with my new phone number. It wasn't before long, I felt well enough to go back on the street corner and make some money. Cate gave up her flat in Crumpsall to live with me, I really didn't like being away from her at the time. It became a problem seeing Beverly, as I was not driving, and well, Cate was always there.

A few months after moving into my new accommodation,

the worst thing happens. I get into trouble with the police in an early morning raid, like they do, a surprise to both me and Cate. This being the first time I was ever arrested, not a pleasant experience. The police asked questions about my drug connections, but I wasn't saying anything, it was my drugs they found, so I held my hands up to possession. The police wanted me for intent to supply class-A drugs, I was released on bail, and later charged with intent to supply. Cate walked with no charges, which was cool, and what I wanted. Within hours of me being released on police bail, I'd purchased more drugs, and was back on the streets.

Having lost most of my money and drugs in the police raid, cash was well low. Changing my phone number a few times over a period in the past, meant my phone was not firing, and I was not in the big league. I was on the lower scale of the drugs industry, selling quarter bags to people who once had a dream or beginning to fade away in a sea of lost faces. A statistic society perpetrates by offering hate, not love.

Being an independent drug dealer comes with some problems and danger. Especially if you haven't got any form of transport. I spent my days at one of two places in the day, as a result, my punters could find me as well as giving out my new number. The betting shop on Moss Lane East was my original headquarters. My father's bad boy pimping girls in his past was a good reference, an added feature, making it safe to sell my gear without having any politics with the other guys selling their drugs.

I didn't have the same influence at Ladbrokes betting shop on Claremont Road, where I found myself more often than not. There were more punters in that area to give my number to, and it was a lot closer to my new flat in Whalley Range. Everyone's watching someone, you never know who is watching you, me, myself, and I. There's always somebody watching everybody, and everyone is looking at you.

A week maybe two weeks after being charged by the police, I found myself at Ladbrokes betting shop on Claremont Road. There was a big horse meeting, and the shop was packed. Noses of short stout men, rubbing up against tall men's backs, backs pressing onto big belly beer bus drivers. Their garage was not far away, it seemed like the bus company staff were all in the betting shop, it was full to the brim. It couldn't have been smokier than *Smokey and the bandits*, it was that smoky. There was a lot of loud noise emanating from boisterous men chattering, the odd drug dealer like myself, weaved in between the crowd, in and out of the one and only main door to lick the shot. (This is a phrase meaning sell the drugs.) I was not as busy as some dealers, and I wasn't known as well as others, so I thought.

After placing a bet, excited along with the rest of the men in the shop, I watched to see my horse running a close second to the finishing line. Intuition, sixth sense, a thought came to my mind in the middle of the excitement, as clear as a newsflash announcement, the words from that thought echoed, *'Some things going to happen, don't worry.'*

I remember tipping my head slightly up towards the ceiling, yet sort of looking at my mind, pondering on a wonder to myself, *'Where did that thought come from? I'm not talking to myself. I was being told.'*

In that moment, someone poked me in my back, I looked down and around, to see a short, younger man than myself, well-built, mixed-race guy looking up in my face, with a command, 'Come outside.'

I didn't take kindly to his manner, approach, or the way he shouted out what seemed like an order over the cries and cheers of anticipation from the men in the shop as the race drew closer to the finishing line. The horse race commentary continued to a climax and excited the crowd, I replied firm but politely, 'I'll see you outside after the race.'

He shouted back in a very aggressive manner, 'Come outside now.'

He was pissing me off, I couldn't see the race, it was thrilling the punters with eagerness, excitement, and jubilation for some, disappointment for others. So, I shouted back, firm, yet well mannered, 'After the race.'

He turned away then disappeared like a penguin diving into a sea of people. I rotated my head to see my horse come in fourth, I was not happy with that. Losing your money, and not even seeing how you lost it. Anyway, I pushed my way through the thick crowd with the other losers to the main door out of the shop, to find the same young guy stood outside waiting. I stepped out of the betting shop, as I did so, he followed up behind me, looking very intimidating. I was feeling on edge, uncomfortable and unsafe with his approach. I turned to face him, I stepped backwards, as I did, he step forward pulling his hood over his head. When I saw that, I knew I was in trouble. Before I could react to the situation, someone put their foot behind my left foot with the first guy in front of me, placing his foot on top of the same leg. I fell backwards, causing my left leg to be broken.

As I laid there helpless and facing what could have been my death, it flashed in my mind, a few men have been shot dead, outside this very spot. I looked up into a face of a man who could have ended it for me. His psychotic approach was identical to a scurrying spider, quickening his pace, as he advanced to pounce, and devour his victim. He stood over me with his cold blank redeyes, which pierced my flesh like a dagger to the chest. He stated with no uncertain terms, 'Don't let me see you around here again.

He bent over towards the right-hand side of my leather coat pocket, then pulled the pocket apart, dragging out my new Sony Mars bar phone. He then turned away, leaving the scene feeling braver than a Saxon warrior, bold similar to washing powder he radiated cool, calm, confidant, and invincible like a bunch of bad boy cowboys that have just killed the sheriff. When I stood up, I could not put my left leg down, I knew straight away they had broken my leg. The crowd of on lookers from the betting shop, looked on, wide eyed like *Spock*, then they were gone, in shock, but not rocked, and horrified not troubled or disturbed. Many onlookers watching the drama I knew as my mother's friends, passers-by in the street stood motionless as the events unfolded.

There was a taxi rank on a nearby street, I hopped to where it was parked, I managed to leap on top of the bonnet and climbed in the cab. I was in absolute pain, agony, and distressed saying, 'Manchester Royal Infirmary please.'

When I arrived at the hospital, I made my way out of the cab, then the pain really kicked in. There was no way I had the strength to hop to the reception of A & E. I held on for dear life to a nearby handrail, feeling helpless, as if I were stranded in the ocean, and in a great deal of pain. The taxi driver had been paid and was gone.

Luckily, an ambulance crewmember noticed my distress, and offered me a wheelchair. Thank God we have the National Health Service, no insurance you're dead. The hospital took an x-ray and plastered up my leg. Then they informed me I had a spiral fracture to my left ankle, because of the manner in which I fell caused another fracture to my heel. They placed me in a plaster cast for six months. Thinking back, I was very fortunate, and wise enough to know when to pull out of the drugs game.

Chapter 28

Love hate is not love

I've met people from all social classes, like most people whenever money isn't involved people present a pleasant persona. Offer them money, you see them double deal, give them drinks or drugs, the real hatred towards society is revealed, not understanding their fear of showing true love makes society hate one another.

When I moved to Whalley Range late in the year 1993, I met one of my neighbours who lived in a flat on the ground floor of the converted house. Fredrick McCloud was a mixed-race Scottish man and was forty-five at the time I met him. He wore matted worn-out clothes, gaping holes in his jumper from tobacco burns, alongside tea and coffee stains on his shirt. White balls of fluff rolled up on his pants, as well as up his nose, his flat was cluttered with all kinds of junk, a rat he named Ben he'd fed some milk. Empty tins of beer covered his sofa, bags of takeaway were home to fat blue bottles, the place smelt of urine with alcohol thrown in.

One night when he had too much drink, and he's not a nice drunk when he drinks, which is always, never enough. Fredrick got his legs crushed in between two cars by a gang of kids who he managed to pick an argument with. What was funny, he was a registered A.A. and Disability Living Allowance decided to buy him a new Peugeot 205. Fredrick gave me the keys to drive him around, he was always too pissed to drive himself, big mistake on my part. Fredrick would knock on my door at four or five o'clock in the morning, asking to be driven to the shop for a beer.

I came home one evening to see his pisshead girlfriend, a worn-out fifty plus overweight white prostitute, crying her eyes out.

While explaining her drama, she pulled up her bloodstained dress to show me fourteen elephant trunk stitches from the length of her crutch just up under her dirty black belly button, caused by Fredrick kicking her, a gruesome sight. He did this because he thought his girlfriend was sleeping with a man, Fredrick was having a sexual relationship with. Fredrick broke his boyfriend's leg, he was pissed when he did it, then he went to bed like nothing happened. Real hate because love is not shared, if God's love were like that, would we be here?

You do not create in order to destroy, God's love is shared, share your love.

Chapter 29

Forewarned is enlightened

The collective mind has a funny way of informing me, information I need without having to look, or do any research. This particular evening on the 14th August 2009 was a boring night, but in saying that, there is nothing more entertaining than a documentary. While flicking through the channels, a show on E4 caught my eye. Guns, germs, and steel.

The show just started to explain the migration of the original African man, through Egypt into the Middle East that extends from the Eastern Mediterranean Coast, on through the Valley of the Tigris, and Euphrates Rivers onto the Persian Gulf, a place called the Fertile Crescent, crescent meaning semi-circle. This area or region is known as the Fertile Crescent because of all the animals in the ancient world, fourteen animals were domesticated farm animals, thirteen of which are indigenous to this region.

Animals such as: pigs, horses, donkeys, camels, sheep, goats, rabbits, chickens, cows, turkeys, geese, cats, and dogs. The fourteenth is a llama, which is found in South America, for this reason, along with wheat, barley, and maze, encouraged the inhabitants into becoming farmers, having animals working and less time foraging, gave parts of the population time to think. Therein making the Europeans seem more intelligent when the reality is, they're not. In my mind, it was beginning to make sense, the pieces linked. The Fertile Crescent was similar as Manchester, which is situated within the Horseshoe Crescent, logic. A lot like *Dan Brown's the Da Vinci Code,* search for symbolic symbols in reverse.

The following morning on the 15th August 2009 was an ordinary day. Ordinary, when nothing happens. It seemed ordinary, until the early afternoon period of the day. I found myself in my kitchen, pacing back and forth most of the morning. My urge to talk to someone was swelling like a waterpipe about to burst, boredom forced me down to the Edinburgh Cellars. It was a lovely summers day; traffic was unusually light around Newington Green as I made my way to the pub.

Upon entering the establishment, I viewed most of my friends through the window seated outside having a drink. As always there were more people outside the pub than in. I preceded to make my way over to where my mates were seated outside. As I approached, I leaned onto the table with both hands, I didn't even say hello to my friends. Then I rudely interrupted their conversation by stating the weirdest thing, 'Excuse me, could you go home to your pets, hold their heads with both hands, then ask your pet, do you know what is happening in the world today? Your pet will nod their heads yes, if your pet nods yes, I think it would be best to have a meeting.'

My friend Jane was seated at the table. I turned to her adding, 'Is that the weirdest thing you have ever heard me say?'

Jane is usually flamboyantly loud, but on this occasion she looked up into my face with a quiet perplexed look on her expression, her big brown glossy eyes glowed brighter, and like a puzzled fluffy cuddly puppy dog, nodded her head yes. Then I went back to my flat.

As I walked down the quiet city streets of Newington Green, the few people that could be seen going about their business were like busy silverback ants, running around in the heat from the sizzling hot summer sun. Within my mind, I was questioning my actions, and what I'd just said. It made sense but was nonsense. My perception was distorted, I was confident with the message in my words, yet a pet, responding to a question, out of the question. My perception was mixed up, confused with reality. I questioned my mind, *'How could I expect an animal, to answer back? If that's the case, how could I convince the world who I am, when the world's perception is just as mixed up as mine! I've got to think straight with my thoughts.'*

Then it occurred to me, *'It was really John talking through me.'*

When I entered my flat, I felt panicked, on edge, and nervous. I made my way to the kitchen, there was building work being carried out on my flat by the local council. The washing machine was pulled out of place into the kitchen space, making the kitchen area smaller than usual. The dinner table was in pieces against the wall, and builder's tools were in a corner. The rest of my flat was in an untidy condition. I started to pace up and down, back and forth in the tight kitchen area, no more than three feet squared, two steps I had to turn right back, I paced at a rapid pace, I paced. I recall crouching down patting the air, repeatedly saying, 'Calm down Islam calm down.'

I paced back and forth; I paced doubling my speed towards the kitchen window. There's a university campus situated at the back of my flat, I opened the window then shouted across the campus in a deep bellow, 'CHRISTIAN WORLD, PHONE PALESTINE, LET THEM KNOW I AM HERE.'

I poked my head back in the window, only to begin pacing franticly back and forth, forth, and back. I seemed to be pacing for ages. As I paced, I began to feel the urge to use the toilet. So, I turned my head-to-head for the toilet, but found myself still pacing franticly around and around in what seemed like a circle. I just could not head for the toilet. I couldn't understand, I felt more panicked and slightly terrified, I stopped. I looked out of the kitchen window, all of a sudden, I screamed the loudest bitch male scream heard, holding my head with both hands, a town crier could not have been louder. In my mind, images of Edward Monk, artistic portrait of the *'Scream,'* engulfed my thoughts. Breathing heavy and fast, sweat pouring down my face, as if I were having a panic attack. I shouted, 'Help, help, help!'

I tried walking to the toilet, but I was still walking around in circles, as if I were a cheetah that just ran a hundred yards dash, chasing a tail I do not have. I rested, slumped over the kitchen work surface, trying to catch my breath. I screamed out, 'Help, help, help!'

When from outside of my flat I heard a neighbour reply, 'Fitzroy, the ambulance is on the way, open the door.'

Still trying to catch my breath, it felt hotter than the midday sun, and I was panting like a hot dog with its tongue hung out. I responded, 'Hello, hello whose there? I can't see, I can just about hear, hello.'

Within my mind, I, Fitzroy was fighting John for control of my bodily movements and speech, in part having some senses, never all five. I tried again to head for the toilet, but I was still running around in circles similar to a dog chasing his tail. Within my mind, I could relate to Jacob, Genesis 31:31 when he has a fight with God, and Jacob breaks his own left leg. Exhausted, I resigned to the fact that I wasn't in control, I rested my upper body sprawled like a beached blue whale on the kitchen worktop.

Not long after, the doorbell alerted me, ring, ring, ring, but I couldn't move, or answer. I was confused within my mind, my thoughts were of wanting to work, but against the idea, turning to crime was not the answer, then on the other hand, denying I was the Messiah, I was, I wasn't, I should, I shouldn't. The conflict within my mind was a wild windy whirlpool of confusion, a chaotic whirling storm blew viciously, the whistling wind battered my thoughts, when normally, there is a calm breeze blowing, the whistling wind caresses my mind with moral order. Bang, bang, whack, the front door caved in, and collides into the hallway wall. I cried out, 'Hello, hello, whose there?'

Still face down spreadeagled on top of the kitchen surface, I could hear a number of bodies moving towards me but found I couldn't move. When a soft female's voice curiously enquired, 'What's the problem?'

There was what seemed like a lifetime pause of silence, while I was struggling, and searching to find my mouthpiece within my mind, so I could answer her question. After a short period of total silence, I countered, 'I think there for I am. Extra sensory perception, I'm trapped in my own mind, fighting my subconscious. He will only give me three senses at a time. Please just touch me, it's hard to explain.'

She timidly approached me, then gently touched my hand, the warmth of a tender touch is an expression of love that brought me back to my senses, in part. The ambulance crew in attendance could see I was disorientated like a dizzy drunken clown, they stepped forward to assist me by holding both of my underarms, I felt weak at the knees, and found it difficult walking straight, I was also confused in my mind, similar to a mad scientist. The ambulance crew led me to the front door, which leads straight down three narrow dogleg flights of stairs. As I stepped down the first flight, both ambulance crewmembers released my arms, my senses seemed normal.

The bright sunlight beaming through the window of the stairwell in front of me, outlined one of the ambulance crew, who was leading the way. The crewmember turned onto his next flight of stairs, opened up my vision to a brilliantly white wall. I felt hypnotised and transfixed to the wall as I walked down the steps then bang, I walked into the brick faced wall. I couldn't see or judge my distance from the white washed wall. The ambulance crew decided to hold my hand and led me down the stairs. I was fine with their help, until the last flight of stairs, my left leg would not move. Sweat began to run down my face, it felt akin to a cold shower in the middle of summer, as I stood there motionless. I was fighting within my mind, just to move my leg, but it was quivering franticly as if it were the freezing season of winter, not wanting to move from its spot. After a minute or so of the ambulance crew slowly encouraging and persuading me down the steps, I finally, reached the bottom, and made my way to the ambulance parked directly opposite the communal front door.

Next door to the flat's main door are shops, and a Turkish social club, where retired men played cards and board games, some of the men were stood outside smoking. As I made my way to the ambulance, I strayed, away from my direction, and walked towards the Turkish men having coffee and a chat. Then in a deep ghostly fashion I approached the men, to be heard repeatedly proclaiming, 'You must hear this man speak. You must hear this man speak.'

An ambulance member held my hand then led me into the ambulance with me continuing to say, 'You must hear this man speak. You must hear this man speak.'

It was all, very bizarre, but I understood that my subconscious was showing me, my sense of I, was not always in full control of my own body or what I may say. I was aware of an extra sensory perception, the sixth sense, or the All-seeing eye.

The All-Seeing Eye, what could that be?
How about a philosopher's puzzle.

Third eye

There are six points of view when looking from the top of a
pyramid:
'1. While walking to the top, I see my own life's journey.
2. Standing at the top of the pyramid, I see God's kingdom, his
creation all around me, and the universe above.
3. I look down to see people below, who should be standing
beside me as equals.
4. I perceive in my mind, there are two minds, and still
maintain twenty, twenty vision.
All-seeing, all-knowing eye, perception.
5. I can look into the past, understand the present, see what the
future could, and will be.'
'6. Perception of vision deduces, I can see there is a problem, and
I'm trying to fix it.'

John T. Hope

Chapter 30

Always proving

The year is 1994, five or six months after my leg was in plaster, and not working for three years, I was too busy selling drugs. It was a good welcome change working, while I awaited trial. A.M.H. Contract Services an agency for builders located in Manchester were sending me on a few jobs shuttering bridges, columns, foundations, etc. Heavy hard dirty backbreaking work. It had been along while unemployed, as a carpenter, and off the tools. I thought to improve my skills, start at the bottom of my trade, then work my way up, my skills developed, and I was gathering knowledge of my industry, working with the new German Doka shuttering system. Much later on, I was also involved in building a four-storey lift shaft.

Subsequently, I know what to do with three years previous work experience under my belt. I was sent by the agency to Manchester Museum, just off Quay Street. Upon arriving, I met two other carpenters from the agency, and one other old timer. This old boy worked direct for the company, and looked well experienced in his field, so I thought.

His face was folded with heaps of leathery cracked creases of skin similar to an unmade bed, white unshaven stubble look like dandruff, and what little grey hair I could see, poked out from his blue hardhat, danced in the cold frostbitten whirling morning wind. The crisp windy wind whipped up a thrash, a lash, as the whistling wind forged around the outside columns of the refurbished museum. He handed out his big dry shovel like hand to offer a handshake, I returned the gesture, and shook his hand, introducing myself as I did. He declared, 'My name is Pete Wells.'

He shook the other boy's hands and led us up to one of the site offices for the normal site safety induction. Usually, the induction is given by the site manager, or the company's health and safety officer. In his broad Irish accent, Pete articulated, 'Wait for the site manager who will induct the group.'

After Pete left the fiberglass cabin, having done the induction, received drawings of the foundation kickers, the face of the concrete was to be a smooth, fine finish. Understanding these instructions and drawings given to all three chippies, we took a plot each to be completed. They were big areas to shutter. After a week of laughing and joking with the guys, we'd completed the project, with only soap oil left to brush on the timber constructions. I spoke up, 'Pete, where can I find the soap oil, or diesel to coat the shutters?'

Pete stated, 'There's no need for that.'

I found his response odd for a professional tradesman, so I reminded him, 'Pete, if we don't put soap oil on the shutter, the concrete will stick to the timber, rip, and breakaway from the finished concrete plinth. We need to put some soap oil on the shutter.'

Who'd believe it, Pete disagreed, and an argument duly ensued. I was not taking responsibility, so I went to the site office to report on the current situation. To my surprise the site agent William Anderson was of the same opinion as Pete. I declared, 'I wasn't taking responsibility for the outcome of the product.'

The site agent, a short pop belly white guy from Yorkshire, did not mince his words, asserted in a cold blank manner, 'If you're not prepared to do the job, you can leave.'

In dismay, needing the work I said nothing. I turned away, then I helped the labourers pour the concrete. The shutters held their positions well, and the labourers finished the top, smoothly. It just needed buffing up once the wooden shutters was stripped. We ended the day without a false word, me knowing full well, there was going to be problems when stripping the timber five days or so later. I was overwhelmed the following day, when Pete said, 'Right guys lets have this timber stripped clean.'

I could not believe what I was hearing. The concrete was still going off, moisture was visible on the surface, deep enough for ducks to have a swim. Having damp chilly air, the night before, did not help the structure dry out. I stepped up to Pete in a commanding manner affirming, 'Can't you see it's not ready, you need to let it rest for two or three-days mate.'

Pete wasn't hearing anything that I had to say, with his stubborn ignorant self, Pete continued with, 'Pass me over that steel recking bar.'

I felt a bit pissed off with the situation, as I gave him what he asked for, and handed him over a smooth cold five-foot long, two-inch thick bar. With his ignorant bad manners, Pete snatched the bar from my hand quite aggressively, he then held the bar above his head, at that stage, he made a strike with the point of the bar in between the timber shutter, and the concrete.

It was a very well swung strike, but missed the joint by two inches, into the concrete surface, breaking the finished top. With an uncaring concern to the job at hand, Pete rocked the bar back, and forth, in an attempt to release the bar, as well as breaking the timber free from the structure, he was making the situation worse. I was right, and walked away, watching from a distance, all I could see were rocky cliff face more than a smooth, skilled job.

In that moment, the stout site agent walked round the corner, looking like father Christmas in a yellow health and safety suit, only to see me stood there with my hands in my pocket, looking over the job. He didn't look impressed with the work, stating, 'What's happened with the top and face of the plinth?'

As he looked round, he rotated his big head to me saying, in a very official manner, 'What are you doing stood there?'

It was cold, which felt more like minus twenty degrees, wet as a baby's bottom, and I was very despondent about the turn of events. I replied, 'Watching them destroy a job that was not ready to be stripped.'

In a firm military tone, the overweight site agent quizzed, 'So what have you been doing?'

At this point, I couldn't careless, I didn't want to put my name to the job. In the same dismissive tone as he gave me, I retorted, 'I've done nothing but watch.'

The last thing I heard from the site agent was, 'Your services are no longer required thanks, I will fax your time sheet to the agency.'

I turned away proud as a peacock displaying his feathers, wiser than an owl, broke like O' Jay Simpson, and tired of moving from one job to another, having to prove every time my worth, I'm not a chancer, or a cowboy. Bowing down to someone who does not know better, makes you a fool. Unemployed again, no music, no interest in life with a lower income came less club nights, missing parties, no socialising, what's life?

During low periods in your life, you discover who your real friends are.

Impatient apprehension brought on tension, constant arguments between Cate, and myself with a trial looming, maximum sentence five years hanging over my head, Cate ended our relationship. But not before I met Annabel, in the New Year of 1995.

Chapter 31

Professional attitude

Jamaicans have an expression called redeye, it means when a person is jealous of what another has, or what someone else can earn. This is not a very good phrase for situations in the workplace. Not all, but some people in a management team overseeing the work of a carpenter, doesn't like to see the carpenter earn as much, or more than them. Especially, if you're in a minority residing in the United Kingdom.

When a white person has been to university to study their field, in his or her mind they feel their seven years of higher education should earn them more money. To see that a minority tradesperson can earn more for their three-year apprenticeship, makes the white person jealous, or redeye. What the white person does not see is their long-term benefits from their post, compared to the carpenter's unstable short-term self-employed contract. If you're in a position to demand a contract, which has never been offered to me, when I ask, all of a sudden I'm out of work.

To be self-employed, or a sole trader, carpenters are left exposed to the trappings of corporate, and commercial law. At the time, a sole trader has to pay for public liability, receives no holiday pay, and no sick pay. As the main carpentry firm employing subcontractors, the law is made easier for the employer to sack the subcontractors, or employ other staff, with no long-term responsibility to their staff, therefore no responsibility to society. They can afford to play a waiting game with the carpenter by offering a low price, with a take it, or find another job policy over the carpenter. The carpenter will and does lose money, finding a new job, as a carpenter does not come easy. The main contractor gives the carpenter the price (time and motion.) This is another way of price fixing, in a market that has far too many carpenters for the amount of work available.

On average, a carpenter earns £500 to £600 before tax, then you have to consider his expenses, which is as follows: holiday pay, tool allowance, insurance for tools, public liability, pension plan, and transport costs. Compared to twenty years ago, the carpenter gets the same for less liability, less responsibility, and received a tool allowance, not today. Any damages to materials, mistakes or mishaps, the carpenter pays the full cost for replacement.

As a result, a carpenter could lose, a week's pay or more on a mistake, which gives them less chance, and less access to the resources.

Whereas the management team, can pencil in, or pass over the cost of their mistake onto the price, delaying tradesmen from working, and default payments. For instance, late delivery of materials means the carpenter cannot earn. So, he receives no pay for his time waiting, which could take days. The complicated applications within the laws of economics is so confusing, how many ways can one find a form of corruption, fraud, and two-faced professional attitude. People will do anything, so one does not get the resources, and if they have the means, try to take it. What a barbaric philosophy, and a senseless demonic ideology for the most intelligent creatures on the planet to be acting towards one another.

I'm driven by a force, I don't fully understand, not knowing it's source, I follow it's command, writing what I should not be saying, expressing what love I have for my fellowman. What I do understand, if not today, they might understand tomorrow. So, I continue to write furiously, not knowing what I'm doing.

Chapter 32

Employment rights

My present-day status in 2009, it's not much fun being unemployed. The feeling of being a reject from society is more apparent when one has no money to take part in social activities. Meeting a woman does not come to mind because the women I like or fancy, prefer to have men with money, in order to provide for their future needs. My prospects looks bleak, dry like a desert, I'm so bored, I feel as if I were listening to a lecture on quantum physics, it's damn right sad. Now I'm older, the expression from a woman's love seems to be a scorecard, there is no value in it.

In 2005, I was made unemployed again, after completing a project in the City of London. The company I was working for were based in Devon, most of their work happened to be anywhere in the country, refurbishing stores for Starbucks. The company offered me a permanent job, but I wasn't interested in traveling around the country in a cramped dirty caravan with four or five builders.

Thinking to myself, I'd find another job quickly, wanting to be independent, I waited until the next job came along. Pride, the stigma attached when signing on, the paperwork involved, sometimes I never bothered. When I did, it was not until my second week out of work, I'd usually sign on for benefit. By the time I had got through the paperwork, and received my signing on date, took me a further four weeks, I'd find a job.

On this occasion, in the spring of 2005, I was working at St Charles Hospital in Ladbroke Grove as a carpenter on price work, time, and motion. I had to start the next day when I heard of this project. It meant; I'd have to miss my signing on time. In so doing, no benefit, rent, or council tax has been paid towards my bills. This occurs from time to time, for one reason or another, the system, and it's flaws. In anyone year, I could work for as many as ten companies or projects. Sure enough, some years are good, more often than not they're bad.

When the job was offered to me over the phone, which is always the case in my field of work, I spoke to a female, I thought she was a secretary, little did I expect a woman to be the site agent when I arrived on site. Her name was Karen Slater, a pretty tiny brunette, she had a low toned voice for her small size, I thought, *'Very sexy.'*

As I got to know her over the next few weeks, I was always curious whenever I saw her. My eyes would wander, down her small body length, measuring her up and down. I made it obvious I wanted to see her figure, which was always hidden under a yellow health and safety coat, it was way bigger than herself. She enjoyed what little attention I was offering, when we were engaged in polite naughty business-like conversations. In a nutshell, we got on with one another, quite well.

The days and weeks passed on the job, as the project progressed Karen seemed to be under a lot of pressure to get the second phase of the development further along. So, informed me that she was taking the other six chippies to the other hospital wings. While I continued with the second and final fix on the main wing, which was nearer completion. With that said, I continued with my work, and things were going well. For the next few days, I got on with Karen, I was under the impression she had a favourable eye for me. The work I was doing was going very well, she was confident with my abilities, never concerned, and pleased, I was also getting good reports from the management team.

Until one day, someone stole my hammer drill, which totalled my days earnings, and the cost for a new drill. Losing my drill, made me a bit on edge, and apprehensive, if you like very anxious about the safety of my tools, a slight misfortune, no insurance, if I did have insurance the cost and the trouble to claim. One suffers or gains less access to the resources for the added cost of replacing the drill, through no fault of my own making. We live by a merciless philosophy.

A few days later, Karen pulls me up modelling her big yellow coat, and adding in an excitable salesman's fashion, 'Fitz, the power on site is going to be switched off on Monday, do you have a 110-volt transformer?'

I thought, *'Another tool to bring to work,'*

I replied, 'Yes, I have one, I'll bring it in.'

The following Monday, I arrived on site with my transformer, and continued my work program for the day. I plan out my workload once I've had instructions, which I received earlier in the previous week. I had jobs on the top two floors, and tools situated in both areas with the transformer on the top floor.

About 8.30 a.m. as usual, Karen walked into the corridor on the top floor of the hospital, where I was working for that moment. She approached with a firm rapid step to her walk, similar to Speedy Gonzales. Karen enquired, 'Morning Fitz, how was your weekend?'

On a speedy course, getting through my busy day and large workload, I was trying to make up for lost earnings. I answered, 'Fine thanks.'

She continued our conversation, 'Fitz are you using your transformer? The carpenters on the other hospital wing need one for an hour or so.'

Now I'm thinking, *'Why haven't the other chippies brought in their transformers.'*

I stated, 'They can get it at ten o'clock when I go for breakfast.'

All of a sudden, her mood switched to a stinking skunk as her pale white face turned bloodshot red. With an angry disposition she replied, 'Fine, I'll be back at ten then.'

She speedily stomped off looking a bit pissed off, but I was too concerned with my workload to be worried about her hang ups. I was on price work, time and motion, as Riddick would say, *'Keep moving.'*

I got together tools I needed for the few small jobs I had on the floor below. I then went downstairs to finish the work, which took about 15 minutes. When I got back on the top floor, only to find my tools had not been moved, but I found my transformer missing. I went from floor to floor, five floors in all, I'm losing money looking for my transformer. I kept an eye out for Karen, I'm thinking she may have taken the transformer. Having walked along every corridor, on each floor, and every room, then walking up the stairs, asking other tradesmen if they've seen the transformer or Karen, I finally bumped into her back on the top floor. I was a bit worried, similar to a father fretful for his son, concerned about his daughter, and anxious. I proceeded to ask, 'Have you got my transformer it's not where I left it?'

In an unconcerned manner, she replied, 'No, but I'll keep an eye out for it. Did it have your name on it?'

I was enraged similar to a bull to a red rag, as it may have been stolen, and I didn't have the money to be buying another. Like a crocodile I snapped at her, shouting, 'Yes, but let me tell you, I'm not doing another stitch of work, until I get my transformer, and you're paying me for every minute I'm waiting.'

I then turned for the stairs and made my way to the site office. It was a fresh morning, outside the office was a chair. Sure enough, I sat down and made myself comfortable, ready for an extended stay. When Karen appeared from one of the fire doors, walking faster than a highspeed bullet train. She slipped into one of the many container offices for various trades located on site.

A few moments later, Karen reappears out of the office with my transformer in her hand. Karen walked towards me looking a bit screwed as she trudged into her office, whereby I stood up to follow her in. Karen then went round the desk to her chair, placed the transformer on the table uttering, 'There's your transformer.'

Now the stage play can reveal the plot. I was annoyed similar to a judge when the witness is lying, and irritated, as if there were ants in my bed. I felt very much fired up, so I enquired, 'What are the bricklayers doing with my transformer? Did you give it to them?'

Usually, Karen's appearance displays bright eyes, a chirpy smile, and has a radiant glow with pink cheeks on her pale slim face, but replied with a red bull anger written on her expression when she answered, 'No.'

I thought, *They had no right to be taking man's tools without asking.*

I responded ready for a verbal war to my tone, 'Right, I'll have words with them about that.'

Karen blared out like a foghorn, 'There's no need for that Fitzroy.'

Pissed off with the whole situation I shouted back, 'Why not? They should not be taking my tools like that; I'm losing time and money looking for it.'

I should have kept my mouth shut, a big shouting match erupted in the site office, within the chaotic exchange of words Karen reaffirmed her authority stating, 'You're sacked, get out.'

That brought a snap shut silence, after a sudden earthquake in the cabin. At that juncture, I turned away with enraged silence. I felt a pressing force behind my wide bulged out eyes at the immediate financial burden, again. I just packed my tools and went home. No employment rights, why is one subjugated to less access to the resources at someone's psychotic whim?

Situations like that force some to suffer or break the unjust secular laws. I'm very resilient, am I. The next day luck, determination, the laws of probability, or the number of hits before gaining a reward, I found work.

Chapter 33

Life's pleasure

Portland nightclub had a capacity of a hundred and fifty, a small venue in central Manchester, situated on Portland Street. Being bored alone with no girlfriend in my life to talk of; a few days after New Year's Eve 1995 celebrations, I was not expecting much of a night, when I decided to socialise, doing what I like. Charlie Monroe, now my mother's ex-next-door neighbour co-incidentally secured the establishment with his muscular stature, and a commanding voice. Accompanied alongside two equivalently sized physique doormen, modelling the usual slightly tight fitted around the arms and chest, black & white penguin suits.

I haven't seen Charlie for a while, so it was nice having a big hug, and a friendly welcome in front of the queuing ladies, who were impatiently waiting to enter the warmth shelter of the venue from the bitter chilly winter whirling wind. It was whipping up a windy rushing whirlpool, as the whistling wind blew down the busy bustling city streets. It made me look important, where reputation meant a lot in what is known as Gunchester, England's capital warfare on drugs and gang life.

Charlie walked me down the flight of stairs to ensure I got in free; it was a turn I needed, I had little, or no money, and no job after an expensive penniless festive season. Lonely, in no meaningful relationship with a lion in between my legs to feed, horny, and a court case dragging on, pussy was dominating my thoughts of time without pussy. Luckily, Charlie true to his word, handled the door price, I was in the club, like a true dog sniffing.

I arrived late not early, early not late 11.45 p.m. upon entering the venue. A few dotted spots of bodies outlined shaded areas of the establishment. The club had a low ceiling, a dimly lit dance-floor dazzled your eyes as random red, blue, white flashed on and off, disco lights. I managed to focus my vision directly opposite across the empty dancefloor, to where I was stood. There I could see two lovely young Nubian queens, what looked like engrossed in conversation, when one of the sexy ladies pointed her finger in my direction. Curiously aroused, when paying closer attention to both tall slim postures in the distance, I could not see their faces clearly. Then they both walked across the empty dancefloor, heading in my direction.

Charlie was still distracted in conversation with the receptionist, as the two girls passed by me, both raising the temperature as hot as the desert sun. While inspecting my stance, their eyes dropped to my feet, shoes first, working their erotic browse up to my face, and strutted off on another level. The aroma of their perfume invited me to tap, tap, tap one on the shoulder. She shrugged off my advances, sharply with a quick snap, pulling back her arm. She added in a dismissive manner, 'What, what, what?'

As my mind looks back at the situation, she seemed scared of my presence, shy in her eyes, timid to a warm touch, delicate as a butterfly, and very inexperienced to a guy's approach, seeing her like that was cool. I busted a joke to mellow out the situation, which worked a treat.

Annabel nineteen to my twenty-eight, studied childcare with hopes of getting into healthcare, worked part time in a takeaway joint. Her friend happened to be her close sister Alisha. Annabel and I sat near the bar, enjoying one another's company with lively conversation most of the night. When the club filled up, I observe cool sexy people meander in between one another, chirping and flirting. Some of the party animals warmed themselves dancing in front of the deejay booth.

Annabel's full lips moved rhythmically to entertaining tunes played loud, yet distantly soft in the background. Her large pearl white eyes were dipped in the centre with two chocolate brown irises, which were fixed in my direction. We engaged in titillating twang of agreeable common taste, but no joy landing a close encounter of heated passion, the final frontier.

She lived in Cheetham Hill with her sister, which was in the opposite direction to my home in Whalley Range, I wasn't driving. We exchanged numbers and called one another over the next few weeks, before really getting together on her first visit to my pad. Annabel, Annabel seductive tantalisingly delightful, I don't think we shut the front door with so much heat, and passion.

Chapter 34

H.M.P. tour of duty

It's been sixteen, or eighteen months since my arrest for intent to supply class-A drugs, five months into 1995, and I'm dating Annabel. I was not taking our relationship serious; Annabel was young with hopes of going a lot further in education, where my future was uncertain, and not in my control.

It wasn't until the last night of a two-day trial; I was with Annabel. I told her I could be sentenced in the morning, after a bad first day in the witness stand. She was shocked as if she just seen her winter electric bill, and devastated, as though her house was on fire. All Annabel knew about me, was working, or in between jobs, unemployed. The trial should have been held in Manchester, but the courts were full. The case was transferred to Bolton Crown Court, a very racist part of Greater Manchester, the odds were against me.

It had been so long since I was involved in drugs, I'd forgotten the difference between a quarter of an ounce to a gram. The barrister for the prosecutor was twisting my words, and it seemed like my appointed legal aid barrister was in league with the prosecution, I sounded like a fool. On the last day, Edwin drove me to court with Cate. I arrived late, like a nervous horse, and very anxious as if I were on an operating table, I asked, 'Cate, could you testify, I brought drugs for my own addiction, and with your help, I was able to sweat out the need for the drugs when I broke my leg?'

In my eyes, Cate may look fantastic, but she showed me then, she can be cold as ice, and as crafty as a fox, when she replied, 'Sign this letter plus 5k.'

Let me tell you, I was shocked like a prisoner being electrocuted, and slapped in the back, surprised this is no jive. When I heard that, I just stood up to face the judge like a man and got three years six months. What I found funny, and cannot understand, if I were so much of a bastard towards Cate to want cash as my witness, why would Cate come to the holding cell, blubbering like a spoilt baby that just lost her dummy?

As I walked to the holding cell, hearing the accompanying court Screws talk of the inmate's sentences as their lotto numbers for this week's draw, rang through my head similar to church bells, when the bloody cell door slammed shut, the echo reverberated louder.

The thundering clash of keys, and slaps of feet banging against the steel plated floor, buffered my ears like an African banging a loud drum. The Screw walked away content with another black bastard banged up, he felt psychologically safer.

My first port of call, on my H.M.P. tour, after sentence was a transport to H.M.P. Strange Ways. It had just been refurbished, after the prison riots a few years earlier. I was not impressed with the cell. After a strip search and an induction, two to a cell, open plan toilet at the end of the bunkbed, one window opened up an inch, the smell. A table, two chairs, and a green woollen blanket over the bottom bunkbed, covered a protruding big lump from a body, there was no movement, I wasn't sure if he was dead. I stepped into the cell; the echoing slam rang out as the bloody door shut, the constant reminder I'm not going home.

Green, lime, yellow, blue I can't remember the colours of the walls, the room was small and the walls, so tall, my breath blew me back against the door. I put my things down, climbed into the top bunk, looked at the ceiling, which stared right back. I was banged up, I had to deal with it, so I focus my mind on the gym. I was tall and slim, time to get lean, trim, like the body builder Ronnie Coleman, and keep my nose clean, similar to an operating theatre.

I wasn't in Strange Ways for long, you learn as you go, fit in, and adapt. The big lump in bed happened to be my first pad mate with a lesson. He declared, 'Hi my name is Anderson, have you got any tobacco? In a few days, when the inmates order their personal canteen, I'll give you back the quarter ounce.'

I thought, *'Fine, he can't go anywhere.'*

Wrong, come the third day having watched him fill out his canteen slip, I felt reassured. In the early hours the next morning, hearing my pad mate maniacal cackle like Muttley from *Wacky Races,* keys clanged, as they shuffled against the cell door, the door opens. A Screw cries out, 'Come on Anderson, get your gear packed, you're going back to Full Sutton.'

Slam, the bloody door shut. With a big grin on his face similar to Bobo the Clown, my cellmate proclaimed, 'Sorry about the tobacco mate.'

Surprised with the course of events I replied, 'Where you going?'

Now I had to listen to this smart arse when I was being nice. Lesson of the day, someone is always scheming in order to survive. He responded, 'I come here once a month for visits, now I'm going back to a cat-A. It's not too bad there, you can cook your own food.'

The door opened, I sat there with my mouth gaped open akin to the dark deep entrance to the Eurotunnel, thinking, *'My tobacco, you bastard.'*

Anderson walked out with I had one over you look on his face, saying, 'Good luck mate, later.'

Slam, the bloody door shut. I'd been in the prison for a few days, I would see a few ex-punters in the exercise yard, but familiar black faces were not to be seen on F-wing's yard. Now, here is a situation that turns out best, for my benefit when I've just been conned, positive karma. A few days later, after being in the cell on my own, my next pad mate was Indian, he'd just got three months for a minor offence. He tried to big up himself, when he confessed, 'I've killed a man in India for disrespecting my sister. So, I came to England to escape trial.'

I thought *'Whatever.'*

At that point, he pulled out a quarter ounce of black ash, we were laughing for days. A few days went by before we were moved onto G-wing together. We hustled for tobacco, or anything we needed, and we shared what we hustled, he was an alright guy. There was a lot of excitement from the inmates because Fred West had been imprisoned, the inmates wanted to give him a kicking. A suicide on the wing, calmed everybody, right down. Fred West went to Liverpool, then he took his own life. Just to get off G-wing I took part in all activities, gym four times a week, and I worked packing junk mail in envelopes.

After a few days, I was moved to a high security wing, A-wing. It was now, I saw lots of familiar black faces. The Screws were a lot more polite with the inmates, a significant difference to the discipline regime on the other wings. I was led up to the top landing, I understood why the Screws had more respect for the inmates when I met my new pad mate, Steven Berwick. He was looking at life for a double murder, which took place at Ladbrokes bookmakers on Claremont Road.

On the other wings, there was talk of T.V. being allowed into prison cells. So, it was a delightful surprise to see a T.V. in my new pad with a new cell mate. The pad was a lot different, pictures of beautiful black women, lined the walls in tasteful underwear, and there was a separate toilet in the pad, a welcome treat. Raymond McDonald an old schoolfriend was gated up on the other side of the bars, in the double cat-A section of the wing. Raymond killed two men at a supermarket in Didsbury, he'd just been convicted, thirty years.

I was not in Strange Ways for long, the night before I was being transferred to H.M.P. Risley, I wanted to watch a movie I've never seen before, *Reservoir dogs,* which was on T.V. for the first time. The night before Steven was facing his sentence in the morning, he was as nervous as a sheep, a bull could not have been as angry, and his high spirit, lifted him off the floor as he talked. All he could chat about was his trial. I was of the mind and the opinion, *'Deal with it, I want to watch the movie.'*

I could not tell him that, there would have been a fight. We didn't know one another on the street, but we knew each other's people. I had to show concern like a nurse, the respect of a judge, and act as if I were listening keenly to radar. I was shipped out to another prison in the morning, never hearing of his outcome. Sadly, I've never had the chance to see the movie, since.

Chapter 35

Exploiting Innocence

About the time Neil and Simon first took over the Edinburgh Cellars in 2007, a young lady walked in one evening with a tall muscular blonde guy. The young lady had big brown eyes, full red lips, smooth looking tanned skin with a tight figure eight for a body, hugging the outline of a short black length coat, revealed her little propped bumper. They sat at a table and had a few drinks in the corner of the pub. As the evening flowed, the night meandered along, people were coming and going, I really wasn't paying any attention to the activities in the pub. I was busy chatting to the bar staff, as it was a quiet night.

The evening was ending, so I started to help out the bar staff by collecting a few glasses that were empty and left on the table. A couple were just leaving the bar, as I approached their table, they exited the pub, I took the moment to have a good look at the woman's bumper. In doing so, opposite me, I noticed big brown eyes watching me looking at this woman's bumper. The woman left the pub, outside earshot, when big brown eyes uttered, 'You shouldn't look at women like that.'

She stated with a polite, deep sultry eastern European tone in her voice.

This was strange I thought, *'She's with her man, and she's watching me.'*

I replied readily for a response, 'I can't wait to have a good look at yours.'

The young man looked on and wasn't saying anything. The young lady stood up, twisted around towards me, and bent over slightly. Then she lifted up her tiny black coat, so I could see her lovely little bumper. The sexy lady turned her head looking straight at me with her full pink glossy lips. In that moment she enquired, 'What do you think?'

She then glided the tip of her tongue across her lips, which caused a slight tight feeling in my pants. I added in a northern manner with a stiff upper lip, 'Very nice.'

As my Adams apple jumped up and down my throat like a slow elevator, her bumper looked lean, firm, and full of bounce, which ran down her upper thigh with a shapely delight, hugging her tight fitted jeans, her legs were not a stick more like a chicken leg, tender and meaty. My throat rose up, my pants felt tighter. She turned towards my direction, then added, 'My name is Vicky what's yours?'

I was surprised at her forward advance for my attention. I answered, 'Fitzroy, you can call me Fitz E. What's your boyfriends name?'

As if she were a contestant on the T.V. quiz show *Blankety Blank,* point blank, Vicky reacted, 'He's not my boyfriend. Do you drink in here all the time?'

Stimulated by her smile and the free-flowing exchange of words, I replied, 'Every now and then. You don't sound English, where are you from?'

I felt a bit uneasy with the situation, the guy she was with was not getting much respect from the young lady. Vicky walked around the table with her every step, looking in my direction. Her eyes took a slow cruise up and down my body length, in the sexiest of ways. The young man she was with, stood up, still not saying a word. In that moment, Vicky informed me, 'I'm from the Czech Republic, I hope to see you in here another time.'

With her words, both of them left the pub, Vicky had a smile on her face, which brought a bigger smile to mine.

As the days and weeks passed, I got to know Vicky very well, she told me, 'I came to England to get away from my boyfriend, back home in the Czech Republic for a few months, which gives me time to think about our relationship.'

She had deep feelings for her man, I didn't want to confuse her young mind by coming onto her. She was only nineteen at the time I met her, and well, my son was older than her.

She went onto say, how she left her parent's home when she was sixteen, and had been paying her own way through college, while doing a part time job. The girl was as independent as an American citizen, her intelligence always provoked good conversations, she was bright similar to the sunshine, and a joy to be with.

The days and weeks had turned into two months, and finally Vicky found a job in Angel, Islington as a trainee waitress. I knew the establishment she was referring to. I was also aware they always had a sign in the window looking for waiters and waitresses, which made me wonder, why they could not keep hold of their staff! Vicky explained, 'For the first two weeks, I would have to work 40 hours per week without pay because I was being trained.'

Thereafter, a sum was mentioned, I didn't like what the job was offering.

Vicky was giving so much and getting little in return, but in her mind she needed the job, this being the first one offered to her since she'd been in England, she had to take the job. I didn't see much of Vicky over the next few weeks, both our working timetables meant we couldn't see one another.

When I did get to see Vicky, a couple of weeks later, she was highly stressed, as tense as the Humber Bridge. Vicky looked as though she was crying with big red puffed up bags under her eyes. She clarified, 'The job was okay, not too busy but there were about six other waiters and waitresses from different nationalities, who always seemed to be arguing amongst themselves for one reason or another. We weren't allowed to keep the tips, and fresh staff were coming and going all the time. After the two weeks training was over, I was given the sack.'

Of course, the loss of her job meant she was unable to pay her rent, which was due the following week. I felt her suffering, but I was not in a good financial situation to help her out, I had little or no money at the time. However, I did offer her my spare room if she was in need. I didn't see or hear from Vicky for a few days.

In time, I phoned her a couple of times, and she didn't return any of my calls. With a bit of concern, I thought, *'It's time to pay her a visit.'*

When I did see Vicky, her eyes were bloodshot red, puffed-up dark bags blossomed under her eyes from tears. She invited me into her bedsit, then told me, 'My landlord would be around in the next few days. He wants four weeks rent paid, or if I didn't have the money, he would accept payment in kind.'

A big old married man wanting to take advantage of a young mind, we expose our kids to this. She went on with our conversation, 'I'm going back to the Czech Republic once I've received some money from my parents in a few days, so I can take a coach back home.'

I offered her my spare room to keep her out of harm's way, she took my offer, and for the next few days she showed me she would make a great housewife. Every day, for the next five days, I woke up to an English breakfast, and a warm meal welcomed me home after an exhausting day at work. The night before she was leaving, I was pleasantly surprised when feeling the warmth of her body slip under the sheets on my bed. Let me tell you, triple X-rated night mate ☺.

Chapter 36

False twist on love, marriage

With nothing but time on my hands to think and reflect on the past, isn't that what prisoners are supposed to do? When I was seventeen, meeting new exciting sexy young people gossip, chatter of clubs, concerts events, unemployed, and she's pregnant again, mate's love affairs with so-called friends, didn't sit nice in my mind but still, a stimulating energetic vibe.

So, when hearing of a friend, who happened to be a few years older than myself, he was twenty-five, and a good fusion dancer, on the dancefloor is where we met. He'd just left university with a new bride to tow. As a mixed-race couple his family being black, made it known in a polite old West Indian fashion, their disapproval of the young couple's union, fuelled by racist ignorance from the bride's parents.

Thatcher is head of government in 1983, unemployment was high, job prospects very low. He gained employment in France, advertising, art, and design. He could only afford to come back to Manchester once a month for the weekends. That being the case, we did not see much of him, he was head over heels in love. She was twenty-two, figure eight fit, very attractive, which is an understatement. She modelled long strawberry blonde hair, pale fluffy white skin, sky blue eyes, and her radiant smile, drove men wild. An admin worker, unemployed at the time, and a wannabe actress with an alluring sleazy demure. I did not know her well, her flirtatious giggles on her nights out with his mates, did not make for good friends to be associated, too closely.

Nine months after being married, six months in France, when he was sending money home to his wife, she was not paying the mortgage, their two-bed semi defaulted, they'd lost their house. On his return, coming back from France, when he was approaching his wife's parent's home in Cheshire, the husband finds his friends bell end, banging his wife's inners, pleasuring the upper reaches of his wife's fur cup, jacked up over the horse stable gate. His wife was a bitch, she bellowed out like a town crier for everyone to hear, her antics when I attended a barbie one summer. The wife informed the guests, how regular she received deep intermit thrusting connections with his brother, and two friends spit roasted her on her hen night.

Believe me when I say, she was as bored as a five-year-old watching the news, a horny page three model, and a lot more explicit, a graphic designer could not have drawn up more exact details.

A few days later, he threw himself from the top floor of a block of flats in Hulme with a rope round his neck. His neck didn't snap, one on looker described him kick dance fighting in mid-air like Bruce Lee. As he kicked, he smashed a window in panic for his life, gripping both hands around the tightening rope, swinging violently, his hands suddenly dropped to his side, a motionless leg dangled as the other trembled franticly to a sudden stop. The volatile swings, gently decreased oscillating like the pendulum from a grandfather clock. The discomforting pivot drifted in the moist warm summer wind, the horrifying scene, embraced a shuddering ambience in the atmosphere, sending a cold displeasing shock of electric down one's back. He passed away before anyone arrived to help him.

Lonely minds

To play games on love can be cruel, it shows hatred towards love not knowing love, sold to an illusion engraved from a false sense of reality.
Too higher expectation on love, is believing this is how it should be, when no one can explain what love is.
Is love misguided, intended for the two of us?
Reproduction of love, there's the pleasure of love, God's gift to us, share one's love, and labour.
Lonely minds, love is meant to create another idea, an education of life for life.
Gaining knowledge, avoiding death, having wisdom to make friends.

John T. Hope

Chapter 37

Sheep follow sheep.

Having left Strange Ways to be transported to H.M.P. Risley, in Warrington, it had a main prison for long serving prisoners and a relocation centre, which is where I was located. The cells weren't much different than Strange Ways. I didn't need to share my pad, but the low indignant way inmates had to slop out every morning was lower than low, in this day and age. The regime wasn't hard to conform to, there was no work, or education available because there was a quick turn over of inmates.

As a consequence, we were banged up every other day, for 23 hours a day. I was never one for reading, so I spent most of my time exercising in my pad. When there was no gym, I'd end up sleeping after training in my single cell. Annabel made every effort to find out, which prison I was in, even when I said, 'Don't bother.'

She was not having it and demanded visiting orders. I wanted to be true to myself, the chances of a ship out too far for my family to travel was high. I told Beverly, and Annabel not to wait but neither one wanted to lose contact. We wrote one another, which was a new experience for me, expressing my thoughts in a letter, romantic not, sex was what I wrote about, the thought of them waiting or wanting me made me feel good. It gave me the sense and reassurance I was loved, and not just, a badman locked up.

There wasn't a lot of inmates on my floor, during association there were about twenty men playing pool, table tennis, passing time. I never wasted my time queuing for the phone, there was never enough time to say anything, and nothing to talk about, being banged up. The only man I knew was from Moss Side Alan Fraser, he was serving two years for G.B.H.

It was everyone's hope to get Buckley Hall Rochdale a cat-C, cat-D prison. It was near Manchester, good for visits but more importantly, it was a new private jail, and the Screws were pussies compared to H.M.P. Screws, so I was told. Like a sheep, I put my name down for Buckley Hall, Risley main wing, and Stafford. I didn't know much about Stafford, it was the nearest from the four offered, and Moorland in Yorkshire was hell, so I was told.

After three weeks of slam, the bloody door, Alan poked his head in my pad with the sorriest face ever. His bottom lip was sliding along the floor, and his head between his legs, as he walked into my pad. I asked, 'You look well pissed off, what's up mate?'

He stood there in his prison blue jacket, and his badly stitched jeans hung uncomfortably loose around the waist, which were too long, they were dragging along the floor like slippers. While his grass green jumper, did him no justice for fashion sense with one side of his white shirt collars stuck out, just under his chin. He had short black cotton hair, a comb needed to rearrange, and his black shiny skin, stood out like a domino spot against the prison white washed walls. Alan replied, 'I'm being shipped out to Stafford in an hour. It's a shithole there, my luck that. I bet you go to Buckley Hall.'

He went back to his cell, and said his bye's fifty minutes later, then he was gone.

A week later, I was still at Risley, I didn't know anyone, the new inmates were not as friendly as the first group I met. When a Screw asked if I wanted to go to Stafford, I just wanted to be relocated, get on with my bird with not so much moving. Six different cells in two jails wow, not forgetting the holding cells. I thought *'Alan is at Stafford a familiar face.'*

So, I said, 'Yes.'

Then I was shipped out to Stafford an hour later.

Chapter 38

Benny's Radcliff

Oh, for the love of memories, especially when you're banged up 23 hours of the day. After Russ and Sherri left 38 Cadogan Street, they moved to one of the flats at Seven Sisters in Old Trafford, directly opposite the derelict flats of William Kent Crescent. Their relationship was on the rocks, me, and Beverly were fine, not.

Saturday nights out with Russ and myself were becoming more regular, the girls preferred weekends in chatting with their other sisters. With Russ driving, we attended the usual spots come weekend. We'd party in the Gallery on Peter Street; the venue had been going for some years. Soul Control Sound System promoted the venue playing R & B, and hip hop. It was packed every week along with the gangster tip, which was becoming more violent. We were more interested in the music, and women. It was time for a change.

Benny's in Radcliff, a very secluded establishment was situated about nine hundred yards off the main highway, down a beat-up mud road, across an unused railway track, through some arch bent bushes and trees. In a clearing, there the club appeared from out of the darkness in big red lights, BENNY'S. It looked like a big barn conversion; red wooden shutters covered the windows with white walls, a queue of lovely ladies in beautiful coloured dresses and short revealing skirts highlighted their legs. This put an extra flutter to my heartbeat with the excitement of pulling a bird.

The venue was a nice L shaped bar, mirrored walls reflected the length of the dancefloor, which had a short width. There were a few columns that held up the low ceiling, they provided somewhere intimate to hide. Brown Chesterfield leather sofas blotted around the club, so you could be seated and have a quiet chat with cool people who had class. We grabbed a drink and started to mingle. It wasn't before long a short blonde, a brunette, and a curly perm from a cheeky tall leggy mixed-race woman caught our attention.

The leggy mixed-race woman happened to be called Lora Wright, twenty-eight, two kids with a nice bumper, we chatted for a bit, she flirted quite a lot, I felt bold, so slapped her on her arse, she enjoyed the moment, and wanted more, but I was not driving, Russ did not know I'd scored. By the time I hooked up with Russ, he was in there with the blonde. At the end of the night, we had breakfast in a cosy bar upstairs. When the evening came to an end, we gave them a lift to Lora's four-bedroom terrace. The brunette in tow was Lora's housemate, Kim. They lived close by Russ's blonde, I think, her name was Helen, she lived five hundred yards away in a one-bedroom flat. I thought, *'Perfect, let's have some sex.'*

Lora wasted no time doing.

Weeks before Beverly moved out of Cadogan Street, and working my last year as a trainee carpenter, it was only Saturdays at Benny's when I was able to see Lora. As time passed, I noticed vodka brought a change to her personality, she was very flirtatious with men, when I see things like that, I tend to walk away, watch, and find a distraction. My distraction towards other women was something Lora made clear she didn't like me doing, but I'm not one to point out how the other's acting, you should know, so I said nothing.

What I found funny, while she was giving me an earwigging about chatting to women, Lora's eyes were wondering away from my direction, down the length of the bar. When I took a closer look to where she was eyeballing, a muscular black guy in a blue pinstriped suit was all teeth, wide eyed, and fixing his tie. I stated, 'Lora, if you want to meet that guy, tell me, I'll introduce you.'

Her mouth dropped like ten tons of bricks were hanging from her bottom jaw. She rotated her head dead slowly to look in my direction, her big brown eyes widened, nearly popping out of her head. Lora answered, 'You what?'

Aroused at the sight of her deep cleavage, and the sweet smell of her exotic perfume, I stated firmly, 'Tell me what you're doing? Giving me an ear full, or eyeing him up? I don't care either way.'

Then she replied, 'No I wasn't.'

I responded, 'What do you mean, you wasn't?'

With a cheeky dismissive tone Lora countered, 'I wasn't eyeballing him up.'

I thought, *'Here we go again, too much drink you little liar, I know what you need.'*

Firm but well mannered, I stated, 'Follow me, come outside.'

I did not wait for an answer, I stepped forward for the main door and she followed up behind, not a word was said between us. Being a gentleman, I let her pass in front of me, as we weaved and pushed our way through the thick crowd of party animals. She looked very sexy in her high heels, her bumper was propped up, pumped up, ready for a shot. There was a slight slit down the side of a black-short French skirt, exposing her mixed-race caramel-coloured legs and her strong firm thighs. Two thin shoulder straps loosely held a white silk top, she never wore a bra, revealing the outline of her dark grape like nipples, oh my word what a thrill.

We stepped out of the vibrant club, to the warm summer air with the soft subtle breeze whipping up the whistling wind, and we crunched, crunched, crunched on a gravel path as we casually strolled. I took the lead walking towards the car park, situated at the back of the building. It was about 1.30 a.m. people stopped arriving and were dancing. She opened her mouth with a curious question to the tone in her voice, 'Where you going?'

Seductively, yet firm and commanding I responded, 'Shut up and come here.'

I continued to walk around to the back of the club, away from the artificial illuminated flood lit front, the club lights were replaced by a full moon. Recesses in the building corners pulled us into the dark shaded areas from any light source that shone on our faces. She walked towards me; I grabbed her arms, then I shuffled her around, causing her to step backward up against a wall, she stopped.

I pressed her even further into the wall and placed a kiss on her sweet cherry lips. Her arousal was immediate, the response she kissed back. I quickly made an advance up her skirt with one hand from the front of her crutch, the other hand was behind her lower back. She was really enjoying the heat, and the passion over flowed. So, I gently rubbed her fur lined cup, which caused her to shiver slightly at the knees. Then she grabbed my butt, at that point pulled me tighter against her firm jelly like breasts. I whispered in her hear, 'You dirty bitch, you love it don't you?'

A moan of delightful pleasure and a deep, exhale of her breath. I lifted up her short French skirt higher, holding her G-string firm and tight with both hands, then I ripped them off similar to Tommy Cooper pulling off a tablecloth. The weight of her chin dropped suddenly onto my shoulder. She quivered at the knees, wobbling slightly back, excited by my actions. I continued to whisper, 'Don't you ever chat to me like that again, you dirty bitch.'

She looked at me with her big puppy seal brown eyes, submissively replying, 'Okay Fitz, teach me a lesson, f--k me hard.'

She pushed me away slightly from my belt, then pulled me back towards her long stride legs, which resembled the Eiffel tower. Before I knew it, my fly was undone, as I lavished kisses along her neck. Both of her hands grabbed my manhood, pulling it hard, and snappy, towards her dripping fur cup. Tenderly, she stroked my extendable thick black throbbing trunk, then guided my length in between her thighs up towards her fur lined lips, hard and ready slip, it was in. Need I say more, she liked it like that, heated, rough, hardcore, yes from behind, K9 style, she was up for anything.

Confess

Ladies you like to do it but you don't like when it's done.
You take your pick then dump really quick.
Let's be honest, you know you just want it, let's stop the lies,
be honest, your just like guys, horny.
How can one deny, then lie, this gift of pleasure,
an expression of love when we're together.
Let's not confuse the issue, it's about the one, not us two.
We're on a mission, enjoy the pleasure, it's part of life's leisure.

John T. Hope

Chapter 39

Two can play

Long journeys in a prisoner's transport vehicle were known as meat wagons. There not very comfortable, the window in the transport are too high from the hard plastic seat, the scene on the trip was my feet. Upon arriving at H.M.P. Stafford, it was one holding cell to another. Finally, I was thrown in a cell on G-wing, situated on the first floor. It was 23 hours bang up unless you were employed. Since I was getting inducted, I had to enrol from a choice. I thought, *'Education always needs improving.'*

I decided to sign up for a business and finance course, first B-Tec Diploma with a new skill to learn, computers. The pads were two to a cell, my pad mate let's call him Ted, he was always in bed, he didn't stay long he was packed then gone, a day had passed on my own, it was nice not having to share, I felt safe, one could shout, 'Rape!'

Nobody would care, luckily I met good pad mates. As I gazed into space, counting cracks in the ceiling paint, the keys clanged against my cell door, a warning of a Screw entering. The door swings open, a Screw shouts out, 'Edwards, new pad mate.'

Entered Deejay Johnathan Edwards, slam, the bloody door shut. The world is so large yet very tiny, you could tell my new pad mate had been in jail for a while. He had broad shoulders, and a wide back, this black guy wore glasses, just like me, I've never met him before, so we started chatting, we had a lot in common. He was from Manchester, born and bred; a few years older than me. I thought, *'Armed robbery, seven years, lucky a low sentence for his offence, but I'm no judge.'*

He was transferred from the main prison wing of H.M.P. Risley for fighting, after spending two years there. He was more concerned about visits from his girlfriend, and their two kids. We both enrolled for education courses, which were full. As a consequence, we sat in our pad, unemployed for weeks. We spent most of our time chatting, playing dominoes, slamming hard till four, five o'clock in the morning. Only to hear the Screws shouting, 'LESS BLOODY NOISE.'

This guy knew everyone I knew in Moss Side, but I couldn't place his face.

In that moment, he reminded me of a club in Trafford Park he promoted with deejays I knew from the pirate radio station. Our heads banged even harder when Cate's name came up, it all fell into place, memories of the evening when we talked of the night, it was the only time I attended. The night mentioned Cate looked as sexy as Sade, her friend Toni Jenkins at eighteen, nineteen had two kids, joined us for the evening. Toni really likes men, but that's another story to tell.

When we got to the venue mentioned, pure men I knew were raving, drinks were flowing with chatter and laughter, the guys could not have been happier. Cate and Toni were buzzing, weed was burning, it was lovely watching them dance, it was all wholesome fun, bubbly with pure jokers. I never worry who my woman's talking with when we're out partying, it's about social-ising, rapping a rhyme with guys or dolls, it's nothing, you're coming home with me, I'm confident, and assertive. I have a lot of respect for my woman, when out and about together, especially if I care. So, I know when to hold my corner and how to square the books. If my girl likes to flirt, I do. If she likes to chat with others, so do I. I never ask a question if I do, I ask once, then there's a response.

Cate drifted around the club with Toni, they danced, and they were provoked, I watched as this bloke approached, she laughed, then she came back to me, we kissed, and then she caressed me, I felt reassured. At the end of the night, I called a taxi. While we waited, she had a wander, when the taxi pulled up Cate and Toni were right beside me. I open the door to let them in, out of nowhere a voice cried out, 'Cate.'

We all looked around to see a lovely black eight series B.M.W. and a guy waving Cate over. What I did not like was when Cate hesitated, she thought twice before entering the taxi. Thinking twice was a mistake, which wasn't nice. The guy who shouted her name was Deejay, he had a lot more to say, he knew her quite well. I felt better, any guilt I harboured concerning other women, had gone, knowing I had pleasure with one of her friends.

Chapter 40

Not a care in the world

Before I was banged up, and not working or introducing myself to women, weekends were fun times with my son when I could afford it. On Friday 21st July 1989, there was a lovely clear blue sky, on a hot summer's day. Just after I returned my son to my mother's new home in Hulme, which was on a new yellow brick housing estate, I made my way to the bus stop on Royce Road, opposite a local pub called, the Spinners Arms. The road was very quiet, less than Sunday traffic, no one could be seen along the dry heat waved road and path. Curving behind me was the empty derelict flats of William Kent Crescent.

The calming silence was broken by a sudden almighty bang. The soothing silence soon returned, as my head twisted, and rotated looking for the cause of the noise. Then bang, bang in quick succession, I'm thinking to myself, *'It could be the backfire from a car, out of sight, behind the block of flats.'*

When in that moment, a tall black man appeared from the Spinners Arms, walking calmly towards me. The ground shuddered as each one of his steps hit the floor firm, sure footed with a straight up right back, a proud distinguished stature. He advanced toward me with a distant glossy glare in his eyes, accompanied by nothing but silent thoughts, and a quiet wind, whipping up a whirlwind with the whistling wind tickling my ears. A shot gun emerged in his right arm, swinging with military honours, passing me politely without a care, or bother. He floated by me like a ship on a calm ocean. At that point, he disappeared in the growing distance as calmly as he'd appeared.

I just caught my bus and went on my way; I was later informed he'd killed Henderson Proverb in the pub.

Two shots to the chest, and one in the head, the splatter of blood, the scene in the pub, dead. How can one live with the thought, he'll have to answer for it?

Or not knowing, the unknown, one has no fear, does that make one brave?

Bravery for me, is one who can risk his or her life for another, in the face of danger, or death, without harming another.

You don't get intelligence for nothing, there is always a catch. We've been told do not kill. A man must defend his life without the death of another. The death of a person cannot be defended, isn't that the discipline necessary when using force?

Chapter 41

Forgive them not

As I sit in my cell, looking back at the past through the crystal ball in my mind, I remember being situated on the first floor of William Kent, meant living above unused garages smelling of urine. Corners of the empty shells were stained black from burnt out fires, and the early evolution of graffiti sprayed on the walls, reminded me of a caveman's drawings. Around the back of the flats, facing the car entrance of the garage, a blue early sixties Ford mobile grocery van that did not move because it had no wheels, provided the needs for the locals. The nearest shop was a bit of a distance. Joe Bing, from the West Indies, projected a bubbly fun-loving owner manager, assisted by his wife, and his four daughters, who attended my primary school.

Just below my window was the Eagle pub, situated in the middle of the estate, close by was Joe's parked grocery van. As they were both positioned below my bedroom window, I viewed the daily goings on, crime, robbery, and pissheads fighting. Whenever I went to the van for my mother, I'd overhear Joe's wife regularly earwigging him about drinking in that pub.

One late night, dimly lit from a distant streetlamp shone on the scene, the noise of men shouting and crying woke me from my slumber sleep. When I looked out of the window, crowds of men look like herds of cattle were just below in front of the pub. At the garage entrance, circling around two men, the crowd of on lookers, watched the two men's arms swing forward and back. When I looked closer at the two men, they had knives in their hands, jabbing, and stabbing at one another. Their shuffling feet danced to the cry of men that sounded similar to warriors going to battle, were all watching the drama.

Then, a sudden pounce, a thrust from one of the men to the chest of the second man, I noticed, it was Joe collapsing like a heap of rubbish dumped by a dustbin truck on the ground. The other man jumped back like Kris Kross singing *Jump*, to watch Joe's body length slowly unfold on the cold floor. Joe was spreadeagled facing the night sky above, I looked into his glazed motionless eyes, the transfix feeling of me falling into a deep dark bottomless pit, drifted me away with him. The reality, his sight lost, and senses no longer functioned, a stab to the heart ended his life.

Not a nice memory for a seven-year-old to have in his mind, it plays a part in becoming a man. Our kids should not have to see, witness, or take part in violence, they become warmongers, like Hitler, and many other political blood lust vermin.

Chapter 42

Booze & Bury

Bang up is pure leisure, there's no pleasure, pussy batters one's mind, thinking back, what a night. There has only been one club, I've had the misfortune of being thrown out, due to Lora Wright. This happened about the time Beverly moved out of Cadogan Street when my apprenticeship was completed, unemployed, and I just started selling drugs.

Lora and Helen invited both Russ and me to the Roxy in central Bury. We had nothing planned, so we went down in his car, and picked the girls up, I thought, *'Thursday night, not so busy.'*

Wrong, I've never been there before, as we walked through a tunnel entrance into a bingo like hall. As you entered the large open space, to your left, long sweeping stairs carried you up to a balcony overhead, which looked over the huge dancefloor below. Towards the back of the large balcony space, led into another dancehall. The place was a maze filled with girls. Me, and Russ looked at one another with glee, we lost our girls quick in a sea of people. Then we went on the search for flirty, sexy women.

As I meandered with the crowd of lovely people, I approached the long sweeping stairs, an image from *Gone with the wind*, where I caught sight of an old friend from four or five years earlier, when I was spinning tracks in Preston. She stood at the top of the steps not noticing me, so I made my way up to say hello. Tracy Millar gave me a very warm welcome, hugs, and kisses, giggling with her friend in delight, about the good old days as she introduced me to her friend. We stood at the top of the stairs with my back to the first step down, overlooking the main dancefloor. I was perched on the handrail with my face looking at the door to the second dancehall.

We both stood chatting for a good ten minutes when Tracy

declared, 'I just moved back to Bury, after touring Eastern Europe with my friends. It is really nice timing us meeting up like this. We're planning a party later on in the summer, is your sound system available to play in a tarpaulin with drinks and food, providing entertainment for one thousand?'

In my mind, *'It sounded really nice, a summer party that paid,'* I thought, *'Yeah this could be great.'*

From the depth of the dimly lit balcony, I could see Lora looking pissed on vodka, advancing towards me resembling a bull to a red rag, Lewis Hamilton wasn't quite fast enough. She approached like a ballistic missile, very aggressively. Pushing Tracy out of her way, bordering on an express steam train, then she had the cheek to push her face up to mine, flapping her lips akin to a camel with, 'I can't leave you for five minutes, and you're chatting to women.'

I was stood on the top step, right at the edge of the stairs, when she pushed me, I lost my footing and balance. I then started running backward down the sweeping stairs. Lord knows how I managed to get to the bottom without breaking my neck. I straightened up to attention, looked at myself, I was fine, I wasn't harmed, I'm cool. Lora followed soon after, verbally loud not unlike a trumpet. I stood away from her and brushed myself down. Tracy came over to me with concerns about Lora. As the night unfolded, it was a surprise when Tracy spoke up, 'I'm sorry if I caused you any trouble Fitz.'

Unhappy with the course of events, I replied, 'You don't have to say sorry.'

She added, 'I'll have a word with her, I'll explain.'

Tracy was off in a rush before I could say a word, the following scene wasn't nice, I didn't hear what was said, but Lora was screaming and shouting, like the bitch she is. Tracy was five foot five, Lora's legs were reminiscent of the twin towers, five foot eleven, did I mention, a big mouth. I could see that the situation was getting heated, Lora's presence was overbearing and hanging over Tracy, similar to a bad dark creepy shadow. Tracy was then forced backward into a corner, Lora struck out, and attacked Tracy parallel to a wild deranged cat. Lora was grabbing Tracy's hair, dragging

Tracy's head all over the place. Lora was ripping off Tracy's clothes viciously, exposing her breasts with a punch to her head, Tracy was in a state. I raced over to stop the fight, but the bouncers pulled me back, dragging me out of the club instead. I did not say a word, or do a thing, and I was out on my ear at 1 a.m. where's my mate.

About five minutes later, Russ comes out of the club with Helen, and Lora followed, very loud, irate, embarrassing the situation for everybody. Helen's flat was not far, I decided to walk, the noise emanating from Lora's mouth was doing my head in. After they took Lora home, I met Russ and Helen, at Helen's apartment. Helen was so nice towards me, she gave me a blanket, and they both left me to sleep on the living room sofa. I got myself wrapped in the woollen blanket, comfy, relaxed twenty minutes into drifting off, when I could hear the muffled sound of a rhythmic beat, boom, boom, boom, and the moans of pleasurable sex arouse my manhood. The knocking beat of the bedhead against the wall, increased its pace, frustrated my mind, I longed for sex. So, I got out of my makeshift bed, put my pants on, then I crept out the door on my way to Lora's house. I got to Lora's crib, then knocked on the door, the response after a moment was not welcoming. Lora looked out of the upstairs window blaring out, 'F--k off.'

I was not giving up that easy, so I went round to the back, down the *Coronation Street* cobbled alley way, and climbed over her garden wall. I got hold of along stick that held up the washing line to tap, tap, tap on her back-bedroom window. The hallway light came on, after a moment the backdoor swung open. There she stood, in a black knee length silk dressing robe. Just like an artist sketching a beautiful work of art, the windy whirlwind whipped up the whistling wind that gently blew her robe in between her legs, defining the outline of her coke a cola bottle shape figure. The silk robe cupped her valley, arousing my desires. She knew what she was doing. In a hostile way, but with a firm sexy tone, she enquired, 'What do you want?'

Lora's hand pressed against her stomach, which held the silk dressing robe in place. I walked towards her, she stepped back yapping like an overplayed record, 'What do you want?'

I pushed her firm but gently, she retreated, which allowed me to walk in, and close the backdoor. Lora stepped back, not wanting to take her eyes off me, she was breathing so deeply her chest puffed up like a balloon. She inhaled so hard, I could hear her heart beating faster with excitement, and heavy, not dissimilar to an impatient train blowing along puff of steam. She manoeuvred herself into the open plan stairway living room. A sofa was situated opposite the flight of stairs, Lora continued walking backwards falling into the sofa. I undid my belt, pulled out my choice black muscular flesh, as I advanced toward her I offered my manhood to her mouth. She leaned forward to accept my proposal; her moist big wet mouth opened up like a pink flower opening up to the sunlight. In that moment, I gave her a raunchy slap in her face with my tool, her eyes rolled round like a white golf ball, her tongue flickered similar to a rattlesnake, Lora's moans of delight cried out for more of the same. So, I slapped her with my black stiff tool again, again, and again. Lora's head rolled from side to side wanting, searching, fighting for my rod to drop in her mouth.

She grew impatient, then grabbed hold of my thick long stiff shaft, engulfing most of my length in her deep moist throat. I pleasured her hardcore, exploring positions on the stairs, the dining chair and back on the sofa. I pulled out at her moment of climax, it follows, I released my juices in her face, she was breathless, panting, gasping for air. Her body shivered franticly, dripping with heated passionate sweat. I put my pants on looking over her, as she laid there exhausted and satisfied. I stood over her, then I declared, 'That's the last time you'll feel that.'

I turned around to do an Elvis Presley and left the building, then I went back to Helen's, and I haven't seen her since.

Chapter 43

Pad mate's story

After a week in H.M.P. Stafford on the induction wing, I bumped into Alan on the exercise yard, miserable as ever. When I introduced him to Deejay Johnathan, they knew one another beforehand. We followed Alan to meet up with a few other Moss Side inmates, I did not feel so alone, they were all familiar faces. A lump came to my throat, when watching a man with his head drooped to his chest, shuffling his feet, as he walked round the yard. It took him a good few minutes to move a yard. I heard Alan say, 'That's the venlafaxine shuffle, a drug they give to sick disobedient inmates. He's just come out of the mental health hospital wing of the prison. Piss the Screws off here, you'll end up like him.'

It was said with a disdain bitter hatred for the system in his voice. I thought to myself, *'I hope I don't become mentally ill in here.'*

Deejay Johnathan and I got on really well, when moving over to the main prison wing together after being on the induction wing for four weeks, we moved onto F-wing, and finally we got started in the educational department. For months we did the same thing, banging dominoes to hear a Screw bellow out, 'LESS BLOODY NOISE.'

Education, gym, sleeping, and slam, the bloody door shut, again. Since Beverly didn't drive I did not see her or my family, but on the odd occasion Annabel wanted to visit, even when she moved to London to take her nursing degree, Deejay's girlfriend gave her a lift on one occasion. Weed was in short supply, nevertheless being friendly with a father and son from Wolverhampton banged up next door, they tended to show me and Deejay love, by offering us a joint from time to time.

I kept my head down and got on with my bird.

There may have been someone with you in your pad, but my first Christmas 1995 inside was the loneliest I've ever been. I was a bit concerned, there were less birds flying around the prison over the Christmas and New Year period. Christmas dinner, and government cutbacks was on my mind.

Midnight New Year's Eve, an eruption from the inmates kicking every door on the wings banging, slamming viciously for freedom. The constant clanging of metal doors against cast iron doorframes was mind numbing, it went on for about an hour.

Being banged up with a pad mate, many stories are to be told, some true, many not so true. That late night evening, Deejay Johnathan tells me his reason for being transferred to Stafford, which did not sound so cool, he articulated, 'I met a fellow inmate who was coming to the end of his twenty-five years sentence. We became friends the moment we met at Risley. This guy was in his late sixties and had been in jail for a long while. When going on his home leave, this old guy was amazed at modern technology, especially escalators. After many times of me asking the guy, finally this old guy tells me of his offence. This old guy had a five-year-old grandson at the time, he was found guilty of raping. There was further evidence showing this old guy was also having sex with a small terrier retriever.'

Deejay was sick as a parrot upon hearing his offence, lost his Fonz's, as a consequence he beat nine bells out of him in his cell.

These sex offenders are disgusting men and women, doing it with animals, sick, and his grandson, Good God. The fact the law sees them as mentally ill, is not an excuse to treat them with kid gloves. An example, days out, home leave, what's that all about?

Chapter 44

My luck or not

Time seemed very much to be at a standstill as the weeks and months dragged into the New Year of 1996. Two foolish inmates tried to escape, they were caught within hours when it was rumoured, one of the inmates broke his leg falling from a nineteen-foot prison wall, slowing their escape, as one was trying to help the other. In the distance, screams of pain echoed throughout the jail identical to a fox being strangled, repeatedly crying out, 'Mummy, I want my mummy, where's my mummy. Mummy, I want my mummy, where's my mummy.'

In the foreground, Tim Westwood was on the radio playing hip hop, as the bellows of a man crying for his mummy put inmates to sleep, placing an uncomfortable nod to one's slumber.

In the morning, the inmates clunked, clunk, clunk down the cast iron stairs to be served breakfast. A thinner than the usual mattress was drooped on the guardrail for everyone to see. When I asked, 'What's that used for?'

An inmate replied, 'They put it over you, so when you get a kicking, there are no marks.'

I thought, *'Very worrying to hear.'*

I wouldn't say I made good friends, but I got on with most people I encountered in education, gym, and the exercise yard. Everyone I knew in Stafford was coming to the end of their sentence, released, or on a transfer list closer to home. Deejay and I, put our names down for Buckley Hall in Rochdale. The transfer was approved in March 1996, but not before an inmate from Manchester, called Ken Milton was transferred to H.M.P. Risley main stay. News got back from Ken to Stafford Deejay was a grass. The problem was, which deejay! Everyone knew me as Fitz a deejay, confusing. At the time, I wasn't aware of the gossip on the wing. Sure enough, excited about my transfer, word of me and Deejay Johnathan leaving got to the wrong ears.

Usually, I would train with Deejay, on this day in question, Deejay didn't want to go to the gym, I thought nothing of it, so I went to the gym. The inmates got to the large gym space, everyone paired up, found their equipment, and got on with their exercise. I teamed up with the father and son from Wolverhampton. There was only one Screw on duty when there should have been two, the one Screw, then decides to go to the toilet. While I was doing bent over rows someone crept up from behind me, like a snake stalking a rat. Then I felt an almighty punch, a blind blow to the right side of my face. Semiconscious, I just dropped to one knee, similar to a lift or elevator that's lost its weights. The pair of 15k dumb bells I had in my hands, slammed down hard, banging on the padded concrete floor, and rolled away from my grip. The father and son ran over to help, all I heard was, 'We didn't see him coming, you're a strong man. Fitz, are you okay?'

I shook my head, in an attempt to come around, as they pulled me up to my feet. I felt dazed like Daffy Duck getting hit over the head with a frying pan, dazzled after a punch from Mohammad Ali, and starry eyed, as if I'd been whacked from Spawn when he clubs me in the head. I got up, made my way to the shower room, on my way, someone pointed out who punched me. I called the stocky white chap into the shower room; we both walked in and closed the door. I enquired, 'What did you do that for?'

In a very aggressive manner, dancing like an American Indian hoping for rain, and prancing not dissimilar to the boxer Sugar Ray Leonard. He replied, 'You're a grass.'

Still not completely clearheaded from the earlier blow I responded, 'I came in on this sentence on my own. The only person I've grassed up was over ten years ago with his family's permission.'

In that moment, a suggestion, or thought entered my mind, which I always follow, I never question my mind, it said, *'Offer the other cheek.'*

Which I did and he took the offer. A terrific punch to the left-hand side of my chin. I folded up, collapsing to one knee, similar to a tower block after being exploded I crumbled up. In that split second, within my mind something was revealed to me, *'Prophecy has been fulfilled.'*

I shook my head, thinking to myself, *'I do not need to be thinking like this.'*

I thought, *'Snap out of it.'*

I shook my head harder again, in an effort to wake up. After a brief moment, I stood up, the attacker had left the shower room, and the Screw was telling the inmates to leave the gym because the period was over. When I came out of the shower room the Screw noticed my nose was bleeding. He called me over asking, 'What happened to you?'

I was still a bit starry eyed when I answered, 'I blew my nose too hard; I may have blown a blood vessel.'

He just looked at me, I looked back, then the Screw shouted out, 'Come on ladies, it's time to leave.'

We went back to our cells for breakfast, I sat down to tell Deejay what had happened. When I started to eat my meal, I noticed I was unable to chew my food when I tried to bite into the meat. I reported the matter to the Screws, a few hours later, they took me to Stafford General Hospital. I was told, my jaw was broken on the left side, then they wired my jaw.

To defend my honour, and reputation, Deejay has a face off in the exercise yard with the coward who gave me a blind punch. Deejay Johnathan knocked him out with one blow, then he ran like hell from the rest of the chasing inmates to the Screws. The last time I saw Deejay he was placed in another cell on G-wing, he came out of his single pad once, only to have the inmates throw sugar in scolding hot water on his face.

After four weeks sucking breakfast, lunch, and dinner through a straw the wires were removed from my jaw, and I was transferred to Buckley Hall.

Chapter 45

The hand of God

Around Christmas 2009, curiosity at my common relationship with God figures caused me to Google God of love. Only because, love was what I was expressing. Whose name comes up, Eros's wisdom, embedded in our mythological history, (myth meaning word of mouth.) Throughout the world in many forms explains, who, how, and what God is. In many beliefs in many social, scientific, and environmental medias. What I found interesting about Eros; he may have left more than the wise words of love. He may have influenced, or spoken to Socrates, or even Plato who wrote a play called *The Cave*.

This play examines perception of vision, and how the mind elevates to knowledge. Great scholars such as Socrates, upheld the meaning of humanity were all in the same school of thought. As was Aristotle whose early research fell into the field of biology, and produced the mathematical theory, logic. This caused me to believe even more, there is a conscious entity guiding men's hand in the search for knowledge and understanding.

When using scientific methods to prove a hypothesis, science requires two forms of evidence, consisting in systematic observation, measurements, and experiments to validate a theory.

'How do you prove the world is round when they believe it's flat?'

'Wait until technology catches up to prove it.'

'How do you prove economics doesn't work?'

'Watch morality fall, social deprivation, and environmental damage.'

'Since man is in the image of God, he is the same therefore equal. Having no supernatural powers, or miracles, how would one prove God exists?'

The Biblical Revelation 13:7:8 He was given power to make war against the saints, and to conquer them. And he was given authority over every tribe, people, languages, and nations.

I put forward my first evidence of divine movement within society, a phenomenon that naturally occurs, science cannot explain. In other words, a miracle, *'The Hand of God.'* I will withdraw the statement if someone can otherwise explain these mysterious events in my life.

14th December 2009 edited publication on social media

Logical reasoning conducted or assessed according to strict principles in validity. The systematic use of symbolic and mathematical techniques to determine the forms of valid deductive argument, logical operations collectively.

Symbol is noted as a sign or a thing that stands for something else. Symbolisms are express as an abstract and mystical ideas. An instance of a form or reasoning in, which a conclusion is drawn, whether validly, or not, from two given or assumed propositions, and premises, each of which shares a term with the conclusion and shares a common, or middle term that is not present in the conclusion. For example: If you were dressed, described, or the same as a judge in wig and robe, you would be a judge.

1. A divine entity would be a bastard king. Fitzroy is an old French, or German word. Roy means royal. Fitz meaning bastard, I am the same.

2. In theology one of the debates is how two minds can be in one head as was our *Lord Jesus Christ.* Brian switch, I, and A, spells brain. I perceive in my mind, there is another mind, I am the same.

3. Edwards is my economic slave name, according to logic, presenting this argument of an economic slave is in the middle term, which is in reference to what I am referring to, and have written about in *Omni's Wordsmith Mantra,* I am the same.

4. The image of a man was first an imagination within the mind of a spiritual entity known as God, then the egg. My name is Deejay Man Egg, I am the same.

5. Eros, God of love was always breaking limbs. For example, his left leg was broken, just like Jacob when he fought God, and broke his own left hip. I have a broken left leg, near the ankle, I am the same.

6. In 1996, someone came up behind me, then punched me. I offered the other cheek, and he took the offer, then my jaw was broken. Our *Lord Jesus Christ* said, 'Offer the other cheek.'

I am the same.

7. In Israel, there is a region called the Fertile Crescent, it is known for this because out of the many animals in the ancient world, thirteen out of fourteen were farm animals, which are indigenous to that area in preliteracy. If we were to take our *Lord Jesus Christ* as half man, half God, or half of an animal from the Fertile Crescent, it could be a horse, we would have the star sign Sagittarius.

I was born within the hills of Manchester, known in old English as the Horseshoe Crescent, I am the same.

8. I was born on the 18th, December 1966 and my star sign is Sagittarian, I am the same.

9. I was born in St. Mary's Royal Infirmary, our *Lord Jesus Christ's* mother was Mary, I am the same.

10. Hyacinth is the name of a mythological goddess, my mother's name is the same as a goddess, I am the same.

11. Logic states you can use numbers, as long as it is used in a mathematical way in reference to the subject. I was born 18th December 1966; we all know 666 from the Bible. The common denominator is six. 18 divided by 6 = 3. 12 divided by 6 =2, there's an extra 6, add 2 + 3 = 5 the fifth element. They heard God's voice, music to your ears. I am a deejay, I come with music, sound.

12. The Temple Mount in Israel is situated in a Christian state, surrounded by Muslims. I live in a Christian country surrounded by Muslims in my local area, I am the same.

13. I grew up on William Kent Crescent, again I am the same as the Fertile Crescent.

14. God's design is precision engineering, my primary school is on the original site for Rolls Royce, precision engineering, I am the same.

15. A symbolic representation of what was first is the blackness of space, I am black, I am the same.

16. St. John cried in the wilderness of the desert, my grandfather calls me John, and I cry for economic freedom in the wilderness of the world. I am the same.

17. I attended a church called St. John; I am the same.

18. I attended two colleges called John; I am the same.

19. Ganesh, the Indian God of Wisdom's right tusk was broken. Our *Lord Jesus Christ* said, Mark 10:20 'He sits on the left-hand side of the Lord.'

I take my scar under my left nostril, as a symbolic representation of that broken tusk, I am the same.

20. Jesus was a carpenter. I am the same.

21. Eros, God of love was a poet, and philosopher. As was Ganesh, our *Lord Jesus Christ,* and Mohammad peace, be upon him. I am an author, poet, and philosopher, I am the same.

22. If science looked at Abraham, our *Lord Jesus Christ,* and Mohammad peace, be upon him, their sudden visions of God, or repeating God's words with empathy, and compassion for humanity, could be a mental condition, or becoming aware, I am the same.

23. There is a statue of Eros, God of love, showing him eating pork. I am the same.

24. My left heel has been broken, just like the man regarded as half man, half god, the demi god Achilles. I am the same.

25 The symbolic representation for the decapitation of John the Baptist's head is the birth of my subconscious mind, John Thought Hope. I am the same.

26. Our *Lord Jesus Christ* was not married. I am the same.

27. I have completed a novel on morality out of creative thought, as prophesised and testified by John in Revelations. I am the same.

28. I have an upper front gold tooth on the left-hand side, as does one of the Pharaoh's of Egypt said to be a god. I am the same.

29. I'm known as Eggy because of my egg-shaped head. Just like the Japanese God of Wisdom and Chance (luck) Fukurokuju. I am the same.

I defy the laws of probability, I am the Lord of Probability, luck, and chance, as I was in the past I am the same in the present. I am Eros, Achilles, Abraham, Jacob, Fukurokuju the Japanese God of Luck, our *Lord Jesus Christ,* Ganesh the Indian God of Wisdom, and an Egyptian pharaoh (I don't know the pharaoh's name, or how to spell it. However, I have seen his uncovered mummies face with an upper gold tooth on the left-hand side on T.V.) To encompass all beliefs, I have the same traits as all Gods of love, and wisdom. Similar to Mohammed peace, be upon him, and Buddha, I have been enlightened by the subconscious mind, and I have left the material world, poor. I am reborn to fulfil a promise. Can you hear me?

I conclude since I can describe myself as a God in over twenty-nine separate ways, I am unique with divine credentials. I believe I can say I am a Seraph, or a prophet from God, and I have divine authority to speak on the entity's behalf, your life is all about my perception.

The future's vision

Once upon a time, I downloaded *Imagine* by John Lennon.
Love's war for resources motivated by faith, and glory.
If history repeats itself, looking at the past allows you to predict
the future to change the presents understanding.
A new story is told at the beginning of the end.

John T. Hope

Chapter 46

Pump up the jam.

Pumping iron in jail, is to be as disciplined as a soldier, and to be focus like a sharp telescope. I noticed the difference in my body when I clunked, clunked, clunked down the prison's cast-iron stairs. I could feel my chest muscles bouncing up and down like Zebedee from the children's T.V. show *The Magic Roundabout*. Centring every push of the bar on women within my mind, memories of me pressing my manhood in between a girl's legs, would rush into my thoughts like the whirling swirl of the whistling wind.

Claire Singleton was one of many brief pleasurable encounters. I met Claire about the time I first started seeing Cate. On a winter's night, six carloads of my friends and myself, drove down to the Pink Coconut in Derby. It was the first time I attended, the venue, and the gaff was big. Two dancefloors, pop in one room, a packed club in the second dancehall, this is where we spent most of the night, the R & B was kicking. Stimulated with the excitement of new surroundings, beautiful people. Me and my friends wandered around, sniffing the air, looking for that stare, when in the air lingered an aroma. I sniffed as I walked, just below me, the delightful fragrance was right under my nose. When I looked closer, a small pear-shaped arse was looking right back, the sexy duck walk was very appealing, I had to announce my presence with, 'Hello.'

My words flowed poetically once I got her attention, the aroma I smelt was not perfume, floral fragrant oil, I was later informed. As the night moved on, there was lots that we mentioned. We all went to an after party, like two snails dancing to slow grooves till six in the morning, cool. In our conversation, she revealed, 'My parents lives in Manchester, I now live in Stoke-on-Trent with two kids. I'm kind of in a relationship, which I feel is coming to an end.'

Stimulated with our tête-à-tête and aroused with her flirtish flirtation. I replied, 'It would be nice to hook up again, can I have your number?'

As Claire batted her eye lids, resembled Daffy Duck's extended eyelashes flapping, and as she puckered her lips, look full, yes sweet cherry whipped cream, full milk chocolate. Claire continued, 'I'm not on the phone, give me your number. Don't worry I will give you a call.'

I gave her my number with a kiss on the cheek, the night was sweet, the good people you meet. Months had passed, I'd forgotten the night in Derby since Claire never called. My relationship with Cate had blossomed, but she never stayed overnight. In time, when Claire did phone a few months later, it was a wonderful surprise. She declared, 'I'm coming to Manchester for the weekend to see my parents, fancy hooking up for a drink?'

My intentions were a lot more, I had to think. As a consequence, to keep Cate at bay I told her, 'I'm working in Leeds on my aunt's house, I'll see you on Monday when I come back.'

Totally surprised with my statement, Cate cried out, 'But it's my birthday weekend.'

I paused for a fleeting moment, then answered, 'I'll make it up some way.'

The next day, Claire came my way, I picked her up from her parent's gate about 8 p.m. then went to chill at my place. Upon arriving, being polite I offered her a drink, I went into the kitchen upon my return Claire wasted no time, she was undressed, yes naked. We had a sex tour all over my place that was one of my best performance, 7 a.m. she was exhausted. Both of us laid back pillow talking, out of nowhere there was a knock on the front door. There was no point me hiding, my Ford Sierra was parked at the front door. Claire questioned, 'Who is it?'

Sure enough, I looked out the window to see Cate standing there, all smiles looking fantastic like the young Diana Ross, sexier than Regina Bell, and more alluring than a hypnotising full moon.

I had to answer Claire with a confession, 'My girlfriends at the door.'

Claire really didn't care, replying, 'What are you going to do?'

Unsure with what I was going to say, I never plan, nor scheme, I go with the flow, so I said, 'I'll be back in a few minutes, just wait here.'

I answered the door to let Cate in, within a minute I had her in tears, when I informed her, 'Beverly was upstairs.'

Not Claire, Cate knew of Beverly and was very worried, she was aware Beverly still loved me and wanted me back. I told Cate, 'We were just talking, nothing happened with Beverly all night.'

To show how I felt, I began to kiss her along her silky neck as a way to comfort her, I started to caress her, to uplift, and reassure her, before I knew it, I was in, screwing Cate. After having sex with Cate, I went back upstairs to hear Claire say, 'You took a long time.'

I told her what happened, she wanted more, so I gave her more of what she was asking for. It was now about 9 a.m. I took Claire to the train station; she knew the score, with a big smile on her face she proclaimed, 'You were great, you can come round anytime, you're more than welcome, you showed me a really good night. I get bored don't leave it too long, I want the same as before.'

When I got back home Cate was in my bed, she declared, 'It's my birthday you know, come here, I'll give you some head.'

With that I thought, *'Good God more.'*

So, I gave her what she was asking for. Eleven a.m. Cate left for work, bow legged, before I fell asleep, what a night, I thought, *'Didn't I do well, I was screwing from 8 p.m. till 11 a.m. Good God, heaven.'*

Chapter 47

H.M.P. Buckley Hall

H. M. P. Buckley Hall was not home from home, after a week of 23 hours bang up, on the induction wing of the jail, it was beginning to be a bore. I was in one of three prefabricated buildings, containing two wings of six. When you entered the building, after passing a turnstile entrance, two-inch thick aluminium bars extended up the length of the building like the Hyperion, the tallest tree in the world. There were steel slabs, the size of a large bank safe, paved on sheeted doors led into one's tiny one bed cell with an open plan toilet. It was a relief to finally explore my new surroundings and walk across the open prison fields for the first time. I felt as if I was in a school playground, so many familiar forgotten faces. Then I heard voices cry out, 'Hi.'

'Hello.'

And shouts out of my name. 'Eggy what's happening?'

'Fitz what you doing in here?'

Like a butcher pounding a slab of beef, the comment battered my mind. I replied, 'Three and a half years.'

After being shown around the prisons medical centre, which was fenced off from the rest of the prison complex, the gym, then onto G-wing, my new temporary home, it wasn't before long I found the black population's games room. It was located entering the main entrance in the lobby way to the adjoining G and H-wing, to one side on the right was the games room. The inmates would playboard games like chess, ludo, dominoes, and cards were played for tobacco and joints. Laughter and cheers from the winning table could be heard, along with the slap, bang, the resonating explosion from dominoes slamming on the table. The sweet smell of weed blocked your nostrils, while the smoke hazed and blurred your vision when entering the small box room.

A lighter, and a used air freshener pad was at hand, only to be burnt to hide the smell of the green bud, when a Screw could be seen walking across the fields.

Two weeks after being on the main wing at Buckley Hall, I was informed, I could no longer take education, I'd completed the first level course work when I was at Stafford. I was forced to work in the warehouse, sorting coat hangers, paying a wage of half a pence per hanger. The time in that warehouse was filled with joke, and laughter, fuelled by a black Jamaican born Yardie, going by the name Mussolini.

One day, I was walking back to my pad after a day in the warehouse, my mind was wondering, free although I was imprisoned, I entered the entrance into the lobby way to G and H wing. Who did I run into, but the same guy who broke my leg, and warned me away from Ladbrokes Betting Shop. I noticed he'd been working out in the gym; his shoulders were like a double humped camel. He was accompanied by a much taller, muscle-bound friend. Their intimidation quickened as they advanced towards me, causing me to back into a corner against the thick aluminium turnstile bars. I wasn't going to run, there was nowhere to run. So, I timidly declared, 'Look ahh, I'm not looking for any trouble, I just want to do my bird, and get out of this shithole.'

They both looked at one another, then left the area as quick as they arrived, leaving me with a sigh of relief. A fight with two beefcakes, just as my glass jaw was getting better was not needed. Being closer to Manchester, meant more visits from my family, friends, Beverly, and Annabel. Since there was plenty of weed floating about the prison, I was passed a fresh brownie, or a queen's head, otherwise known as a tenner, on all my visits, and my training was going well.

After a few months in the prison, one of the main white guys Jason, was being released, I became a cleaner on the wing. The prison was left with an inmate's political void upon Jason's release, which came to a head when Todd Wilson, short but packed with muscle, and was also the brothers' trainer. On this particular day, Todd was walking over from his wing to the games room, he

190

crossed the path of two other white inmates, who were close friends to the ex-main man Jason, who'd just been released. They made a comment, Todd did not have an agreeable expression on his face. Todd entered the games room with a slight tempered tone. He informed the inmates, 'That cunt, has just told me to go back to my own wing, you black bastard.'

Everyone in the games room went into silence, similar to being in a library, shocked as if we'd touched an electric eel, and surprise but not surprised, we are still seen lower than second-class citizens. This type of comment, in this day and age, couldn't, and would not be tolerated. Someone cried out, 'Kick his face in.'

Cheers of unified agreement by all attending, 'Yeah, f--k him up.'

All the men marched out in order, shoulder to shoulder in a military fashion, roaring in uproar in total agreement, and a unified plan to the main door. Someone added in an angry tone, 'Call him over when he walks back round the yard.'

The two white boys casually approached, unaware of our intent, when Todd called them into the entrance of G and H wing's lobby. The two white guys bravely walked in through the turnstile gateway in front of the games room lobby with brazen courage. One of the bold white guys exhaled with a screwed-up face, and in a bad-tempered manner, 'What do you want?'

His militant tone was not suited to the occasion. Todd replied in a defiant mood, 'Who the F--k are you calling a black bastard?'

The black figures surrounding the two white boys stepped back to create more fighting space. Swallowing lumps of fresh air, the two white boys Adam's apple danced up and down their necks, similar to a sliding trombone. The white guys looked at one another, then the quieter white dude took one step back, joining the brothers who were behind him.

As soon as he'd stepped back the distraction gave Todd the opportunity to a pre-empt strike with an upper cut to the loud mouth's left cheek. Reminiscent of a rocking chair, the white boy was rocked, again here's *Spock,* he's in shock.

Todd wasted no time, he jumped onto the white guy clamping his legs around the white guy's waist, grabbed hold of the white guy's head with both hands, then bit off the white guy's ear. A scream bellowed out of the white guy's throat identical to a roaring lion, as he ran off picking up his ear, fleeing into the distance with his so-called friend. Laughter and cheers from the black men in attendance, pats on Todd's back placed the brothers on top of the jail, running drugs and tobacco were now on sale.

Chapter 48

Mounting stress

Around September 2009, after I was discharged from Highgate Mental Health Hospital, a court ruling imposed an order for me to make payments of £15 per week for overpayment of housing benefit, plus a further £3.25 per week for my rent arrears. I was only paying £60 per month. Adding to the fact, I received a letter from my housing office on my birthday, demanding full payment. Now the Christmas festive season was over, I didn't have any money, no phone credit, and no landline. It was time I paid the housing office a visit.

As I meandered through the streets of East Islington, passing built up areas of houses, a school, then along the high streets to Upper Street housing office. The brisk chilly winter wind blew a gust, whipped up a thrash, a lash another thrash, the whirling swirl of the whistling wind placed a firm speedy step to my walk. I felt confident, cool, calm, and determined I was not going to pay any more money at the risk of losing my flat.

As per usual, the queue could not be beaten, at 10 a.m. there was standing room only in the housing office. Luckily, I just wanted the phone, which was freely available to use in the reception. When speaking to my housing officer, I explained my situation in a very cool manner, but our conversation started to get heated once I did not agree to pay the extra £3.25 per week. Before I knew it, I was screaming uncontrollably down the phone. Sweat was pouring down my face with rage, I have never felt like this before. I finally shouted, 'Take me to court, I'm not paying a f--king penny.'

Engulfed in anger, I slammed the phone down, as I did that, I turned to make my way out of the building, all protruding eyes were on me. Some of the people in the office were jaw dropped shocked with surprise at my exhibition. I just headed for the main door out. Then I turned back into the housing office just before leaving. I shouted, 'I AM A MAN WHO CAN DESCRIBE HIMSELF AS A GOD in over twenty-nine different ways and SAY I'M A PROPHET FROM GOD. IF YOU SAY I'M NOT, I CANNOT SAVE YOU.'

Everyone looked at one another with nothing to say, I just turned away and left the building. That was not me in the housing office, I never shout out in public areas, I'm calm, cool, and considerate in my manner towards people, I'm polite, and respectful towards my equals. I needed help, I found myself on the way to social services, which was a few hundred yards up Holloway Road.

Joanna was in the office, and she invited Dr. Douglas a consultant who has been involved in my case to join us. We sat and talked about how I was feeling, I explained what happened in the housing office adding my financial situation. I expressed myself politely in a humble fashion. Dr. Douglas knew what buttons to press when she offered over a solution, 'Why don't you go back to work?'

A sudden cold sweat developed, the Meghalaya Island the wettest place in the world was flooding under my armpits. It seemed she didn't understand the black exploitation I was under, and I was trying to explain. I just gripped tightly onto the armchair I was sat on, then a childish outburst of a temper tantrum broke out, I hit the roof with anger, as I jumped up and down in the chair I was sat on, like I was a kid on a bouncy castle. I repeatedly conveyed, 'No, no, no, I'm not doing it. No, no, no, I'm not doing it.'

Dr. Douglas and Joanna pinned themselves further back in their seat startled, surprised, and shocked, upon hearing my deep bellowing voice echo in the small box meeting room. They sat watching my antics bouncing in the chair for a moment, then they left the room with me still bobbing up and down in my chair, shouting franticly, 'No, no, no, I'm not doing it.'

After a minute or so, I calmed down, but breathing as if I'd just dashed two hundred meters. I placed my head in between my legs and found composure.

I waited for Joanna for a moment, not seeing her return, I went home because it seemed like they'd both finished with me. The following day, on the 6th, January 2010. I received a phone call from Joanna, asking me to come into the office, which I did. When I arrived at social services, a doctor was in attendance with Joanna, they placed me on a section two. I was then escorted to Highgate Mental Health Hospital by police officers. On one of my ward rounds Dr. Lester asked about my problems. Once again, I had to explain to the doctor, 'I was an economic slave, and the black exploitation was too much to bear.'

I went onto say, 'I'm not paying a thing, if they take my flat from me, it would be an inhumane act and a contradiction because it goes against what society is trying to achieve. Furthermore, I'm prepared to sit outside Westminster, dressed just in my underpants, so I don't break the law with all my poems on a board for people to see. Regardless, of the freezing weather.'

Dr. Lester understood what I was saying. He replied, 'You won't lose your flat Fitzroy, there are a few options to consider. I'll speak to Joanna, then get back to you.'

Despondent, dismayed, downhearted and feeling down in the dumps with my current situation I answered, 'Fine.'

Because of the hospital regime, it was not until the 24th, January 2010 when I was able to post a blog, explaining my current predicament but not in so many words.

Chapter 49

Determined

It's the 23rd, January 2010, two weeks into a strict hospital regime, when Dr. Lester felt I was well enough to go home for an hours leave. I never took note of what he said, I took as long as I needed, which always ran to three or four hours, to the frustration of the hospital staff. All I ever wanted to do when I got home was watch the news and write comments on current affairs. I was also expecting to see two payments from the benefit agency, a monthly total of £595 at my flat. My intentions was to place a deposit of £350 to self-publish my first book, costing a total of £700. When I came back with a postal order receipt, the staff from the hospital were impressed with my determination to achieve my goal, and understood, the empathy I was feeling towards humanity.

Chapter 50

Girl Tuesday

While looking at the blank expression from my cell ceiling look back, I'd review my life from a screen in my mind, free as it were. Tuesday nights are usually very quiet, but being horny drug dealers, my mates and me, found a nice secluded club somewhere out of the reach from local gangsters. We'd always show up at the venue two or three cars loaded up with big black Moss Side men. We would never approach the door all at once, going in one at a time, like we're not friends or we don't know each other. One must remember, too many black boys entering a club is not a good image for some establishments. Being the only black guys in the club, we didn't want the five or six white doormen looking at us for trouble, and we were not lacking attention from the ladies.

The deejay played a mixture of tunes, pop, and R & B. We'd watch the girl's do their thing on the dancefloor, there was every chance you'd score, take your pick, the lass is yours. Looking around the venue, there were pure options from a number of women. One young woman, who pushed herself on me, every week, Joyce Hall. There was not much I fancied about the woman, she didn't seem capable of managing her drink, and well, as nice as she was, there were other girls who were more appealing. So, I always said, 'No.'

Honestly, most nights I would go home on my own. This particular evening, a rabbit on heat couldn't be as horny, and things were not looking so good. All my mates pulled a bird, and I was lonely Jack, nothing was happening. It goes without saying, persistent Joyce pulled the back of my jacket looking for attention. Being frisky as a funky cockerel, horny like a jet-propelled rabbit on heat, and playful similar to a kitten playing with a ball of wool, I responded to my natural urges; I disregarded my thoughts.

As I turned to face her, she wore a very nice black pencil skirt, a white shirt, open top revealed a lot of her deep cleavage with pink cherry nipples, stuck out, just a little. There was movement from my third leg, you know, my middle. Without delay my mate dropped us off at her place. Trust me and my mate, the girl he picked up was Joyce's friend. They were arguing all the way to Joyce's place, then started a fight outside Joyce's gate. Both of them were kicking and screaming then they dented my mate's car, he went ape. Six foot two, eighteen stone, breeze block fists, and a big broad back, he's not a twat, calming him down took some chat. He stepped back, got his girl in his car, he was off, not even a look back, or a wave goodbye.

I looked at Joyce, she knew the score, we were in the door, kissing caressing as we slowly climbed up the stairs. I stripped off her shirt, she seemed alert, she proceeded to take off my jacket before I knew it, we were outside the bedroom door. She paused to hold my hand as she led me to her bedroom. Then, she sat down, slowly relaxing her body length on the double bed. While Joyce was looking into my eyes, I was watching the movement of her seamlessly large breasts. Joyce really did have a lot more to reveal, Good God, my eyes popped out, big ripe watermelon tits, imagine the scene.

I followed her lead, I spread my weight evenly balanced over her tasty warm figure in between her legs, kissing her neck, moistening her lips. In one hand I gathered up a full cup of her firm large breast, stroking, rubbing, and flicking my tongue over her nipples, I was turning them pink, firming them up, they turned bright red, I flickered, sucked, and licked. Her moans of delight echoed in my ear, as she puffed up her chest, arched her back, the pleasure she felt an exuberant, energetic inhale of delight. I felt excited by her arousal, impressed with my techniques, the heat that grew was too great, what a treat. She then placed her hand tenderly against my lips, indicating I should pause, not so erotic, so I stopped. Joyce twisted her body over to the edge of the bed with me on top, then she threw up, there was vomit all over the floor, I declared, 'Good God.'

She heaved once more, splatter, splatter, splatter, a waterfall hit the floor as vomit gushed out of her trap door. Joyce finally stopped throwing up, rolled back with me still on top. My head was in my hands, thinking, *'What the f--k.'*

Then she licked the stinking sick off her lips stating, 'Come on then!'

Spock turns up, I'm shocked again, surprised there's no prize. I looked up, then replied, 'Aren't you going to clean up? Never mind washing your mouth.'

Joyce licked her sick stained lipstick, then answered, 'No.'

Sickened of her cleanliness and repulsed at her behaviour, I responded, 'Watch this.'

I got up, waving in front of her, what was once a rock is now a large limp black cock. Disappointed with the evening, I put on my clothes, zipped up, then I went out the door, I was lucky enough to find a cab to the train station and I found my way home.

The following day, the evening's events came up in conversation, my mates took the piss, wouldn't you take the Charlie. Hey, the joke of the week was me. No problem, looking back, what fun, but the story isn't done.

A week passed it was boring, as a result a few of us went to the club for a treat, we were doing nothing all week, there was only my two mates, myself, and a geek, who always seem to get into fights. A bit of a freak the geek, he wasn't my mate we met a few weeks beforehand. We got in the club, it was a quiet night, not as many people as usual, it wasn't much fun. The three of us sat down and mellowed out, having a chat, we weren't looking for girls, we had women problems. Who walks over, Joyce with her argumentative friend from last week. Joyce exhaled, 'Hi Fitz, sorry about last week, I had a few too many, and I had things on my mind. Do you want to come back to my place tonight?'

I thought, *'It was a nice offer but after last week, no thanks.'*

I didn't want to offend her, so I replied nice and politely, 'Sorry love, not tonight, I'm chatting business with my mates, later.'

As she walked away my mates blew up with laughter, she was well in earshot, embarrassed maybe she was, she pissed me off.

After a bit of a giggle, me and my mates continued to talk women problems. Fifteen minutes into engrossed conversation with my mates, I felt a tender touch, creep seductively up my back, curiously stimulated and sexually aroused by the erotic suggestion, I turned to be surprised by the sight of Joyce enticingly caressing my back. She wasn't so tempting, her breath smelt like last week's drink. Joyce's voice suggested, 'Come on Fitzroy, let's have some fun.'

Firm but politely I stated with a wizard's tongue, 'Sorry no thanks, can't you see I'm busy, please leave me alone.'

I turned to my mates, their expression, my impression, *'Wow that's pressure.'*

Joyce turned away with a puffed-up face, give her this, she's persistent this miss, did I say a bitch. She came back five minutes later, puckering up her lips as if she were a baboon, about she wants a kiss. I responded, 'Move from me sis, you don't get it. If you can't wash out your mouth, what is your underneath like?

That was a fat controller moment, her face went beetroot red, allowing her eyeballs to extend out, steam escaped via pulsating nostrils, and through her ears. In her navy-blue outfit, she turned with a wild twist to her pleated skirt, marching off in a naval officer style, stomping her feet hard against the carpeted floor, totally distressed towards a group of white guys drinking champagne, laughing it up. We thought nothing of it and continued to sup up.

At the end of the night, we made our way to the main door, I should have stayed at home, it was hell, I don't know what happened, why or what for. Here's what happened next at the main door. Eighteen stone of muscle led the way to the exit, I walked naive in the middle, the fighting geek was walking behind me, as the crowd quietly made their way to the exit. In that moment, the geek cried out, 'Ahh, what the f--k.'

I turned to look behind, when I could see four white guys floor the geek on some nearby steps, attacking him with fists, feet, and a chair was in the air.

As I made an advanced to help, I had no time to respond, an arm was around my throat, I received a few punches to the stomach and my face, I got battered like a fish, the doorman pulled them off me and rescued the geek. I could not see my other mate in the chaotic arena.

Subsequently, both of us ran out to the car, he wasn't there. When we dashed back to the club the front door was locked, we sprinted around to the back entrance, kicked open the fire door, barged into the club to see a crowd of people around a guy lying on the floor, shivering franticly. When I took a closer look through a gap in the horrified people, his lower jaw was detached from his face. The blood poured out similar to a cold running water tap; it was tragic. A doorman shouted frantically, 'Quick, quick get out of here.'

We ran for the main double swinging doors, as we pushed the doors, they opened out into the fresh air, I could not believe what had happened in there. I declared, 'Where's my mate?'

In the distance I heard, 'Over here, get in the car.'

We never looked nor went back, not knowing how it started. When we asked the geek, he answered bewilderedly, 'A guy just came up behind me, to slam a chair in my back.'

Not sure of his story, or if Joyce instigated an argument, we watched the geek, we had a pleasant surprise next time he wanted to start a fight.

Chapter 51

Free I thought

On the 19th, February 2010, after informing the hospital staff I'd made a final payment towards my book £350 from my benefit, Dr Lester was not pleased. I remember Dr. Lester probing me with curiosity, 'I can't understand why you have done that Fitzroy!'

In a defiant manner I replied, 'Dr Lester, you have advised me that I should not, cannot work before now. I have no intentions of applying for a job. This book is the only way, I can earn some money, and pass on my message without getting involved in the material world. This book is my future.'

Dr. Lester bent over while sat in his armchair, holding his forehead in both hands, totally displeased with what I said. He slowly raised his head to proclaim, 'Fine Fitzroy, I have concluded you have no responsibility towards your financial affairs. Therefore, I want you to sign over your benefit, so the hospital can pay your bills, you'll have to live on a budget, we set.'

I was left with no choice, what little money I was getting to express free will was being taken away. As a consequence, I had to sign over my benefit before being discharged. Only to continue posting my blogs.

Chapter 52

Confrontation

While I was stuck in jail, I'd look back on my life and as I remember it, I did not come into much contact with the police. Only as a passenger when I was involved in two serious car crashes, I was lucky enough to walk away from. When I did come into contact with the police, I had to think quick on my feet. During a drugs drought period in Manchester, I became friends with a young lady from St Paul's Bristol, Liz Weekes. She was pregnant to a man from Old Trafford, he had been transferred to Nuneaton Police Station because of the H.M.P. Strange Ways riots, which kicked off on the 1st, April 1990. She wanted to visit her man, so suggested, 'Since there's a drugs drought in Manchester, and you don't know anyone in Liverpool, I could introduce you to a dealer in Bristol, if you drive me to the jail in Nuneaton for a visit.'

I thought, *'It was an idea, the supply of drugs was needed, it was summer, Cate looked as hot as the weather.'*

Having no driving license, but being able to arrange a hired car, a drive out with my girlfriend so far was a nice idea. In so doing, we went for a drive. We got to Nuneaton Police Station in suitable time. It follows, Liz pulls out a surprise, a quarter ounce of weed, requesting, 'Fitz, could you give this to my man on the visit?'

This was a bit of a bombshell. Now here is a situation where my reputation as a so-called bad boy drug dealer is on the table. More often than not, one acts stupid to prove a point. Hence, not even knowing who I was visiting, like a foolish clown I took the drugs into the police station.

Imagine the scene, having been led into a small ten feet square box visiting room, there was just a square table, four chairs, pale blue walls, a square window with bars, me, and the pregnant girl sat down. After a few moments, in came a Screw with her Boo. Liz and her man both held hands, touched lips, and cheek to cheek, he was opposite me, they sat in their seats, the Screw sat to my left, breathing quite deeply, as if he had emphysema. The two love birds could not stop talking the talk, and the chatter, they had a lot to say, good thing really, I didn't know what to say. After five minutes of them chatting the chat, chat chatter, the officer looked bored and distracted. I took the moment to ask, 'Do you want a cigarette?'

My comment took the prisoners gaze slowly away from his woman's eyes, the jailbird looked across the table toward me with a puzzled perplexed expression on his face. Him not knowing me he politely answered in a deep husky voice, 'Yes please.'

I passed him over a twenty pack of Benson along with the quarter ounce of weed, blindside to the police officer's vision. The muscle-bound jailbird took the packet from my hand, his instinct mismeasured the packet stumbling the pack slightly, then he realised he needed a bigger handgrip to receive a parcel, he was a professional. The puzzled perplexed expression turned to a warm welcomed grin. The glitter in his eye, was it a tear that welled up, or was it his nerves. I thought, *'It was time for me to disappear.'*

I left the box visiting room to sit in the car with Cate. While we waited, I was sat in the front passenger seat showing Cate how to use the clutch and shift the gear.

Leading up to the entrance of the police station there is a ramp rising quite steeply, taking twenty yards or so to get to the entrance. Exiting the local constabulary, Liz was only five foot three, the eight-month pregnant woman tried to run down the ramp, but her knees kept knocking her belly front. She had difficulty controlling her speed of descent, down the steep slope, the young woman's heavy load caused her behind to protrude favouring the waddle of *Daisy Duck*. Liz shouted out, 'Quick, quick start the car they might be onto us.'

I could not move fast enough being in the passenger seat

showing Cate around the steering wheel. By the time I'd move my leg in reaction to what I was hearing, a large garage door slid up below the building of the police station to where I was parked. Out of the depth of darkness from the garage, what seemed like hundreds of white shirts with black shoulder tabs were ten to fifteen police officers, approaching my car with two or three dogs, quite menacingly. They requested, 'Could you step away from the car please sir.'

Which I did, I never question authority, the dogs were out sniffing the car before the police asked my name. We were all taken back into the police station, searched with questions concerning £2,000 I had in the car to buy the drugs in Bristol. After I explained, 'I'm buying a car in Bristol.'

They confiscated, a quarter ounce of my own personal weed, no charges. Then the police let us all go. I was braver than Robert the Bruce, as bold as King Arthur, and a stupid court jester. After a few trips to Bristol, I got to know an elderly black gentlemen by the name of Derek Jackson. I didn't know him very well and I can't remember our conversation, but I'll never forget his words, *'The best thing to find in the world is peace of mind.'*

The only other time I had the pleasure of confronting a police officer was when I first became mentally ill in 1993. I was more inclined to escape from Withington Mental Health Hospital, then make my way to Crumpsall, where Cate was living at the time. I always stayed too late at Cate's hostel; the time would come when I had to go back to the hospital. Public transport stopped operating, so I'd call the emergency number 999, since I was on a section, the police had a duty to pick me up, and give me a free taxi ride back to the hospital, which was clear on the other side of Manchester in Withington.

The police had enough of my games, as they walked me away from Cate's hostel to the back of the police van. One of the officers menacing comment made me worried and the expression on Cate's face indicated the same concerns. I can't remember what the officer said, but I do recall saying plain and square in reply, 'Just don't kick me in the head.'

As I walked out of the hostel in the custody of two officers, one officer opened the backdoor to the van, the second officer forced me down to the floor, then his leg rose up to be unleashed in my face. In that instant, I heard a loud cry coming from the steps of Cate's hostel, 'Hey! Watch what you're doing.'

When I looked up, there she was Cate stood outside the hostel with a housemate overseeing the scene. I was then placed in the van, then taken to Withington Mental Health hospital.

Chapter 53

H.M.P. Riots

During my term in prison, the general rule for inmates, if one's sentence was under four years, one would do half the sentence. If while one's in custody and was found guilty of a further offence, one could lose up to six weeks from remission. This sentence can be claimed back, if the inmate receives no further charges over a six-month period.

After a few weeks at H.M.P. Buckley Hall I could understand why inmates preferred privately owned prisons, the Screws had no backbone, a bit like a snake. The antics that occurred were a joke, a laugh every minute, the warden was taking remission left right and centre.

In the summer of 1996, the warden invited a band to perform for the inmates in the open air, on a two-foot platform in front of the gymnasium. It was a lovely hot summer's day, I had my Saturday visit from Beverly, and the show was due to start 6 p.m. that evening. Everyone in the prison was looking forward to what turned out to be a good, bubbly energetic show. The performance started late, ended later than planned, 9.25 p.m. I made my way back to my cell with a few other inmates, knowing full well bang up was at 10 p.m. and hearing the Screws shout out, 'Inmates time to make your way back to your wings.'

The concert had some real excitement and energy that spilt over to the mischievous and ill-behaved prisoners, unbeknown to me of the events unfolding outside. Approaching bang up time, my main concern was having everything I needed, rolling paper, lighter, weed etc. At that point, slam, the bloody door shut.

Relaxed in my pad, content with another torturous day in prison over, fifteen minutes or so into enjoying a joint, the sounds of cheers similar to a football match, drew my eyes away from the spot on the cell ceiling. When I looked out of my barred window, three Screws were running into the distance, but I could not see who they were chasing. A split second later, I could hear the roars from many voices, then inmates appeared in my vision, twenty maybe more prisoners were chasing the three Screws. Conversations then started from barred windows to disobedient inmates, who would not go back to their cells, jokes and laughter rang out from the yard of the prison.

Soon after, the increasing fast sound of the snap chop chopping from helicopter blades could be heard. Shadows of bodies weaving in between beams of light, seemed to dance Calypso on the field. After an hour or so, the chaotic antics bored me. It was time for another joint, then bed.

The following morning, me, and a few other inmates walked to the canteen, as we passed the medical centre, the door and windows of the centre had been damaged. We entered the unusually quiet mess hall and sat down for breakfast to see a man's head fall into his plate. We asked an inmate from another wing, who was sat on a nearby table, 'What's the problem with him?'

The other inmate declared, 'Some of the guy's raided the medical centre, and got hold of a few diazepam's with some other drugs, there's the result.'

The commotion in the prison came on the local T.V. as the headline evening news. The reporter reported on the community radio, 'The jail was out of control.'

That summer, in the 1996 European Cup, England were playing a late fixture, and the game went into extra time. In all of the excitement a Screw cried out, 'Bang up time lads.'

That didn't impress the inmates, they kicked the Screw out of G-wings T.V. room, at that point they barricaded the door. I could not believe the situation into which I was forced. The Screws could not get in the T.V. room, what could I do but watch big men act like disobedient school boys. It wasn't until 12 a.m. when bang up was at 10 p.m. and the match was over, when someone asked, 'Has anyone got any weed?'

Seeing no one had any drugs on them, made the inmates decide to go back to their cell, what a joke.

Chapter 54

Just to get a rep

One of the familiar faces at H.M.P. Buckley Hall was fifty-six-year-old, tubby old boy Lee Robins. Tubby in my mind, only because of his big barrel belly. We met many years earlier, when my father introduced me to Lee on Broadfield Road, Moss Lane East Manchester. As a young boy, I would see him on the frontline in his American jeep, one of the first men to have one in the area. I'd make my way from secondary school to visit my grandma on Great Western Street. Lee was always parked on Moss Lane East, playing joke, smiling, flirting with the ladies, doing his illegal business. This sentence was not Lee's first imprisonment; in fact, he was an old hat in the criminal world. He may have been well overweight, and long in the tooth, but that didn't stop him from training with the younger brothers when the mood suited him.

In jail, you can well imagine, you have low days, with Lee it was more often than not, which made him seem miserable when he's not. There was a fellow inmate on the wing, half Chinese Jamaican from Birmingham, slightly younger than Lee, going by the name Sun Leung, he modelled three upper front teeth, and two front facing lower set. Sun tried many times to crack a shaggy dog story, when he was a joke, very much a dickhead. Lee never got on with the toothless Chinaman, Sun loved to chat crap, miserable as hell, and constantly moaned.

One Saturday afternoon, Lee received a visit from his loving wife, a white woman and from what I understand, they've been married for over twenty years, Lee being black. While Lee was on a visit, Sun saw Lee in the visiting hall with his wife. When Sun came back to G-wing from his visit, only to be heard saying, 'I don't know how Lee can lay down with that woman, never mind lick out her underneath.'

Word got back to Lee, and everyday Lee came over to my pad, talking about what Sun was gossiping. Lee was annoyed and anxious, then he expressed, 'I feel infuriated, disrespected, and totally insulted.'

Every day for a week I'd tried to cool Lee down when I replied, 'Lee, he's not worth the bother, you've not got long left to do. Just hold your corner.'

I thought, *'I got through to him.'*

No, I was wrong. The following Saturday, as usual, I was up before the Screws opened the door, you never know who could run into your pad, and beat you up, while you're still sleeping or getting dressed. The main T.V. room wasn't open, as a consequence I found myself sat next to Sun in the small box T.V. room. It was a quiet morning, there didn't seem to be much movement on the wing, when Lee walked in with a puffed-up face vowing, 'You'll never talk about me and my wife like that again.'

Sun looked up from his seat into Lee's face to see Lee raise his arm. Suddenly whack, Lee unleashed a strike across Sun's face. Sun swayed back on his seat, as if he were on a rocking chair, he made a quick move to hold his mouth as blood started seeping out in between his fingers. Whack again, to Sun's lower jaw, and whack, across his face. Lee turned to walk out, dangling in his righthand I could see his choice weapon, a sock with two pool balls. I thought, *'I couldn't see myself coming back to jail to be fighting in my old age.'*

It was not until the late afternoon that day, Sun came back onto the wing from the medical centre, modelling a swelling above, and below his left eye. This allowed a slit of fiery red iris to reflect the light, and Dunlop lips with a purple ruby ball grew on his chin. He tried to smile when he overheard a joke, revealing the only five teeth that could be seen in his head were no longer there.

It was time to have my own annual dental check-up. I noticed all the brothers were getting free gold teeth, I have a healthy set, but my front tooth on the left-hand side has never dropped out. In so doing, my adult tooth grew around my milk tooth and left a white patch, so I had a free gold capping over it.

The warm summer sun turned into a cold bitter winter, the whistling wind swirls, and twirls around in the prison complex. As I looked over the prison wall, the chilled wind sings a wild windy whipping song, as it whisks along, howling like a wolf as it travels over the naked branches on a few trees, and ruffles the green grassy hills of the Lancashire County countryside. Just as I was coming to the end of my sentence, alcohol was thrown over the prison wall, when we came out of Christmas 1996. Coming into the New Year of 1997, I was always pissed, or should I say, I was as sober as a judge. I was asked, 'Fitz, take a visit for one of the inmates to get some weed into the jail.'

Up until then, I'd kept my nose clean, but I was obligated to take this visit, if anything, to keep what little reputation I had as a bad boy drug dealer. In the hope I would receive an afternoon visit, being New Year's Eve, the visiting room would be full. Therefore, the Screws would be too busy to see what I was doing. But no, my mate gets to the visiting hall at 8.30p.m. closing at 8.45p.m. when there were only two other visitors, four or five peering cameras with six Screws watching. To top that, the parcel was a big half-ounce block of black ash, and the cling film would not stick to the block, I had a real problem, having to cheek it in between my butt. After the visit was over, I'm sure I looked quite funny, I was walking like a cowboy with a pencil up his arse to the holding cell.

In all the time I was in prison, I was never asked to do a strip search, until then. There was one inmate leaving the holding cell after his search, sat next to me was another inmate. We both looked at one another, he could read my eyes and see, I had a slight problem. So, he went in for a search before me, while I tried pushing this parcel up in between my butt cheeks without the parcel going into the no entrance sign, exit only.

It was now my turn to strip, I went into the holding cell changing room, took off my top, then I placed it back on, no problem. I undid my pants, allowing them to slide down my legs to the floor, my underpants followed in the same fashion. The Screw declared, 'Okay Edwards, get dressed.'

In my mind, I was relieved, no problem. I then bent over to pull up my pants, big mistake. As I bent over the parcel popped out of my butt, only for the Screw to see the wrapped block of ash bouncing on the floor as if it was dancing like Fred Astaire. The Screw got to the package before me because I was still dressing myself. I thought, *'I've got to get the drugs.'*

So, like a foolish court jester, I bent the Screw's arm up behind his back, pushed his body and face into the wall, in the hope he would drop the weed, oh no, not this Screw, he held onto the weed for dear life, even when I threatened him, 'Drop the drugs or I will bite you, I've got Aids.'

Stupid, so stupid, for one I haven't got Aids. Secondly, if I did bite him, knowing I have Aids, it would be a murder charge. Me manhandling the Screw didn't last long, six or seven Screws ran into the holding cell to apprehend me, then I was spreadeagled by four Screws. Subsequently, I was taken to the block, carried through two gates, and across two fields for the whole jail to see.

The Screws were not satisfied with the catch. They announced, 'We want a further strip search Edwards, get your clothes off.'

Standing proud in a defiant mood in the prison cell block, I replied, 'F--k off.'

In that moment, I made a quick dash for the bed, and tried to crawl under it, in an effort to fight them off but that did not work. They grabbed hold of me, only to be spreadeagled again. The Screws took my clothes off, while one Screw took a closer inspection in between my butt. As a result, I farted in his face. They dropped me quick enough, then they left me on my own in the block, how low can life get?

That evening, midnight 1997 struck, the distant eruption of cell doors being battered by soles of inmate's feet, thunderous roars of men's anger were like raging bulls, cries sounded off as if you were spectators in the Roman arena, and shouts for freedom echoed around the prison site in the Lancashire county valley. After half hour of the mind-bending noise, dead silent, like a calm ocean after a vicious storm. It was now time for bed.

After the following seven days alone in the block, I was stood in front of the warden with two Screws standing either side of me for adjudication. Having heard the charges made, the warden said, 'Do you have anything to say before I pass sentence?'

I knew I could not claim my days back, I had less than six months on my sentence remaining. So, I stood up for myself like a man in a rebellious mood. I replied, 'Yes, for five hundred years and more, you've known black, I will not stop smoking weed.'

The clean-shaven bald-headed warden, sat across two long chestnut brown mahogany veneer government tables that had thin square metal black legs. He looked me up and down, over his round turtle shell lens NHS glasses with his devilishly bloodshot redeyes. At that juncture, the warden stated, 'Six weeks remission lost, get him out of here.'

Chapter 55

Free am I not

Losing remission meant an automatic ship out to another prison, a week after adjudication, the relaxed atmosphere of H.M.P. Buckley Hall had been exchanged for the disciplined regime of the military, and no respect for human dignity, when I was transported to H.M.P. Moorland's block. When I walked into my sky-blue double cell was just like Strange Ways or Stafford. I ended up banged up with Christopher Boyle, a mixed-race guy from Manchester. Although he was from Moss Side, ten years younger than me, I did not know him or the people he moved with. We were banged up for 23 hours, we'd spend our time chatting, playing chess, or we would play some music. When I wanted to sleep, and he didn't he'd always decide to play his radio, loud. I'd still fall asleep anyway no matter how deafening the music was.

I arrived at the jail with no tobacco, Christopher was kind enough to share what he had, until I received my canteen order, which was due in a few days. When we did finally runout of smokes, for the first time on my sentence we had to shout out of the barred window for tobacco. Luckily, in a cell right below ours, an Irish voice replied, 'Drop a line mate, I'll sort you out.'

We lowered him a string line, weighed down with a lighter, when we pulled up the line to open an envelope it revealed what one uses toilet paper for. Disgust, revolt, swear words the lot were exchanged out of our window between us, and the strange Irishman below. We shouted out of the barred window, 'Wait until exercise.'

Me and Christopher could hear his laughter, the joke was on us as far as he was concerned. The following day in the prison yard, the only time we were allowed out of our cell was for an hour's exercise, the Irish dude was not to be seen. We asked other inmates in the yard, about the Irish dude in cell B2-5. An inmate answered, 'The Irish guy is on numbers, in other words protective custody. He raped a young offender who'd just been transferred from Moorlands Young Offenders Prison wing to the adult wings.'

I thought, *'Poor young man, he must have pissed off the Screws to be banged up with a man like that.'*

Being on the block meant, I could not work or go on educational courses. Hence, I was only paid £2.50 a week, for being unemployed, plus a further £2.50 from my personal account, which I could spend on my canteen. I had personal cash, but a psychological game was being played on me by the Screws. After I filled out my canteen slip, the Screws informed me, 'My personal cash did not arrive in my account when I was transferred.'

In my mind, this didn't sound right with only £2.50 to spend. I had to look after my pad mate for his kindness first, before thinking about myself, I was indebted to him. Having paid Christopher back for tobacco that cost £1.90, rolling paper, matches and a first-class stamp, I had nothing for myself. This went on for another two weeks, it was beginning to irritate and infuriate Christopher because I was always asking him for tobacco. Christopher was constantly in my ear ranting, 'Weak pussy, weak pussy, the Screws are taking the piss out of you, weak pussy, weak pussy.'

I knew the game the Screws were playing, I could not risk losing my cool to give an excuse for the Screws to beat me up. At that point, it came to my mind, I told Christopher, 'I would write to Annabel, and ask her to send some money.'

Which she did, when Annabel replied to my letter, she posted a postal order for £20. This took me into the third week without a full canteen. Now when you get a canteen slip, the slip will state how much prison wage one is paid and can spend, and how much personal cash one has in their account, with how much one can spend depending on which one of the three regimes one might be on. Being on the block, as mentioned earlier, I received my £2.50 unemployed, and the slip stated £20 personal cash from Annabel. I thought, *'Cool, I played a smart move, £5 in total to spend.'*

Wrong, when I got my small brown canteen bag, there was only £2.50 worth of goods. Christopher was rubbing my nose in it, and laughing his head off, doing a Chuckle Brother, 'Hehe he, weak pussy, weak pussy, they're playing on your patience mate, weak pussy, weak pussy, Hehe he.'

He was right, the Screws were taking the piss, I had to insist on my right to have a full canteen. So, I started banging on the secure cast iron door. Suddenly, the increasing volume of an erupting earthquake rumbled from the soles of many leather boots, beating down on the metal girded prison gangway.

I sat back on my bed knowing, the noise of the Screw's boots were getting louder, and closer to my door. I felt nervous, if you can imagine being at the dentist, or waiting in anticipation to walking on the stage to perform a play, and similar to standing at the edge of a cliff ready to jump, but as confident and defiant as Malcom X. I looked towards Christopher he was in his bed; all I could see of him were the white of his eyes looking on at the scene with a woollen blanket over his head. The Screw's keys did not even clash against the door, it was straight in the keyhole. The door swung open with speed. Eight white faces, managed to fit their big heads into the small doorway. One of the Screws looked straight towards me cried out, 'You f--king black bastard, did you bang on this door?'

I was shocked but not surprised by his remark, in fact it underlined his intent. I just sat there, on my bed, and confidently replied, 'Besides what you think of me, and what I think of you, when am I going to get a full canteen?'

All the Screws straighten their backs from their attacking stance and stood to attention like guards on parade. They looked at one another a bit bewildered and taken a back. They turned to leave the cell, slamming the bloody door shut behind them. Christopher sat up on his bed looking bemused, baffled, and bamboozled, after the drama that just unfolded, stating, 'I'm amazed you didn't get a kicking.'

Five minutes later, a Screw returns to my cell, proclaiming, 'Here you are Edwards.'

The Screw offered me a large brown canteen bag, adding, 'It's an order from another inmate who was released today, enjoy. You're alright Edwards.'

The Screw left the cell, slamming the bloody door shut. I opened the bigger than usual heavy brown paper bag to see pure food, snack bars, tobacco, phone credits, it was like Christmas. After weeks of scraping the bottom of the barrel, for the next few days it felt nice to have the resources one needed.

After six weeks in total on the block, it was a relief to get back on the main wing with four months remaining on my sentence. I stayed unemployed in my single cell, and for the first time, since I became an adult, it gave me the chance to read the Bible with great difficulty understanding. I only came out of my cell for association, or the gym, until my release.

Chapter 56

Back in the swing

Having never received any home leave before my release date on the 11th, June 1997. At 9.01 a.m. it was nice to hear slam for the last time, as the bloody main prison gate closed behind me. Outside, the taste of fresh air was the air of freedom. In front of me were a few buildings, and a green open field. The blue open sky did not have a cloud, the sun cast a warm glow in the atmosphere, and the warmth of the cool fresh breeze, brought a gentle whirl from the whip of the wind. It triggered the soothing sounds of the whistling wind whisper a comforting melody.

I walked over to the bus stop, which was nicely placed, across the road from the prison gate. Only to discover, I'd just missed the bus. The timetable displayed, half an hour for the next bus, I wasn't waiting. I started to walk home only to see my old friend Theo Robinson arrive in his new B.M.W. After a warm welcome from my friend, I remember saying before driving home, 'I feel totally sin free.'

Theo, along-time schoolfriend replied, 'It's about time you put on some weight, you don't look so skinny.'

Now I was thirteen and a half stones, compare to the eleven stones when I went into jail, I knew the training paid off. No need to mention the warm welcome when I arrived in Manchester, I was elated to see my son and family members. However, I didn't want to be noticed by my friends. As a consequence, once I'd seen my family, I stayed with Beverly for a week. I've never planned anything, never had insight of where I was going, never mind with a woman. Seven fun days passed; something was not right in my mind. I asked, 'Beverly, are you seeing another guy?'

Her honesty is why I still love her today, she answered, 'Yes.'

I just stood up and left, I never went back or called. I thought,

'If that's what you want, I hope you're happy.'

In many ways, it worked for me, a decision I didn't have to make with a conclusion. I liked the way Annabel was towards me, while I was banged up. The evening I broke up with Beverly, Annabel was on her way to Manchester from London where she was studying.

Annabel's welcome home was with a warm rapturous energy, I really thought sex would be number one, on the I really miss that list. Nope, sorry ladies, number one on the list was my mother's rice, peas and fried chicken with coleslaw. After a short weekend visit, Annabel went back to London. The words of a man I met in Bristol stayed in my mind when he stated, *'The most important thing in the world is peace of mind.'*

Throughout my sentence, those words were the last thoughts on my mind before I fell asleep. Since I had nothing, it was time to re-establish my life with the intentions of staying out of the drug scene. I followed the advice from my parole officer, 'Stay out of trouble, book myself into a hostel in Ardwick and try to find some work.'

My friends are so good to me, knowing of my stolen record collection, Theo gave me a very large box of records. His taste isn't the same as mine, but the box help kickstart my new collection. Theo also set me up as a deejay promoter in Withington where he was working as a doorman. At the time Theo made the offer, I was not interested in the club scene, I'd been out of the deejay world over four years by now, but after a bit of encouragement, I agreed to do the gig on the worst night, Tuesdays. It only lasted a few weeks, and I didn't make any money. The club went bust soon after, but it gave me the hunger, and the want to be a deejay. With a new attitude towards the club scene, it was just too expensive to party every night of the week. So, to enjoy the nightlife, become a deejay.

As a dear friend, Theo went one step further, he sold me a 1.8 litre injection Ford Orion for half its value. That helped, money was tight, and I needed cash for my tools as a carpenter. To be honest, I was not really looking for work the first few weeks after being released. It's kind a funny but somehow, I felt out of step with the rest of society, a lot further back from where my mates were, who seemed to be ahead in life. I had to catch up and make some money, now I was out, and about. A friend I have not seen for years, welcomed me with open arms, but added, 'I've got some cheap drugs to sell. Come and work for me, selling drugs.'

It was no good, everywhere I went, drugs. I had to move from the Moss Side area. I informed my parole officer how I was feeling, he decided to move me to the very same hostel Cate was living a few years earlier. Two or so weeks after moving in, Annabel comes to visit. That evening, we were wrapped up warm together in each other's arms, there was a flicker of light given off from the T.V. Then, news flash, the reporter's statement stated, 'Princess Diana the queen of hearts, died in a car crash tonight.'

I was in shock like a baby being slapped at birth, horrified there's *Frankenstein*, and surprise, surprise is there a spy, cascaded my mind. I quickly questioned conspiracy, the reporter's comment was a quotation from the Bible, *'The queen of hearts.'*

This particular week was a week of mixed fortunes. It so happens, it wasn't before long I found work on a building site, just outside St. Helens Merseyside. The night before starting work, about 11.30 p.m. I was driving from Theo's place towards my new residence in the hostel. The evening was warm from a hot summer's day, the roads were quiet on my journey with only 400 yards before arriving at the hostel in Crumpsall. Travelling at 28 to 29 miles per hour, I hear whoop, whoop, whoop, I get pulled over by the police. I parked up like a civil citizen, in my mirror I could see flashing blue lights, as I watched two policewomen approach my car from either side of the vehicle, I opened up my window to hear one of the officers greet me with a question, 'Good evening sir, is this your car?'

I had a problem, no driver's license, and under covered on my insurance, I was looking at jail for breaking my parole conditions. I nervously but confidently replied, 'Yes officer, this is my car, why have you stopped me? I wasn't speeding, was I?'

In a very official capacity with a subtle tender tone, the officer answered, 'No, as it goes, you weren't speeding, which gives us a reason to pull you over. You were driving under the speed limit. Would you please step out of the car sir?'

I didn't question the police officer, I came out of the car thinking, *'No speed is the right speed if you're black.'*

I walked over to the pavement with the officer following up behind, I stated, 'Yes officer how can I help?'

She looked me up and down replying, 'Do you have your driving documents?'

Feeling apprehensive, tense as a thriller by Alfred Hitchcock, and uneasy about the turn of events, I answered, 'Sorry officer no.'

She continued with a flat monotone voice, and quoted a familiar line, 'What's your name, date of birth, and address please?'

The other female police officer was looking over my car, while doing a P.C. check.

I responded to the first officer apprehensively, 'Fitzroy Edwards 18th December 1966, 65 Rectory Road, Crumpsall.'

She proceeded to write, while asking, 'Do you have any proof of identity?'

I couldn't fool my way out of this situation, I can be deceitful, but I'm not a good liar. So, told the truth in part, 'To be honest with you officer, it's not been long since my release from prison. I've been at my friend's house in Hyde, his excuse for him drinking tonight was my friends celebrating my release. He was too drunk to drive me home, and I start a new job in the morning. I needed to be home to pick up my tools.'

I'm not sure what it was, either I leave a lasting impression, or coppers, never forget. The police officer looked me up and down. She responded, 'That cut didn't leave much of a scar.'

At that moment, I was totally surprised, similar to a woman being proposed to, and puzzled like a contestant in a quiz show. I came back with, 'Excuse me?'

She looked me up and down once again, but in the darkness of the night, lit by a nearby city streetlight, there seemed to be a sparkle in her big blue eyes, when she replied, 'You don't remember me, do you?'

Still puzzled and charmed by her manner towards me, I answered politely with a flirtatious stare, 'Sorry officer no.'

She looked up from the paper pad that was in her hand, her big blue eyes widen to absorb the light, she continued, 'My name is W.P.C. Jane Kent. I'm the officer who took you to the hospital, when you received that cut under your nose.'

My memory suddenly clicked into place. I responded quite surprised, 'Oh yeah, I remember you. You're a bit far from Moss Side, aren't you working out of that station?'

She replied, 'No, I'm in Cheetham Hill.'

After a slight pause she continued, 'Listen Fitzroy, I'll have to give you a producer. You have five days before an officer comes to your address.'

Then she handed me a ticket, I understood what the officer was saying, she was trying to warn me. I answered, 'Okay officer, thanks.'

We parted company, me knowing full well I didn't have much time, I had to change address quick.

The following day, I didn't have much money and needed to sign on at the benefit agency that morning. I arrived on site 11.30 a.m. later than expected, only to find the site had no power, and the materials had not arrived on site. The site manager stated, 'You need to have a generator and the materials would be on site in the morning.'

I was a bit discouraged; the site agent could have told me over the phone, I needed a generator. It didn't help, not having materials on my first day working on price. I was back in my car, heading home by 12.30 p.m. a wasted day.

My problems were mounting, when I went to my mother's house to see my son Nicolas, my mother was beginning to feel the stress of bringing up an eleven-year-old boy. Nicolas was destroying my mother's house by breaking up the furniture whenever he was told off. This was not the first time I had to talk to my son about his temper. In fact, it was the third time on the same subject. My mother felt I was not hard enough on him. So, for the first time, I was forced to beat my son with my belt.

Three times, the belt slashed his skinny black flesh, he never did that again, but my mother was still not happy. She was tired, getting old, and my mother wanted her own time. As a consequence, we decided that my son should live with me once I'd found a flat.

The following day at 8 a.m. I arrived on site with a new generator costing £250 with no materials on site, all I could do was fit a flight of stairs, until the delivery of timber arrived. It didn't take long to fit the stairs. After I had an early breakfast, the timber arrived on site. Since there were no labourers on the job, I had to unload the flooring that was being delivered. Only to be shown an assorted mix ten-kilo box of nails, I was not impressed. I asked the site manager, 'Am I getting paid for this labouring?'

The site agent was a tall slim white guy from Liverpool, middle aged with a lazy boy attitude, he replied, 'You're on price mate.'

At that juncture, he handed me a box of mixed sized nails, going through the mixed array of nails wasn't a professional approach towards me. I felt my integrity as a carpenter was being undermined. As a consequence, I nailed the floor with a mixture of nails.

I surprised the site agent with the speed of my fitting, but when he took a closer look at the floor, the assorted nails in the flooring changed the expression on his face to a red tomato, favouring the devil in Tom Cruise's movie *Legend*. The site agent questioned, 'What have you done?'

I queried the ten-kilo box of mixed nails, by 12.30 p.m. I was on my way home, never to return to the site. I never asked or received a wage for the work done. Luckily, with all the effort trying to find work earlier, a recruitment agency called me on my mobile to offer me a job, starting the following day. It went well for the two weeks I was employed on that particular job. Because of the police producer, I rushed around to find a flat in Middleton, Langley. Two bedrooms were just too expensive from private landlords. By Friday of that week, I was in my new one-bedroom flat.

Chapter 57

Uptown girl

When I moved into my new one-bedroom flat at 12 Lever Street, Langley, Middleton, things seem to be falling into place with a carpentry job, and deejay work in a new local bar opening in Middleton, the Life Café Bar every Saturday night. It didn't pay much, forty quid from 9 p.m. till 1 a.m. but it allowed me to buy the music I needed. My love, appetite, and reputation for playing fresh new tunes caused me to always spend over budget.

The fact, Annabel was living in London, my loins were always crying out for a woman. After playing my set in the Life Café Bar, I would find myself driving into Moss Side for the night life, if I did not pick up a girl in a bar locally.

The Big Western, a very large Edwardian pub in the middle of a seventies lemon yellow brick housing estate, in Alexander Park. The boozer stood out at five stories high, it looked similar to a dark dreary haunted gothic church. The bar had red Mancunian bricks with white windows. It sat in between two warring gangs, Doddington, and Gooch Close. Outside the pub 24 hours a day, you were guaranteed to see the local drug dealers fending their turf.

After the clubs in central Manchester had closed 1, 2 a.m. the late night would continue till 4, 5 a.m. in the Western. The vibe of the underground would come to life 2 a.m. People would join the party to hear tunes, but the bad boy business could kick off at any time from time to time. The locals dressed nice, looked sexy and smelt divine. Men and women from all walks of life, would attend the venue to hear classic reggae tunes downstairs, in a large seedy dimly lit function room upstairs, is where I spent most of the night. The R & B bassline would rumble around the walls, helping the heartbeat pump, all the more excited by the ladies, dancing their dance on the dancefloor.

The ladies modelled tight fitted jeans, if not, a short skirt, or a racy dress, firm bumpers would squeeze up against man's front, as lovely, sexy girls tried to weave through the energetic, cool, and excited crowd. As the night proceeded, coming through the main entrance into the dancehall, I noticed a lovely tall strawberry blonde being harassed by a bunch of horny black men. The cool classy way she politely turned down the men's advances, appealed to my desires as she made her way to the edge of the dancefloor. I could tell from the look in her eyes, she was enjoying the attention, but yet to be impressed. I stood from a distance for 15 - 20 minutes, intrigued by her figure eight figure, and captivated by her graceful flow to the rhythm of the bass. As time passed, the attention she was receiving was not as noticeable. It was my time to make my move.

I'd like to believe like most men, I didn't know what to say, or the best way to introduce myself, but I was as confident as a judge, and I felt as horny as a bull elephant on heat. I found myself pushing and weaving through the thick crowd when I approached her from behind. As I got closer, I could see she was wearing two thin straps holding up a very low-cut back, a honey-coloured dress outlined her hourglass figure invitingly. I moved in closer to her right ear, and I was very surprised with myself when I whispered, 'I would love to pour chocolate down your back, and slowly, lick it off.'

As I said that, I turned away, back into a sea of people around me to join my mates. I stood back from a distance to watch her turning her head, swivelling around and around like a lighthouse, looking every which way now and then. Her eyes were searching in a sea of swaying bodies and rocking people. The look in her eyes were probing the crowd, looking for someone, not knowing who.

Everyone in the venue was dancing the night away, I allowed two, or three records to be played, while I watched her stylish stance. I admired the elegant way she flowed majestically to the rhythm of the beat, I yearned to caress her soft pearl skin. As I glared at her long hair and stared in her face, she was still shaking her head no to men's advances. I decided to walk over facing her, and as I approached I held out my hand to offer her a handshake. Her small soft smooth warm hand naturally fell into mine. I gently pulled her closer, as I leaned into her ear. Over the loud music I whispered, 'My names Fitzroy, I would love to pour chocolate down your chest, suck your nipples, until their nice, and firm. What's your name?'

Over the loud rumbling bass, and the soothing romantic music of R & B, she uttered back, 'Tiana Whitlock.'

In my deep husky Barry White voice, I replied, 'It's nice to meet you, have fun, we'll chat later.'

Her big hazel eyes shone like the flickering stars at night, a twinkle in her eyes and a wink there's a surprise, she replied, 'Okay.'

I returned the gesture by giving her a wink before disappearing into the packed venue towards my mates. From a distance, we watched one another rocking simultaneously with the rhythm, staring past on lookers, only drifting from each other's gaze when someone wanted our attention. The night came to an untimely end at 4 a.m. Me, and my mates, found we were standing alongside my car overlooking the party people. Exiting the venue in amongst the sexy crowd, I could see Tiana saying, 'No, no, no.'

Giggling like she's heard a good joke, laughing in a fun-loving fashion with the men waiting wanting her attention. She made her way gracefully through the thick crowd of unsuccessful men not noticing me, as she walked chatting with her friend. I announced to my mates, 'Later guys I'm on a mission.'

I jumped in my car to pull up alongside Tiana and her friend, just around the corner from the venue for them to hear me say, 'Hi there Tiana, where you going?'

She bent down to look into the car, all I could see were her big hazel eyes, I could have fallen in love with her there and then. Her deep cleavage appeared in front of my vision, revealing she had a lot more than a surprise. Her big cherry sized nipples pierced her silk dress nearly steamed up my car. Tiana replied, 'We're waiting for a taxi we've booked to go home.'

Feeling excited and very enthusiastic about the prospect of

having some sex, if not who knows what the future may hold, like a gentleman from the royal household, I asked, 'Where abouts do you live?'

Giggling along with her mate, not dissimilar to a bunch of immature school girls, Tiana countered, 'I live in Moston, my sister is on the way in Longsight.'

Time waits for no one, I answered, 'Get in, I'll give you a lift.'

The two women knew the phrase and wasted no time getting in the car. Once in the vehicle, Tiana's perfume drifted to my nose. This forced me to have a closer look at her shapely legs, which led up to her slim stomach, closely following up were two well rounded breasts, her pretty face, and full pink lips, revealed a glowing smile. Tiana introduced her sister Susan, who sat in the back seat very quietly. I was forced to ask a question, 'How come you two sexy ladies aren't out with your man tonight?'

Tiana was blunt as a knife, brash like a smug banker, and straight to the point replied, 'What man? Who needs a man?'

Tiana turned to face her sister who was sat in the back seat when Tiana muttered, 'That reminds me, I need some new batteries.'

A sudden burst of laughter exploded between the two of them. I understood what she was in stitches about, I responded to her remark, 'I've heard a lot about these rabbits.'

The laughter stopped as quick as it erupted, all I could feel were all eyes on me. I followed the comment, 'And it just doesn't have the same weight behind a thirteen stone thrust.'

From the corner of my eye, I could see Tiana's eyes widen to the size of a tennis ball, her hazel iris turned as black as night, then her eyes dropped down to look in between my legs. She retorted in an erotic manner, 'Is that right!'

Tiana slowly licked her lips, as she looked up into my face, I continued driving to her sister's house. As we proceeded we had small chit chat, Tiana revealed, 'I'm twenty-eight with a nine-year-old boy and I'm studying English at Manchester University.'

It wasn't before long we were in Longsight, I dropped off Susan to take Tiana home.

Now Susan was not around to hear our conversation, I felt horny, self-assured, and straight to the point when I declared, 'You live too far away.'

We only had a 15-minute drive to Moston, Tiana replied, 'What do you mean? It's not that far.'

I couldn't help myself; I was in no doubt Tiana liked my company, I fancied her as if she were Nia Long, so being bold similar to Rosa Parks, and courageous as if I were Nelson Mandela, I pulled no punches when out of my mouth came, 'I want you right now, on top of my bonnet with the engine running, what you saying?'

From the corner of my eye, I could see the tip of her tongue slowly cruise across her full pink lips. Her eyes opened, her pupils widened into blackness, absorbing what light there was. Tiana instructed me, 'Turn left here, then second right.'

I followed her route stating, 'This isn't the right way to Moston, where you taking me to?'

As I drove to her directions, she leaned in closer to my left ear. In a seductive manner Tiana whispered, 'Do you really want me on your bonnet?'

Tiana's course led to a dimly lit dead end, underneath a railway bridge.

I parked the car under the overpass out of sight, and the slow-moving sounds of a train running on the tracks could be heard passing overhead, chugga chuggar, chugga chuggar, chugga chuggar. I turned to Tiana, her eyes were fixed in my direction, her lips were painted with pink fresh glossy lipstick, which invited a tender kiss. I leaned towards her, gently held her chin, and pulled her head over to my lips. Tiana came closer towards me, similar to an airship making a soft landing, her lips touched mines. They were soft and as sweet as a ripe mango, I had to make a move for her large breasts that felt like a cluster of grapes. It was beginning to steam up in the car, the passion in our kiss was stimulating and arousing. Suddenly, Tiana pulled her lips away from mines, muttering, 'I thought we were doing this on the bonnet?'

I thought, *'Your keen, you horny bitch.'*

228

We gazed into each other's eyes, simultaneously we both exited the car, rushed to the front of the vehicle to continue where we left off. The engine was still running and sounded like a cat purring as it ticked over. I held Tiana in my arms, then I caressed her lips tenderly, her response she kissed back. She made a move to release my belt, in that moment she stop kissing me to sit on the car bonnet. Her smooth silky legs slowly spread wide open invitingly, need I say more.

After meeting Tiana, and a few other women, I was in and out of work for short spells. Time came as agreed between me and my mother, Nicolas moved in with me, before the new term of school started. The weekend before my son went to school, I registered us both with the benefit agencies, housing groups to be rehoused in cheaper accommodation. I received my last pay, and unemployed.

Tuesday of that week, Nicolas was due to start his first day in secondary school, I wanted him to feel the most comfort. As a consequence, he slept in the bedroom, while I slept on the settee. Unsure when I'd be working again, the Saturday before Nicolas started school, I spent £150 on meat, pure food, and new clothes, anything Nicolas wanted. We both unloaded the car, running in turn up to the first floor, down the one flight of stairs to where my car was parked in view from the balcony above. We had a fun time bringing in the shopping, with the car unloaded both of us started unpacking, only to find there was no meat in the bags, fifty pounds worth of meat disappeared; I was pissed off with my misfortune.

I resigned to the fact, and let Nicolas play out. Fifteen minutes later he returns stating, 'Dad, this woman's laughing about our meat that's gone missing, I think she's got it.'

My blood was boiling similar to a hot kettle, no need to mention the big fighting match of words between me and the thief, which engulfed the flats and surrounding area. Looking back, it was not something my son should have seen. The woman I was arguing with and her four or five kids, looked worst off then me.

In my mind, it didn't look like a good start between me and my son. He was a good lad, every morning, he was up and out, on time travelling over six miles to school. Over the next few months, I was in and out of work. The Life Café Bar was getting better on my nights but was failing the rest of the week. The owner of the bar said, 'You're booked for a party that starts at 8 p.m. till they go home.'

Till they go home was an open clock, the longest set I've done was four hours, using vinyl, there was no mp3 and CD's are not really a deejays tool. We agreed £15 per hour, after my normal rate.

The deejay booth of the club was situated on the third floor, as a consequence, I was not aware they were charging at the door. On the night, it was packed nose to nose with people, at 4 a.m. gunshot fired off. There was a sudden rush into the dancefloor, screams from girls amid the chaos and among the confused dancers. The lights came on, the party was over. I later learnt the door was raided, over £800 was stolen from the door, I was unemployed at the time.

Now, I had a further problem, two doormen had been paid, the bar staff did not have to worry about a weekly wage, but I did. I was expecting £100 for 8 hours straight spinning tracks, a top night, cheap. The owner, gives me £5 taxi fare home, uttering underneath his breath, 'I haven't got any money to pay you.'

After a big shouting match between the owner of the bar and myself, like a dog that has just been kicked, I left the venue with my tail in between my legs. No pay, no further deejay work at the gaff, and unemployed with a young boy to feed. A few weeks later, the establishment went bust, and closed shop. I'm always financially used and abused.

Chapter 58

Headache, heartache

It's September 1997, I was drifting in and out of completed work, I was also due to change address to 18 Balmoral Street, Gorton Manchester. A two-bedroom Mancunium red brick terraced house, which was a lot nearer to my family, and more importantly, Nicolas's school. Two weeks before moving in, I just started a new job not too far from my new home. First fix, refurbishing some terrace houses in Ardwick. On my start day, I noticed a lone figure standing across the road at a distance from the site, looking over the job. Two hours later, he was still there. I asked the other tradesmen, 'What's his problem?'

A bricklayer replied, 'He was a chippy on the job, he didn't get paid for his work.'

Working for an agency I thought, *'I didn't have a problem, as long as my timesheet was signed.'*

On the Friday of that week, it was time to sign my timesheet. The site agent who was telling me what to do, would not sign my hours off because I was employed by a subcontractor called Brian Bidwell. Now, I knew I worked for another company, through my agent, but I have never seen this Brian Bidwell in the five days on site. I had no choice, but to believe my timesheet would be signed off and faxed to the recruitment agency.

The following Monday, I arrived at work, phoned the recruitment agency, they confirmed receiving a signed timesheet, but they didn't inform me of the hours submitted. I continued working feeling reassured about my pay. On the Thursday, Brian Bidwell shows his face for the first time, stepping out of a new Land Rover Discovery. He approached me wearing jeans, and a white businessman's shirt looking as smug as Niles Crane from *Fraser*, similar to a *Dragons Den* bidder he was confident, and with a flippant statement declared, 'You've not done a lot of work.'

I was not very pleased with the comment and tried to explain why, 'I was delayed, which was due to the floor layers, and other tradesmen.'

Bidwell was not fazed by my comment, and with a dismissive attitude he affirmed his authority, 'Okay, your services are no longer required, I will fax your timesheet.'

I wasn't happy with that either, so I tried to get him to sign my timesheet for that week, he just walked away, got in his car, and drove off.

Things just got from bad to worse that same weekend. I was due to move to my new house, I was also expecting money from a few quarters, and I was looking forward to getting my deposit back for the flat in Langley £1400. So, me and Nicolas cleaned the flat. I received a wage slip in Saturday morning's post, £28 minus tax, I was screwing a ton. I was expecting £450 wage to buy a cooker, fridge all the basics. I was unable to save with irregular work, I needed the cash.

Monday morning, my blood was boiling, not dissimilar to viciously cooking Basmati rice. I made my way to the building site, after Nicolas went to school. On confronting the site agent, he was unable to speak with Brian Bidwell over the phone. When I contacted my agent, the recruitment agent accused me of punching Brian Bidwell, I could not believe what I was hearing. The only people to date I'd hit was my father and son. When I asked about the hours signed in for that week's pay, the agent said, 'Nothing had been received or faxed.'

Uncontrollable rage rushed through my mind and body, full blown stressed out. I thought, *Fine, watch this.*

Sure enough, I got out my skill saw from the boot of my car, and cut through all the work I'd fixed, doorframes, trusses, four flights of stairs everything I fitted. Then I went onto pick up my deposit from the letting agency. Nothing ever runs smoothly, there's always a problem. When I arrived at the letting agency, they didn't want to give me the full amount of the deposit, which was £1400. The letting agent commented, 'The flat was not clean, and it would cost the company £100 to get a cleaner in.'

This is one example of many swindles, which are not claimed because it seems a small amount to do the paperwork and pay the court fees. I had to leave £100 short, so I did not involve the police. I managed to get what I needed for the house, but not what I'd planned for. It was another two weeks before I found alternative work. I ended up losing that, two weeks into working because the police paid me a visit at 6 a.m. concerning the Brian Bidwell job. I was placed under arrest for vandalising property and given two hundred hours community service.

The first day of my community service, I walked into a carpenter's workshop, they wanted me to do repair work on windows and kid's toys. I thought *'This is cheap slave labour, to do that work for free, and not have been paid from Bidwell, you're taking the piss.'*

I told them where they can put it and walked out, I haven't heard from them since.

Throughout this period, Annabel was still travelling from London at least once a month to see me, as well as her family for the weekends or holidays. Me being constantly in and out of work played on Annabel's mind. She had a concerned comment, 'I cannot understand why you can't find steady work?'

I explained, 'Employers don't take on full time staff, not unless you know the boss personally, when that person goes on holiday, or a company needs a temporary tradesmen that's when a recruitment agency offer me work. Until the job is completed, or the staff gets back from holiday.'

In Annabel's mind, I could see my unstable working life was a mark against me, but at the same time she understood my situation.

Chapter 59

Chasing a dream

The weeks and months passed at Balmoral Street; Nicolas was a lot happier but difficult to talk to. Although work was not constant, I got by with the added bad luck along the way. Tiana wanted to get a bit more serious, in turn there was a little bit of a drama when I just did not call, ending a nice and sweet but short-lived romance.

Things did not help when my car broke down just before it's M.O.T. I was unemployed, the stress of it all, for four weeks my car sat outside. Finally, I got a job, come the second Friday payday that evening after work, I pumped up the wheels ready to drive to the garage. Excited about my car going to the mechanic's it was a shock to see the car was not where I parked it the following morning. I phone the police to report it stolen. The police informed me, 'We have it impounded because the tax date had expired. If you want your car back, there is a fine of £180 plus £25 for everyday storage.'

I just couldn't find that kind of money so fast, I had to right off my car. On top of pressing bills, bills, bills, the new job I'd started was not going well at the newly built Trafford Centre. I was on price work, plaster boarding the auditorium for the cinema screens at £1400 per wall double skinned. Me and my mate were doing good for time, fixing the plasterboards. It took us a week to do one wall at £700 each, we were on a good earner. The foremen disagreed with the standard on one wall, and would not sign it over, we left the job pissed off. Six months later, forgetting all about that job, I get a P60 through the post, informing the taxman I received £700 before tax. I was on the phone to complain, two weeks later I received a cheque. It just shows, if you don't keep your books straight, someone will try to stitch you up, or have one over you.

Just over a year had gone by, when I received a letter from Middleton Council, demanding payment for council tax, and housing benefit overpayments. The entire system is constantly chasing you for money. I had to pay back a total of £1,600. This hole was getting deeper, and I was not having much of a social life. From home to work from unemployed to home, going to jobs, meeting six or seven carpenters and the job, only requires three chippies, wasting my day with no pay. It was a relief to see Annabel when she did come to Manchester.

I tried promoting a bar in Manchester city centre, at Lineker's Bar on Mosley Street. I paid £200 for doormen and a further £150 on flyers. Only to be told, 'Someone was following up behind you Eggy and binning your flyers.'

Twenty people attended my first night, at a venue that could hold two hundred. I just couldn't afford another night. Although everyone was saying, 'Try again, it was a good night, we'll tell people.'

While I was working at Boots in central Manchester, constructing a four-story lift shaft, Nicolas calls me on my mobile phone, 'Dad, your turntables, and music have been stolen.'

I could not believe it, for the second time my music was pinched. There was a force against me that I just could not see.

People say things and don't think twice or take responsibility for what they say. I remember one evening my sister Sharon made a comment to Nicolas, 'If you find you don't like living with your dad you can come and live with me.'

If it's one thing you don't do with kids, is give them too many options. Bearing this in mind, Nicolas's attitude changed for the worse, he was beginning to question my authority as a parent. It came to a head with me, and Nicolas now thirteen. I came home from work about 9 p.m. I needed something from the shop, exhausted from a hard long 12 - hour day. Nicolas was playing outside with his friends, so I called him in, to go to the shop. Nicolas had the bear face cheek to answer, 'No, get it yourself.'

A war of words between me and my son broke out, I could not believe how he was chatting back to his dad. I had enough, my final words, 'I'm the father you're the son, you do as I say, if you don't like it there's the door.'

Stubborn just like his dad, Nicolas walked out, making his way to my sister Sharon. Sharon called me that evening to tell me, 'Nicolas was at her place.'

A whole week went by, no phone call from Nicolas, or Sharon. I thought, *'It was time he came back home.'*

Without even discussing the matter with me, Sharon was of the opinion I was wrong, and defended Nicolas.

This pissed me off no end, Sharon was undermining my authority as a parent. I lost my cool, and in a fit of rage I broke my sister's window. Dismayed with my family's current affairs, I sat outside my sister's doorstep, until the police arrived, then I was placed in a cell for eight hours. All I kept thinking is this isn't what I want, constantly arguing with my family, I did not feel needed as much as before I was imprisoned. My younger sisters were older, independent, and dominating when I'm looking for peace of mind. Contemplating what to do, I remembered Annabel saying, *'Why don't you come to London, you've never been to visit me, and there was a lot of building work.'*

After being released from the police cell, a week later, I was in London.

Chapter 60

Looking forward

While I was living in Manchester for just over a year after my release from jail, more often than not, I was working for a recruitment agency called A.M.H. Contract Services. I asked A.M.H. if they had any offices in London, which they did. As a course of action with plans to stay in London for two weeks, they arranged for me to start working the Monday following.

The weekend I left for London, on the 29th, October 1999, I arrived in London on a Friday evening to be met by Annabel, and a loud lively G20 protest of some sort. Annabel was living in a small box room in the student's hall of residence, at St Bart's Hospital with only a single bed. We slept on the floor, in a pump-up camping bed. Monday morning, I was on site at a medical centre in Summertown, Euston at 8 a.m. ready for a long 12-hour day. Upon arriving on site, the site agent was not there. I met four chippies from Australia, one mentioned, 'The site agent was always late, just wait.'

10 a.m. the site agent arrives on site, just as the chippies were on their way out for breakfast. I've never seen anything like it, the site agent look similar to a hairy mammoth, he was unshaven, long uneven haircut, very unprofessional for his position, he smelt of alcohol, and couldn't walk straight. At that moment, he pulled out a small bottle of brandy, before inviting me into his makeshift office, whereby we duly introduced ourselves. Paul Conrad went onto ask, 'What have you been told about the job?'

Feeling very keen about starting a new job in a different environment, and excited at my possible future in a new city. I answered, 'I was told a second fix job working 8 a.m. to 8 p.m.'

There was a slight pause in our conversation while Paul drank a large glass of brandy. Then he said, 'That's if anyone asks, we finish at 5 p.m. Here are the plans for the stairwell, I'd like you to plasterboard the area as indicated on the drawings.'

I thought, *'Cool less hours more money.'*

Something that was never offered to me in Manchester. I replied keenly and enthusiastically, 'Okay.'

At that juncture, I went straight to work. It wasn't a difficult job, just a lot of fixings and cuttings around the riser and tread. Paul disappeared from site by 10.45 a.m. we didn't see his face until 3.30 p.m. where he seemed more pissed than earlier in the morning. Paul stumbled around the building site shouting, 'Right lads pack up, lets shut shop.'

The site agent was stumbling as he wobbled, more wobbles, than the *Wombles of Wimbledon,* he wobbled. The lads wasted no time packing up, I was at Annabel's place by 4.30 p.m. smoking weed.

The constant changing to plans for the stairwell, made it look like I'd did nothing. Every day, for three weeks, I was home before Annabel, no later than 5 p.m. booking in for Saturdays, and never having to show my face, meant a large pay cheque. Two or three weeks into the job Paul's boss entered the scene, this being the first time I'd met the contracts manager since I started. After driving from his head office in Birmingham, he was throwing his weight around, in a very aggressive high-strung manner, and shouting at the contractors on site because the job was behind schedule. I didn't like his attitude towards the tradesmen, any delays to the job was due to the site agent's lack of interest in the job, and his love for alcohol. I phoned A.M.H. to comment on the current situation, and relayed I was not happy. A.M.H. found me another job for the next day.

After three weeks in total, Nicolas moved back into my mother's house, a week after I arrived in London. The offer Sharon made to Nicolas, *'If you have a problem with your dad, you can live with me.'*

Was withdrawn.

Things seemed to be going well between me and Annabel, we

would go to Manchester once a month to see our families, we were out and about with meals at nice restaurants, the cinema, clubs like Leisure Lounge were night spots we raved and partied. Bringing in the millennium at a number of venues in Notting Hill and Ladbroke Grove. The misery in Manchester with no social life was exchanged from two, three weeks unemployed to working three or four weeks working, all that had changed to one, or two days out of work, a week in three months. At long last, I thought, *'Some consistency and continuity.'*

I was able to buy more power tools, with a heavier toolbox, meant I had to take out a £5,000 loan to buy a car. I was also getting a lot of attention from the student nurses in the halls of residence, but funnily enough, I really wasn't interested. I decided unconsciously to have just Annabel. Bearing that in mind, honesty is the best policy, but when sex is involved, we all act like fools, and don't think.

For example, one evening Annabel was on top of me, riding my pleasure zone when I received a phone call. I was enjoying the moment, and did not want to answer, but Annabel insisted, 'Answer the phone.'

I answered, while Annabel was still gently riding. It was someone I'd not seen for months, Tiana with, 'Hi Fitz, how you doing?'

Annabel was still, forcibly inflicting more gentle enjoyable pleasure on my manhood, I replied, 'I'm fine.'

With the biggest smile on my face, Tiana added in a seductive manner, 'Fitz I'm bored, why don't you come round for a bit of company?'

The intense pleasure I was receiving was distracting clear thoughts, my honesty shone through when I stated, 'I'm busy at the moment.'

Curious cats always bite back, Tiana reacted, 'Doing what?'

Not thinking straight and biting my lip because of the intense pleasure I was receiving, I retorted, 'Doing what you want.'

Annabel stopped moving her waistline over my manhood, I thought, *'Shit, I did not say the right thing over the phone.'*

Tiana replied in a cold uncaring manner, 'Bye.'

With an angry disposition, Annabel got up, pushed her face right up to mine's, and was barking like a drill sergeant, 'Who was that?'

I was bang to rights and guilty of all charges. I've always adopted an honest approach, in part a bit of deceit, I answered her question honestly, 'A girl who fancies me in Manchester.'

Annabel got up, then she stomped up and down in the small bedsit, the annoyed judge was in attendance, an angry rock wilder appeared, and she was aggravated similar to a bad-tempered cat. Annabel reacted quite fired up, 'What do you mean fancies you?'

You know the story, I tried to explain, how we met, underlining nothing had happened between me and Tiana, but I felt Annabel did not believe me.

That was the end of a pleasurable evening, instead of waking up wrapped in each other's arms, it was the start of back-to-back sleeping. In time, we'd both put the Tiana moment behind us, and for the first time, I was able to book a short holiday to Jamaica, in order to see my grandparents Mr. and Mrs. Walker. Annabel got her degree in nursing, and she was offered a bedsit, which she took, and whereby we decided, I should give up my house in Manchester to live with her at 56 Penfield House, Islington the spring-summer of 2000.

Since none of my family wanted or were interested in my input for my son's wellbeing, I left them to it. Only to be told, Nicolas has been charged for street robbery. He was going to learn the hard way. It was not what I wanted to hear, but what could I do, if he is not going to listen to his father, why should I provide for him. Nicolas was sentenced to two years imprisonment. I did my bit, driving to places I'd not heard of before to see my son, the expense, and inconvenience of it all was stressful. Stealing, just to get the resources.

The heart

The intimacies of the heart do not have thoughts
on knowledge and wisdom.
There is an irrational thinking behind a heart,
it's not like the mind that has a rational thought of conscience,
quite wise is the mind that sits next to conscience.
Knowing the emotions of the heart, is a primitive part of love
for the mind, the love one searches for is guided
by a mind of conscience.
Like a rod of iron, the mind will never bend,
if the heart one loves is not a friend.

John T. Hope

Chapter 61

Built-up stress

In all the time I was in London, I was developing a good reputation with A.M.H. Contract Services with unwanted breaks for a week, or so. Travelling from site to site, I was able to see the sights of London's attractions but never experiencing exhibitions or museums. They never reflected my culture, why bother. Besides, my unstable work pattern meant I couldn't really plan too far ahead. Tension was beginning to mount between Annabel and myself. Arguments over what seemed like nothing started to occur, I assumed we needed space.

While I was wandering the streets of Camden escaping from the tension, my legs brought me to a club called W.K.D. After speaking to the owner Aitch, I had the opportunity of paid deejay work, over the Christmas, and New Year season 2000 - 2001. The few nights I span the tracks, I was rocking the dancefloor with energetic vibe. The manager was impressed, but still relieved me, after the season was over because he preferred promoters. Aitch the owner manager of W.K.D. suggested, 'Why don't you come back later on in the New Year with a promotional idea, I might have some booking dates available then.'

I thought, *'Cool, something to think about.'*

Annabel was really doing my head in; one or two things made me think twice about our relationship. We were shopping in Wood Green arm in arm, enjoying one another's company, while weaving through the hustle and bustle of weekend shoppers, when a short skinny looking African man just appeared out of the crowd. He walked up to Annabel, which stopped us from our leisurely stroll, proclaiming, 'Hi pretty, my names Roland, can I have your number?'

I looked at Annabel she looked at me with a big grin on her

face, I just held Annabel's arm, then pushed pass the bad-mannered African. It was something I'd not seen a man do, he was very much breaking an unsaid code of conduct between men, but I notice people down south, don't have much respect for one another as they do up north. I thought nothing more of it, Annabel was very attractive. I mean, it was to be expected, my point being, never act jealously possessive, but it happened again. I was driving through Westminster, I pulled over to a black taxi rank to ask for directions. I couldn't see Annabel's face, she was sat in the front passenger seat, her head turned facing the taxi driver, he was sat in his cab, shouting out directions. After informing me, which way to go, in that moment, the taxi driver asked a question, 'Excuse me love, are you two married?'

Annabel turned to look at me with a smile all over her face, again. I thought, *'The taxi driver was out of order.'*

I put my foot on the gas, and drove off, before she could answer. In my mind, I was wondering, if Annabel was encouraging these situations by winking to these men out of my vision. I didn't say a word, I started to have more late nights without the company of Annabel, picking up the odd girl here and there. Arguments were increasingly more aggressive, my temper caused me to break furniture, having to take a slap in my face, which forced me to turn my back. If that was not enough, Annabel pulled out a knife, if I was threatening, I did not realise until that moment. The situation was something I did not like or want. I chose to head for the front door on many occasions, in order to cool the conflict down, one must remember, love was not meant to hurt. Annabel didn't like me leaving, she stated with a vicious tongue, 'You're always running away instead of sorting out our problems.'

She did not understand, I didn't like arguing about nothing, it's too stressful. At the same time, I managed to find more deejay work at a pub in Ladbroke Grove for a few weeks, around the same period, I was working on a building site in Kilburn, I met up with a Liverpudlian by the name of Bob Ashford. After talking to Bob about my deejay work, we met up with Aitch, we agreed on a night me and Bob could promote. We both pooled together £200, arranged for flyers to be printed, then we were both out and about promoting in Camden, Morning Crescent, Kentish Town the whole area. Annabel never said anything, but I really didn't think she like the idea of me in the club scene, she was not as supportive as my previous girlfriends.

Excited about my new venture with three days before my big night, I get into a serious argument when Annabel tells me to leave her bedsit. After investing a hundred quid Bob was screwing a ton when I told him, 'I'm going back to Manchester, I don't know anyone in London, where could I stay, even if I wanted to stay.'

Having little money saved, I was forced to give up my job in Kilburn, go back to Manchester, and move into a hostel.

A.M.H. really showed me their worth, having surprisingly leaving the Kilburn job, A.M.H. understanding my predicament had another job lined up for me in Greater Manchester, the day after arriving. The job was building a church roof in Cheshire, it was going well, but I just wasn't happy being in my hometown. I felt as if I was taking a step back in my life, and I was really missing Annabel, we chatted on the phone kissed and made up from a distance, two weeks later, there I was, back in London. I was seeing Annabel, but I didn't move back in with her. I found an expensive bedsit in Hampstead Heath, £180 per week plus bills, and council tax, expensive. It seemed like a real mistake going back to London.

A.M.H. found me a job in Golders Green, an area mainly populated by the Jewish community. I was recruited to refurbish a shop with instructions not to arrive on site until 10 a.m. I pulled up at 9.45 a.m. parked a bit of a distance from the job, but I thought *'Go on site, introduce myself, then unload my tools.'*

I entered the building at 9.55 a.m. I was met by a tall slim white guy in a blue boilersuit. I politely stated and enquired, 'Hello, I'm Fitzroy Edwards, a carpenter from A.M.H. is the site agent Richard about?'

It could have been a winters night, he was cold as ice, and

not unlike the welcoming from a receptionist doing overtime, he remarked, 'Sorry for wasting your time mate, my firm's chippies have finished a job earlier than expected, and they're on their way here. Your services are not needed, thanks.'

I was very disappointed, a large rent to pay was a louder African drumbeat in the back of my head. The insecurity was stress, I did not need. Cool and calm I said, 'Okay mate, cheers.'

I went back to my car, called A.M.H. to inform them of the current situation. A.M.H. commented, 'Wait for a few moments, I'll return your call once we've spoken to the contracts manager for the shopfitting company.'

Ten minutes later A.M.H. called me back, 'Listen Fitz, we have a signed contract with this company. Go back, get that guy to phone his contracts manager, or A.M.H. It's your job.'

Feeling a bit more confident about my new position, calm as the deep blue ocean, I replied, 'Okay.'

I went back to the shop to be met by the same boilersuit. I explained, 'Excuse me mate, I've just spoken to my agent, he informs me your company has signed a contract for me to start work here, could you phone your boss to confirm my position please?'

He pulled out his phone, walked away and made a call, just as another tradesman with a small bag of tools walked into the shop. I politely asked the stocky chap, 'Do you work for A.M.H.?'

A deep semi tone voice with a slight Eastern European accent replied, 'Yes.'

I responded, 'I think there's a contract problem here, there's a chance there is no work.'

The boilersuit returns as he placed his phone into his pocket walking towards us stating to me, 'Sorry mate you're not needed.'

I turned to leave the shop without a goodbye, back to my car to call A.M.H. I declared, 'They don't need a carpenter.'

A.M.H. seemed surprised when stating, 'Fitz, we don't understand this, we have a contract and they've just called asking for more carpenters.'

Now in situations like this, it could only be one thing, it clicked into place, in all the time I have worked for A.M.H. I've not met the team. I wouldn't say I have a chip on my shoulder but when A.M.H. heard my response they were shocked, when I said, 'He doesn't want me working there because I'm black.'

A.M.H. came across supportive, I felt reassured when hearing, 'Fitz, don't worry, we'll find you another job as soon as one comes in the office. Whatever you decide to do about that company A.M.H. are behind you.'

That comment was very suggestive, take the bastard to court entered my mind. It was funny, all of a sudden work at A.M.H. seem to dry up. A week went by nothing had been offered to me. Since they always had work for me within a few days, I never applied to other companies, or explored other positions. I was forced to apply to other builders. After a brief period out of work, I found a job with a repair firm, something I've not done before, but it gave me a chance to see London, driving from house to house with petrol money within my mileage rate. After one or two days, the tank was taking more than the rate paid. Traffic around London didn't help me get from A to B transporting materials in a white four door Honda Civic. The stress was building, I was working on price, and making, nothing.

When I finally got to a job doing some repair work on the flooring, the tenant of the house calls me over stating, 'Watch this on the T.V. it's something out of a Hollywood movie.'

I couldn't believe what I was seeing, the second explosion hit the Twin Towers, a close up revealed an airplane, I was overwhelmed with shock, when I viewed the two towers burning. My thought spun straight to the Bible in Revelation 10:2 *'His right foot in the sea and his left foot on the land.'*

That attack was an act of God in my mind.

Chapter 62

Yesterday, today

In the winter of 2001, after leaving Annabel's bedsit in Islington, I moved to Hampstead Heath, and I gained nothing but short-term contracts, a week working here, unemployed for two. Since I wasn't working and getting up early enough for the number of parking tickets plastered on the screen of my car, I could not afford to run my four door Honda Civic. To raise cash fast, I had to sell it cheaper than valued, and I didn't have much of a social life, anything I made went on bills, what a life.

It mentioned on the letting agency contract, I must clean the accommodation when I leave at the end of my six-month term. It could not come soon enough, it all seemed to be timed perfectly for Nicolas's release from prison, but the letting agency, would not give me back my deposit of £1800 because housing benefit were behind in payments. When they did get paid by housing benefit a month later, the letting agent had to say, 'The bedsit was not cleaned your deposit is less cleaning cost, which was £150.'

People with money can afford to wait, applying times pressure on those who do not have the funds. This is a prime example of psychological economic domination over an equal.

Now fifteen, Nicolas was being release from jail, at the same time my contract for the flat was ending. Our situation gave us access to the council's resources when Nicolas was released, we moved into a hostel in Stamford Hill. While we were living in the hostel, the fact me and Nicolas were placed in separate rooms meant as a parent, I wasn't aware of a minor's movements. Being sociable, in time I became friends to a few residents in the hostel. One resident told me, 'I saw Nicolas with some boys chasing the dragon.'

I was furious, a steaming war of words were exchanged between me and Nicolas. I believed him when Nicolas disclosed, 'Dad I wasn't using it.'

However, my fear for him forced me to implement some rules, Nicolas thought a lot different, he packed his things, and was on his way to Manchester. After months in the hostel unemployed with past tax contributions to my nation, I was trying to beat prioritised Afghans on the housing list.

When the council heard of my argument with my son, I relayed to the council my prioritised reasoning, concerns, and restrictions when performing my duty as a parent. The council understood what I was saying, they offered me, a two-bedroom flat within a week, and where I am today, Newington Green, Islington. Things were just not working out between me and Annabel when I got my new flat, I finally stopped seeing Annabel.

Chapter 63

Joe's story

You meet all sorts of people in the world moulded by society, if they could be different, they would. Joe Barrett was twenty-eight when I met him, an ex-soldier doing varied numbers of jobs, like most people in our unstable gig economy. He was living with his girlfriend, who had five rude kids, rude isn't a strong enough word to describe their kids. His girlfriend having four children to previous relationships with one more on the way. They lived in a two-bedroom council flat, creating pure chaos on the Newington Green estate, plus the added companionship of a family pet, a shaggy dog. Only ever having one other woman before his present girlfriend, like it's an excuse for having no manners. Yet his frustration I can understand. One must remember, manners makes a man. What do I mean?

Well, I was not impressed when he came to my flat uninvited. I watched amused at his efforts coming onto my Croatian girlfriend, who happened to be there at the time of his unwelcome arrival. A few days later, he noticed I'd deleted him for his bad manners from my social media page. He came over to my flat with a drink to say sorry for his behaviour, after speaking my mind when he phoned me earlier in the day.

In conveying his heartfelt story, he began saying, 'I was unable to find work, or a trade, and I'm not one for education. So, I joined the armed forces when I was seventeen in an effort to escape from my abusive father, who did not seem to have much self-esteem. After my father was laid off work in the mining, then the press industry, he began to drink and wasn't interested in work. My father battered me and my brothers for one reason or another.'

When Joe joined the armed forces just before being deployed to the invasion of the second Iraq war Desert Storm, his regiment became aware he was still a virgin. Sure enough, they introduced him to a local prostitute. A fine way to experience your first sexual encounter.

Nightmares of war haunted him, horrific traumatising scenes of explosions and mayhem. He recalled watching his friend scream blue murder, when a tank rolled majestically over his fragile legs, his mate tried to crawl away leaving his legs behind. As a witness, Joe watched his pal biting through his own bottom lip from the excruciating pain endured, when his legs were severed by the tank.

A sudden explosion mutilated his friend's torso. Rolling along the floor, there was just a helmet strapped around his head and chin. His mouth gaped open, allowing his tongue to drape out. The blood red hole from his eye socket stared back with a perplexed hypnotising spell. Connected to his head was an untwined coil of optic nerve attached to his eyeball, which rested on his blood-stained cheek. The same blast provoked his other mate to stand up, holding up both his upper arms, exposing bones, both his forearms hung below, and swung from side to side, on inches of muscle and flesh. He walked aimlessly, stumbling bewildered into the line of fire, thud, thud, thud, in quick succession, three shots to the chest, puncturing flesh, and arteries. He collapsed face first, splashing into a pool mixture of mud, blood, bricks, and rubble. Dead isn't the question on Joe's mind he was dead.

As Joe told his story, his eyes welled up in an ocean of tears that never fell, his pupils widened, his blue iris disappeared, as if he were walking into a big black cave. The whites of his eyes turned devilishly red with rage, and suitcase sized bags puffed up under his eyes. A prickly pale unshaven white skin punctuated his sickening disgust, mountains, and valleys of red spots, sat uncomfortably on his slim underweight face.

With each deep inhale of breath, in between each word under-lined remorse, hatred, and confusion at the insane acts of war. A belly pit of sorrow echoed in his voice as if he were shouting in a deep cavern. When he questioned the word humanity, Joe stated, 'If war is humanity, death is a welcomed friend.'

In time Joe and his family found larger accommodation, somewhere in the concrete city of London, I just haven't seen him. Is winning a war worth fighting, when the real fight is helping these boys when they come home.

Whose war

'Wealth buys armies to fight their battles.'
'He's more of a coward if he can't fend for himself.'
'Defending a culture imposed on others.'
'Wealth, strength doesn't make you right, it's our way of life that's
wrong, there's no love from the strong, rich, and stupid.'
'Strength doesn't make one wise,
intelligent shouldn't you be kind?'
'The strong, rich, and stupid are in fear of their
own psychotic shadow.'
'Primitive.'

John T. Hope

Chapter 64

Never ending

In 2004, it had to happen again, while I was refurbishing the new N1 bar in Islington, I met Dave Dunn a foreman from the same area as the last shopfitting company I came across racism, Leicester. The foreman's racist jokes pissed me off no end, I pulled him to one side over breakfast, nice and politely, then I stated, 'I don't like your jokes, pal.'

With a cocky manner, like he was a proud immature bull displaying his small horns, he replied, 'Sorry, I thought we were mates.'

I've only known the dude for two or three days, I'm thinking, *'He doesn't know how to show respect.*

I spoke up, 'If you were my mate, you'd know you couldn't crack those kind of jokes.'

The next day he was on the same tip, in one ear and out the other. A new recruitment agency found me the job. When I told them what was happening, they weren't too pleased. They would not employ me thereafter, with that, less agency work. Hence, I was forced into price work. Here's where you learn how many ways you can lose money and the company gains on your time.

Having worked irregular work patterns, I could never afford too many party nights over a three-month period. In effect, I was not meeting as many women, and when I did, they were all ticking boxes, flirting with options they had, or trying to dominate me. I found myself having one nightstands. When I did feel comfortable with a woman, the word marriage pops up. I've never been to a wedding; I've never thought of marriage. When faced with it as an option in order to keep a short-term relationship together, it was too much of a promise to give, not even the fact this Australian woman told me she was pregnant.

A year or so later, I was stupid, I met a young woman from Croatia, I really liked the woman, but she had immigration problems. The thought of the government's law stopping my affections from growing again, made me ask her to marry me. Believe me when I say, everything in the universe was against us. She went back to Croatia for a brief period of time to bring more of her belongings, but on her return, she was detained by immigration.

By this time, I was driving once again, but was unable to get her from the detention centre because my car broke down. I was working on a refurbishment at Woolwich Arsenal industrial park, in east London. Weeks passed, no payment for work I've done, or delayed to payments of wages for one reason, or another. When I went to a local garage in Woolwich where my car was being repaired, they charged me £25 per day for parking. I lost my car, and my future wife was banged up for weeks, then sent back to Croatia. How can I stay in credit with this constant instability. No materials on site, so you don't get paid for the day, or arriving on site, not to be required, and then to have your tools stolen, what the f- -k!

Stolen tools, it's happened to me a number of times as well as on this present job in Woolwich. More often than not, you find to do your job, tradesmen need a large number of tools on site for the varied amounts of work that's needed to carry out the job. Therefore, over £2,000 worth of tools are on site, but because insurance companies will only pay out a maximum of £1,500, I was always forced into buying cheaper replacement tools.

She called off the wedding because I was not man money enough. To date at twenty-five my son is starting his third prison sentence, all for the want of sharing the resources. This isn't living, the stress is overwhelming, and why I write as an appeal, when I never write a word. A quote from Mr. Cameron, 'We can't dream of having homes like this.'

Only because governments around the world, will not give the people of the so-called free world, the resources. Political leaders, and the elite are savagely barbaric, primitive with the social intelligence of a spider, or an ant's colony.

Chapter 65

Divine Authority

Revelations 12:10:11 Then I heard a loud voice in heaven say, now have come the salvation, and the power, and the Kingdom of our God, and the authority of Christ. For the accuser of our brothers who accuses them before our God day, and night has been hurled down.

As I write and edit this chapter on 16th February 2011, citizens in Libya rise up for democracy, freedom, and humanity. Could these edited blogs in the novel *The Chronicles,* be an influence?

Again, valuable information finds its way to me, without any research being applied by myself. Below important periods in history was sent to me by email on the 3rd, February 2011.

8th April 2011 is an edited publication on social media

Abraham Lincoln was elected to Congress in 1846. John F. Kennedy was elected to Congress in 1946. Abraham Lincoln was elected President in 1860. John F. Kennedy was elected President in 1960. Both were particularly concerned with civil rights. Both wives lost their children while living in the White House. Both Presidents were shot on a Friday. Both Presidents were shot in the head, now it gets really weird. Lincoln's secretary was named Kennedy; Kennedy's Secretary was named Lincoln both were assassinated by Southerners. Southerners named Johnson succeeded both Andrew Johnson, who succeeded Lincoln, was born in 1808. Lyndon Johnson, who succeeded Kennedy, was born in 1908. John Wilkes Booth, who assassinated Lincoln, was born in 1839. Lee Harvey Oswald, who assassinated Kennedy, was born in 1939.

Both assassins were known by their three names. Both names are composed of fifteen letters. This is where it gets weirder. Lincoln was shot in the theatre named 'Ford.' Kennedy was shot in a car called Lincoln made by 'Ford.' Lincoln was shot in a theatre and his assassin ran and hid in a warehouse. Kennedy was shot from a warehouse and his assassin ran and hid in a theatre.

Booth and Oswald were assassinated before their trials.

Dead Presidential Authority

On the previous page, I put forward my second evidence of divine movement within society, and a phenomenon that naturally occurs, science cannot explain. In other words, a miracle, the *Hand of God*.

Republished titled chapter 45 *The Hand of God*.

Fitzroy Brian Edwards and John T. Hope, divine credentials are in chapter 45. Since there is conflict in the world, I believe, I have the authority to write divine laws. As of this day, the Ten Commandments are null, and void. And not the will of our *Lord Jesus Christ*, Good God Almighty, God of Love Eros, Nature.

PROCLAMATION; *The New Ten Commandments*

1. Defend your logic.

2. Whoever love's the Father, Nature, God must love one's neighbour.

3. Thou Shall Not Kill.

4. Free will.

5. Go forth and multiply.

6. Natural law does not say you should be married. Men, and women have proved they cannot live up to their promise. Therefore, it is forbidden to be married.

7. It is a sin if you do not revert back to Natural law, or aim not to use, and abolish the monetary system. For the reasons I have explained throughout the books *Omni's Wordsmith Mantra,* and *The Whistling Wind.*

8. It Takes Many Minds to Make A God and No One God, Is Greater Than Many Minds. Humanity aims to be equal no one should be titled above anyone as royal, religious, or political dynasties, it is forbidden.

9. Note, Moses is the only so-called prophet from God, where I do not have any identifying marks, or scars on my body. His symbolic descriptions from his visions and receiving the word of God, differs from that of Abraham the father of all nations, our *Lord Jesus Christ,* and Muhammad peace be upon him, through the mind. The odd one out Moses, a corrupt prophet, who killed. Moses's laws and teachings are a contradiction of reason, barbaric, primitive, and psychologically insane. After reading the afore-mentioned barbarism from Moses, he should be known as a false prophet.

10. Respect your parents.

The Father is harvesting his field. Men's will is to do freely because free will allows that pleasure, yet men still kill not fearing man, when it is written in all spiritual, and religious text, *'Thou shall not kill.'*

I am very merciful; my hand will not harm another; one can act freely. Fearing God, the divine demanding faithfulness and worship is a rage that is misplaced. This appeals to the primitive, irrational subconscious minds of men. There is only one God, why would he be jealous?

God's rage derives from the frustration of trying to complete or solve a mathematical problem, this rage is focused on disciplining the creative and intelligent minds of men.

Remember the French philosopher Rene Descartes, *'I think therefore I am.'*

In my opinion, what he was trying to say is as follows; you still have a mind with imagination, although you are dead. As we seem to forget, I will remind you of Nature, Good God Almighty, Eros, God of Love's powers as written in mythology. He controls the movement of the universe, life and death, the mind, body, and the fortunes of men. The so-called free world is being judged.

1. Our *Lord Jesus Christ's* door is closing, becoming the main road from all paths to me.

2. I introduce myself as the new gatekeeper.

3. Not upholding *The New Ten Commandments* means, you act for the Father above. In so doing, I remind you; The Father is not as forgiving as me.

The Natural lawgivers.

The Holy Trinity

Please note: No one man can rule the world. Therefore, I cannot lead any nation, I can only offer my wisdom, or entertain as a deejay, I am not a dictator. Obey *The New Ten Commandments* from Nature's natural law. I will take back the words in this book, if any man, or woman can describe themself as a god, or a goddess in the same numbers, manner, or fashion, if their scars were inflicted before the birth of John T. Hope's mind on the 3rd May 2009. One could say, 'A virgin birth from the mind of a man.'

May I add, if no man or woman can do, what I have done, then I'd say, 'I'm quite unique, if you agree with my closing argument, good for you. If you don't agree, I cannot save you.'

Chapter 66

The journey

Christian pagan philosophers have the belief, one is oppressed, and suppressed by the influential elite. In so doing, religious dogma about the afterlife, placed fear in the minds of primitive naïve men. So, the strong sociopaths and psychopaths, having no belief, can control the believer. This section of the book tries to understand how divinity deems the actions of men, and the cycle of life after death.

Mundane existence

The end all and be all for your existence,
you must earn a wage to live your life.
If a wage has no importance when you're dead,
why should it have importance in life?

Many living in the world have the belief
of survival of the fittest.
In death, many take that thought into the afterlife,
then face God with a challenge to be champion.
Of course, their all defeated by God's might,
because he is number one.

Guilt

Conscience forgives innocence's guilt, ignorance's consciousness
should it be forgiven?
Conscience awareness always remembers because guilt never
forgets.
Principles prevail over the virtues of misconduct; guilt exists
because of your conscience.
Conscience guilt fears more than men can deliver.

The evil one may not like being considered a beaten number
two, but even he knows, there's a God.

Get there

'*Our Lord Jesus Christ described what it looks like, the name of the place and who would be there.*'
'Oh yeah, sounds nice, how does one get there?'
'*One believes one knows where it is.*'
'Great, how does one get there?'
'*There isn't a road to where we're going.*'
'Okay, how does one get there?'
'*It does not appear on the map.*'
'Fine, how does one get there?'
'*One saw it in a dream.*'
'Oh, how did one get there?'
'*Not reality, so it seems.*'
'How did one get there?'
'*Oh, dear Lord, it's hell here on earth.*'
'How did it get there?'
'*A question for heaven, how does one get there?*
'Why look for a place that's still unknown, heaven is right here on earth we can make it a better home, let's find our way back to a location everybody knows. One knows, how to get there.

The journey

Since life seems to be a race to death,
why can't in death be a race for life?
From the void of nothing into life, why would life die,
then fall into a vacuum of nothing?
If nothing can produce something,
why would something plunge into nothing?
Why produce something, if only to end up as nothing?
One must be here to do something, or there would be nothing.
Striving to create life is to the death,
by Nature's will with the sun life lives on.
If life moves on, then death has not won
because time marches on.
Escaping from death is one's thought of life,
abstract art could explain that thought.
One's belief, one strives to live life from death.

In the natural world, everything has a biological or mathematical signature. From the start of life, you're vulnerable, as you grow you learn to fend and protect your ground. Since life is much too short, no matter how long your life may last, the one thing that should give you hope and comfort for everlasting life, is the natural world wastes nothing. It tends to change into a new biological or mathematical signature, constantly contributing to the natural world.

Shakespeare said, *'To be or not to be that is the question?'*

A very famous quote, intelligence plunges into a void of nothing, not to be. Intelligence has proven to strive for life from nothing, to be. Faith is trust in the knowledge someone is wise enough to remind you how to be. My article of faith declares, there must be one with greater knowledge and intelligence to show me how to be. I have trust in our *Lord Jesus Christ.*

The minds of men are truly ignorant into how a divine entity of all knowledge, wisdom, and love, reasons. You must remember, one of God's powers is to control the minds and bodies of men, to do as he sees fit. To implement the enforcement of economic law over natural law takes away the authority God has over men, to be placed into the hands of a psychotic tyrant with a superiority complex. Men being in the image of God, anything man can do, God can do better. For example, there have been many occasions, when someone has done a wrong to another, they wish, *'I hope to God you get your head chopped off.'*

The quote above is from the movie *Highlander,* the quote underlines, how society uses God's name. Indicating, as well as being described as a Good God, if you end up doing the wrong thing in God's eyes, he has another side to his persona that does not sound too welcoming. Fearing God, you pay homage, and respect life. Men prefer to kill instead of living in the peace of God's grace.

God has made the earth, so believers in his creation can eat from the sacrifice of the lamb. Those who have no belief in God, his prophets, our *Lord Jesus Christ,* and the prophet Mohammad peace be, upon him, cannot eat from the land, sea, or air. WARNING: If anyone undertakes the responsibilities of God's charge over humanity, one will be SEVERELY REPRIMANDED, for using a tool that enslaves humanity, to the will of one, who irresponsibly distributes the resources, and neglects the environment. Our *Lord Jesus Christ* is all forgiving, his door is closing. God uses a double barrel meaning to the words Merciful Father. Men of faith, love, knowledge, and wisdom understand God's words.

The title Good God Almighty gives a description of God's nature, and behaviour. Good in the first instance, refers to a feature, he has good intentions over humanity, having almighty power to do so. The fact God has almighty power over men, shows he has psychotic rage, directed at disciplining his foes, such as the evil one, and his followers, evil nonbelievers. Displaying psychotic rage over men is not a good example to set in front of humanity. So, God sends prophets, who convey the words of peace, and love, as an example to men. It should be understood, as a messenger of God, he must not kill in the name of God, why should any man have that right?

It is written, on the day of Judgment, Luke 3:16–17, 'God will harvest his fields, and separate the wheat from the chaff.'

In effect, God is in search for representatives from his own mind. You represent a cell from God's mind. In other words, he is in search of like-minded thinkers.

If life, and death, is not a cycle, why must men only have the privilege of being a man, and an insect never becomes more than what it is?

Christian Pagan philosophers believe, if an insect can be reincarnated into a man, it makes sense, a man can be demoted to an insect. On the other hand, projection of perception implies, when the universal entity sends you to your deepest fear. Abiding to a righteous path, heaven is gained with a good heart. It's funny, how men live by secular law, but God judge's men using, natural morality.

What to expect

Not knowing, what to expect in life,
what can one expect in death?
One's fear of death, is one's disappointments in life.
Life is hard because one expects others to do one's bidding, hell.
One's fear of death is due to the fact life is made tough.
Life could be roses, if one shared one's labour for love, heaven.
Since there is pleasure in life there must be joy in death.

When I started writing, I've drawn on my own personal experience, when expressing my words. I extend these feelings when I say, the first time I conceived a child was an unbelievable experience with a mystic presence, or my sixth sense alerted to a manifestation from within my mind and body. Unaware of what I was experiencing at the time, I came across the same feeling when I have a psychotic episode, but with more intense apprehension, and fear for the authority of the Good God Almighty's entity. Now, I know and I'm aware of this mystic presence, no one can tell me God is not involved in the intimacy from the act of sex, or love. When two are joined to make one. Another form of the Holy Trinity, God's entity is present, or touches humanity in order to ordain life.

Smile

Happily smiling, smile is to be happy.
Is the memory of a smile, the memories of death?
Does the memory of one's smile, bring a tear to one's eyes?
Is the memory of one's smile, loneliness?
Does the memory of a smile, say, 'Hello.'
When extending a fond fair well, 'Bye, bye.'
Is the memory of one's smile make you happy,
or sad, and gloomy?
Does the memory of a smile make one laugh,
while others cry?
The memory of one's smile should
bring happiness to one's mind.

Life and death's pleasure

'What is the worrying thing about living,
is it the pain love brings, or the pain of death?
Is it the pain of what's left behind, or the fear of the unknown?
How can one be afraid of the unknown if
one knows he's all forgiving?
Why worry about the pain of love when it
brings so much joy, and pleasure living?
Being full of love is there any reason to fear death?'
*'Only the guilty should be afraid, while innocents
awaits the pleasure one has given.'*
'The expression of love is the key, and the gateway to the
joys of life living, death is but a passageway to
the pleasure of eternal life, loving.'

One's duty

One must remember, although one has the creator's authority
to speak on his behalf, one does not have authority over
nations, or the people.
One can, and should teach of God's logical reasoning, in line
with nature, and his relationship with mankind's humanity.

If

If you can hear the birds sing, and the tree branches thrashing
as the whistling wind drifts without direction,
listen to nature, then praise a Spiritual entity.
If you can walk or wander in lush green fields, to dense forests
that continue up steep mountain passes, descending down
bendy rock filled rapid rivers, and bountiful trees,
then praise Divinity.
If you can smell the fragrance of flourishing floral pigments in
wide open valleys, stroll in harmony with nature,
then praise a Supernatural power.
If you can see the vibrant colours of the rainbow, the deep blue
sea, and the sky-blue sky up above,
tell others of his wonders, then praise Nature.
If you can talk the talk, exchange words of peace, and your love
for nature, then praise Good God Almighty.
If you can feel a sensitive touch, express the sentiments love
loves to share love, then praise our *Lord Jesus Christ.*
If none of the above applies, then praise God you're alive.

John T. Hope

Chapter 67

The whistling wind outro

Whilst I walk the busy London streets, I'm accompanied by the subtle sounds of a whirling windy wind, whip up a whistling whirlpool, as it blows it flutters like a butterfly, whipping up a song as it drifts along. The whistling wind pushes the few dark clouds aimlessly in the spring chilled air. An opening in the grey clouds reveals a gloomy evening in the depth of the atmosphere. It made my mouth gape open with amazing awesome awe, when I look to the heavens at the blackness in the night sky, the odd shooting star shoots by, then it fades away to the depth of space, or disintegrates in earth's face.

The full moon glows dim, there's a little amount of light flickering in the night, just a shimmer, and a glimmer from the distant starlight's. Creeping creepily into view, eerie floating fluffy grey clouds appear, moonlight disappears, car's headlights brighten the roads, and late-night shop's lights blink bright red lights. As I stroll along in the urban streets, the city's artificial streetlights replace natural light. Excitedly dancing in between the rush of headlights and red, amber, switching to green go traffic lights, seems to dazzle my eyes, a colourful mesmerising sight.

The whirling windy wind blows up a twirling whirlpool, as the whistling wind twists turns and swirls, it's all over the world. In the distance there's moonlight, a pleasing sight, it cast fast moving spooky shadows with the highspeed traffic lights. By sound, when you put your ears to the ground, the city streets hears the vibrating juddering judder of car's deep rumbling engines, echo vroom, vroom, vroom, their horns blow beep, beep, beep, and whoop, whoop go the emergency sirens with flashing blue lights.

The rush grows as the nightlife rolls with R & B soul. The clubs and bar lights, flash on with green laser lights, switching off red lights, there's no fireworks it's not Guy Fawkes night, it's bashment night. After a good dance, there may be a playful advance, the girls look fine, dressed divine, guys line up ready to dine, it's a flirtatious rhyme, or a chat up line, you're mines. When the evening comes to an end, in the early morn, close to the break of dawn, a wild windy whirlpool whips up the whistling wind, end to end on street bends from beginning to end. From the soothing sounds of the musical underground to the violent howling whirlwind. It swirls along singing a song, breaking the sound barrier. As it twirls and whirls, it strums a chilling raucous of a chorus, the roaring song conducted by the whistling wind.

The wild windy wind thrashes branches from old oak trees that bend, and sing, creak, creak, rickety creak to the force of the windy whirling wind. The vicious thrash, a sudden lash of a twirling spinning windy wind kicks a tin can that clackety clangs, it bounces off the walls, knocking a door, and clashing not smashing shop windows. The tin can tumbles and stumbles along, clash clackety clang, clash clackety bang, in harmony with the relentless whirling sound from the whistling wind.

As the whirling wind roars, the whistling wind pushes the grey stormy clouds away. Then there's the heavy beating rain, pitter patter pitter patter, it pounds your brain. The loud rolling rumble from a deep bellowing thunder, explodes like an atomic bomb with a crack, a whip, a boom, and a lash, flashes of illuminated electrical light when lightning strikes. It suddenly disappears, it's oh so clear, the heavens opens up with no tears, there's no fear.

While gazing across the horizon, at the spectacular spectacle through a clearing in a fastmoving grey cloudy sky, the blackness of space appears before my eyes. The pin pricked twinkling lights are stars sparkling back in the mirror of the night. In the colourful rainbow of the Nebular clouds, a marvellous array is displayed in the milky way. The spinning rings of Saturn sings, a love song that makes Neptune's blue rings ring, ring, ring, sounds like blue bells ping, ping, ping, then a flash whoosh, a shooting star burns brightly. As it speeds passed it streaks straight into the early morning sky.

In turn, the windy wind blows, and clears the sky from the dark dreary clouds to the warmer vibrant spring colours of the rainbow. Peering over the opposite side of the horizon, an orangey red glow, semi-circles a yellow sunrise, brightens up parts of a built-up city skyline. The purple rays, brings a purple haze, a relaxing phase from an emerging clear blue-sky. The whistling wind recites a flowing poetic rhyme with the scarlets' song, and the squawking magpies squawk along, the birds fly high sing hello to the sky, as the warmth spreads over the city.

The traffic lights are not so bright, the roads are clear, no one's in sight, the rolling rubber wheels from automobiles, rarely pass by to peel the wet road. As I wander the streets of a metropolitan city, the windy wind follows my lead.

While I ponder in my mind, the windy whirlpool subsides, it's calm in my mind, pure clarity with my vision, and cosily quiet outside. Then the calming windy wind, whips up a whirlpool whirling wind, the whistling wind whispers, *'I'm not confused, I'm clear in my thoughts, and my mind is made up, I know who I am.'*

THE END